MANAGING AMERICA'S ECONOMIC EXPLOSION

ANNUAL NATIONAL BUSINESS CONFERENCES

HARVARD GRADUATE SCHOOL OF BUSINESS ADMINISTRATION

Planning the Future Strategy of Your Business

Management Guide to Overseas Operations

Management in a Rapidly Changing Economy

Management's Mission in a New Society

Business Responsibility in Action

Managing America's Economic Explosion

MANAGING AMERICA'S ECONOMIC EXPLOSION

Edited by

DAN H. FENN, JR.

Editor, Harvard Business School Bulletin

McGRAW-HILL BOOK COMPANY, INC.

New York Toronto London 1961

MANAGING AMERICA'S ECONOMIC EXPLOSION

 Library of Congress Catalog Card Number: 61-8653.

20418

PREFACE

NOT LONG AGO a clergyman received a Christmas card from one of his parishioners. Attached to it was a chatty little note from the man's wife, which ran along these lines: "Our 12-year-old is having problems with his arithmetic; Mary, who is 8, is having problems with her teeth; I am having problems with the League of Women Voters, but George has no problems. All he has is a lot of those pesky challenges."

I must admit I sympathize with the poor lady; I presume, among other things, she was reacting against the tiresome repetition of the words "challenge," "problem," "demand," and, perhaps, "opportunity."

But boring as the terms may be, the facts they reflect are hard and real. There is an urgency about these times which we have not yet recognized; there is a time fuse sputtering, buried but not extinguished by the mush of complacency, which we have not yet heard. And one of the most decisive questions of our time is: who will hear it first?

One of the nation's most publicized economists is perfectly frank in saying that it will be the politicians, following the lead of the intellectuals. Here, he says, is where the real innovations will be nurtured and launched; here is where the technological revolution of the future will be conceived and born; here is where the great ideas which will shape American society will find their outlet.

We will continue to have private business in the future, he surmises, but mostly as a cover for the activities of the federal government. Some people will be made to feel better and the transition will be eased if we maintain the corporation as the contractee for the government instead of building enormous, exclusive in-house government capacity. But the big people and the big dreams and the big plans in the future will come from Washington.

He could be right.

Or, worse, we could be swallowed up as a people, along with the principles we are trying to implement as a nation, because we saw too little, too late.

I don't believe that we are going the way of Rome and Carthage, but I do have an enormous respect for the pragmatism of the American people when they are aroused. If they see something to be done, they are driven to get off and do it; if the existing patterns do not seem capable of producing an adequate solution, they are not loath to change them. American political history is filled with instances where the people used their government to do a job that needed doing, a job business was overlooking or refusing to take on. If there is insufficient self-regulation, regulation is sure to follow. If there is insufficient service to consumers, government participation in the economy is inevitable. If business refuses to take care of its employees, the government will.

The business community fights all this, of course, but they fight at the wrong time and they fight the wrong battle. Instead of wasting their time and energy trying to halt the inexorable march of events set in motion by their own failures, they should be diagnosing and remedying those weaknesses before they become grave social and economic problems. Instead of taking the leadership in opposing in the world the kind of evolutionary, modernizing change which they encourage in their companies, they should be shoving and elbowing the politicians along just as the intellectuals are doing. Instead of writing volumes of books and speeches justifying the role and achievements of the business community twenty-five or fifty or even ten years ago, they should be working so their successors can justify it a decade or two from now.

Unfortunately, business and an initiative enterprise system have, apparently, been granted no inalienable right to exist by American society. It exists to the extent that it does the job that needs to be done. This may be hard, but it is, in itself, the ultimate expression of the philosophy of competition.

In this volume, the participants in the 30th Annual National Business Conference look at our economic explosion and the complexities of managing it fruitfully from the standpoint of some of the specific administrative decisions involved and the goals and interests of the nation. I am sorry to have to warn the reader that they use the words "challenge," "problem," "demand," and, perhaps, "opportunity" a great many times. But that's the fault of the times, not the authors or the editors. And that's the message, I suspect, which they are trying to convey in these pages.

Many people have contributed to this volume, and I am most grateful to them for their time and effort. At the head of the list, of course, come the men who prepared the papers on which this book is based. Secondly, the participants who enriched the ideas in the chapters with their questions are due a bow. Finally, Mrs. Alan Lebowitz who managed the publication details and worked on many of the manuscripts, and Miss Elizabeth Knox who carried the burden of the typing, have earned the gratitude of the reader, as well as mine.

Dan H. Fenn, Jr.

CONTENTS

Part Three SOME LARGER ISSUES FACING BUSINESS

INTRODUCTION

Stanley F. Teele

ONCE AGAIN the volume based on the yearly national business conference held at Harvard directs its attention to an issue significant not only for the business community but also for the country and the world. We cannot hope to present final answers to the many perplexing aspects of our central theme in a single volume. We do, however, trust that the thoughts and ideas expressed here will stimulate minds, delineate the major paths along which solutions are to be sought, and encourage us all to pursue that step-by-step process which is the hallmark of informed democratic decision making.

Each of the four words of our theme, "Managing America's Economic Explosion," has its own forceful meaning and must call to our minds a series of questions around which the discussions here will build. To me they come in this sequence. First, *should* America have an economic explosion at all? In thinking about such a question, one inevitably must wonder whether our emphasis on economic matters, on material well-being, has detracted or will detract from those values which in the long run are far more important.

Then we must ask what kind of economic explosion should America have? Here one's thoughts turn to the propositions advanced by many observers, but no one has stated the case more pungently than John Kenneth Galbraith. He has expressed the belief that we are being crippled by an economic imbalance which over-

Note: Mr. Teele is Dean, Harvard Business School.

emphasizes private goods and underemphasizes public goods like roads, schools, recreational facilities, and clean streets.

But we may also question whether America *will* have an economic explosion. Concern that our economic progress has been stabilized at a relatively low rate of increase, at least in terms of percentages, has been expressed in many quarters. Among the Russian economists this possibility has been proclaimed with vigor and enthusiasm. What combination of government and business actions can we fashion that will make both the concern of our own economists and the boast of the Russians unfounded?

Again, can there be an economic explosion in America alone? The immense gap in material well-being between the rich countries and the poor countries that already exists seems unlikely to be tolerated for long. If an economic explosion in America widens the gap still further, can we expect the less fortunate areas of the world to sit quietly by and watch? Will we not inevitably need to turn our minds to managing a world economic explosion if we ourselves are to enjoy sustained growth? Furthermore, in this age of increasingly independent economies, is it feasible to maintain an island of plenty in a sea of poverty?

Finally, is there a contradiction in terms between the words "managing" and "explosion"? What can we do by way of managing an explosion, except to set it off and then jump to a safe spot?

These issues, then, form the subject matter of this book. They are vital concerns, and it is our hope that the reader will focus on them with us in an effort, not to formulate answers, but to clarify thinking so that the best courses of action will become possible.

Part One

GROWTH: PROSPECTS AND PITFALLS

GOVERNMENT'S PARTNERSHIP IN ECONOMIC GROWTH

Stuart Symington

THERE ARE many facets of economic growth upon which one may focus—it is a vast subject. But here I would like to concentrate on the role of the federal government in the effort to strengthen the American economy. This rather oversimplifies the case, for it must be clear that no one sector of our nation has a monopoly, either of knowledge or responsibility, in the vast area of growth. It calls for the best that we all have to give: the combined efforts of responsible free enterprise and responsible free government, the private and public actions of our entire responsible citizenship. Partnership is the word to stress, and in this chapter I will examine the problems of growth with this emphasis always in the foreground. Let me begin

Note: Mr. Symington is United States Senator from Missouri.

with a few remarks on the general nature of economic progress—what does it involve, and why is it desirable?

Although statistical measurements act as tools and help identify the objectives, the problem of economic growth is not a mere numbers game as to how much the gross national product grows from year to year. Any study or definition of economic growth must also carefully consider how we use this production and how a free society can strike a balance between individual initiative and national purpose, between action by government and action by others. In fact, the subject of growth is related to all of our needs and ideals as a great nation and a great people.

While we may use what we produce wisely or unwisely, it is simple common sense that the more we produce in general—and especially per capita—the more we shall have to devote in wise proportions to all of our purposes as a nation.

Let us look at several of these purposes in terms of economic growth. In our private economic lives, some 40 million families still have incomes below the commonly accepted minimum requirements for an American standard of living. Correction of this deficiency must come primarily from further economic growth, rather than from redistribution of the current national income. Through such increased growth, all American families should have the opportunity to improve their living standards. This is not only good for them; it is good for the American system.

Our domestic public needs also call for accelerated economic growth. We all know the glaring deficiencies in education and health services, social-security protection, urban renewal and some types of housing, basic research, and resource development. These all require a combination of private and public efforts.

Another national purpose is to meet the challenge posed by world-wide events. Those who divide up our national product into cloistered chambers may argue that all we need to do is to make a different allocation of what we now produce. In that way we presumably can support indefinitely a heavy national-security burden and also meet our inescapable obligations to the underdeveloped peoples of the free world. That, however, is a negative approach, and one to which I cannot subscribe. In our free society, we do not want to commandeer resources as dictatorships do. We do not need to sacrifice our basic freedoms to attain our objectives.

While the totalitarian threat is ominous, I do not feel that we should become obsessed with it. Even if that threat were to vanish overnight—which it will not—we would still have an overwhelming need for increased economic growth. However, I do want to make a few comments about the comparisons of our growth rate with that of the Soviets. We cannot dismiss these comparisons in airy fashion, by saying that a less-developed country can grow more rapidly than a higher-developed country.

The Soviet population and labor force seem to be growing less rapidly than ours. If their economy has a so-called natural capacity to grow faster than ours, as some allege, it would reside in the Soviet capacity to improve technology and productivity more rapidly than we can. But it is not self-evident that a less-developed technology can be improved faster than a more advanced one. I see some signs that modern technology reaches what might be called a breakthrough point at times, which accelerates rather than decelerates its capacity for further advance. The facts are that American technology and productivity have advanced at an accelerating rate, when the incentives of reasonably full use of resources have been present.

More important, regardless of comparisons between us and the Soviets or the Chinese, there are firm grounds for the widely held conclusion that our economic growth rate has been unacceptably low since the end of the Korean War. (I take this time benchmark only because actual wartime provides certain galvanizing forces for growth which differentiate such periods from the nonwar situation.)

This brings us to another question often asked by students of the nature of growth—how much should we have?

The conclusion that our economic growth rate has been too low in recent years is not based upon selecting some arbitrary growth-rate figure—whether 5% or otherwise. Rather, it is based upon the evidence that our growth rate has been insufficient to avoid recessions and to absorb the growing labor force and the advancing technology.

We do not expect our American type of economy to grow in a perfectly straight line. But I think most of us would agree that the frequency of ups and downs since the end of the Korean War has been debilitating. Moreover, the 2.5% average annual rate of economic growth in real terms, from the beginning of 1953 through the end of 1959, has resulted in an excessively large rise in unemployed manpower and plant. Leaving out the recession periods, the true level of unemployment in the United States—including both full-time unemployment and the full-time equivalent of part-time unemployment—rose from about 4% of the civilian labor force in 1953 to about 5.8% in 1956, and to about 7.3% in 1959. It has averaged approximately 6.6% through June 1960, seasonally adjusted.

Our productive resources of plant and equipment were in reasonably full use in early 1953. But, since then, increasing percentages of such resources have been idle. During 1960 it seems that close to 10% of these resources were not productive. Since the beginning of 1953, some estimates indicate about $200 billion *less* in actual production measured in 1959 dollars, and about 15 million manyears *less* in employment opportunity, than we would have had with reasonably full use of our total productive resources. These estimates may be challenged as to exactness. But they could be varied 10 or 20%, one way or the other, without changing their essential significance.

Similarly, it is estimated that, during the five-year period from the beginning of 1960 through the end of 1964, over a 5% rate of economic growth would yield close to $350 billion *more* production, and about 18 million manyears *more* employment opportunity, than if the average annual growth rate of the past seven years were continued. These estimates may well understate our reasonable potentials. But, as I have already suggested, the important thing is not whether we think in terms of a 4% or a 6% growth rate. In fact, it is not in harmony with our system to ordain any preconceived rate of growth.

The important thing is whether we set in motion the forces required to use our resources reasonably well on a sustained basis. The difficulties now standing in our way seem to me to lie not in the objective, but in the means of attaining it—and, having done so, of retaining it. What are some of the possible means available to us, and how effective are they?

There are those who say that a sustained and satisfactory growth rate depends primarily upon a high enough level of business investment. Assuming that our resources are kept in reasonably full use, this is obviously true. For the more we invest in improved plant and equipment, the faster productivity will increase—and the rate of this increase sets the upper limits for economic growth. But this approach alone is too narrow; investment must be balanced by private consumption and public demand.

Recall that improvements in technology and productivity during the 1920s outran the distribution of goods. And the distribution failure led to the debacle of the early 1930s. Again, the investment boom of 1955–1957 was out of step with the slow progress in other parts of the economy and thus contributed to the ensuing recession.

There are other commentators who place primary emphasis upon expansion of private consumption. I think most businessmen feel that we do need a vast expansion in this area in the years ahead. Nonetheless, excessive stress upon private consumption might substitute inflation for stable growth. It might lead us to neglect our essential public services, both domestic and international.

Another approach, and now quite a popular one, is that we should expand our public outlays greatly and obtain a large part of the resources required for this purpose by deliberately holding down the rate of expansion of private consumption. While some types of public outlays indeed should be expanded, I think that this approach misjudges the requirements for balanced economic growth.

To illustrate, I have already referred to a deficiency of some $200 billion in our total national production during the past seven years. It seems to me that, in order to have taken up this deficiency in balanced proportions, we should have used about 25% of it for a further expansion of private investment, 60% for further expansion of private consumption and living standards, and 15% for further expansion of public "goods and services" outlays at all levels of government. Incidentally, this higher rate of economic growth would have yielded, *at existing tax rates,* about $65 billion more of public revenues. This would have been enough to cover the additional public outlays for essential purposes. And enough would have been left over to balance the federal budget, instead of running the actual net deficiency of about $19 billion during the 1954–1960 period.

What, then, is the soundest way of increasing economic growth? Where should steps be taken, and who should take them? Looking to the future, it seems to me clear that we cannot absorb the new technology and the new automation through unbalanced development of one or two sectors of the economy. Between early 1960 and the end of 1964, a reasonably high growth rate would yield about $350 billion more in total production than would a 2.5% growth rate. This increase should be judiciously distributed into private investment, into private consumption, and into public goods and services.

This would provide abundant public outlays to do the great things we need to do through public instrumentalities. But it would still leave us in 1964 with a federal budget *much smaller* in ratio to the size of the total economy than it has been in recent years. And the approximately $100 billion in additional public revenues which the high growth rate would yield at existing tax rates would enable us to balance the budget over the years—a virtual impossibility with a low growth rate.

The government can promote balanced economic growth without invading the established areas of private enterprise. Moreover, under conditions short of total war, I do not see any need for new government controls. But I do insist most vigorously that the government must do a more realistic and effective management job in its own sphere than it has thus far been doing.

First of all, if private investment, consumer spending, and public outlays are to develop in balanced proportions, then both business and government must have some common concepts or general goals to indicate what these balanced proportions are. Assuredly, the government must understand its part of the job before it can do that job well. Without clearly expressed concepts and goals, the government's management of its own business will continue to be hit or miss. And it will continue to be guided excessively by inertia or pressure politics, rather than by sound economics.

The Employment Act of 1946 now states that the President should set long-range goals for employment, production, and purchasing power, and adjust the government's policies to them. This sound legislation was enacted on a bipartisan basis. Modern techniques of fact gathering and analysis enable the chief executive, in consultation with private economic leaders, to develop these general perspectives with great benefit to all.

For example, the long-range spending programs of the federal government should be based upon two considerations: (1), a sober appraisal of our productive potentials as a nation, and (2), a realistic judgment as to what part of these potentials should be allocated to those national priorities which the government serves.

This would be a sounder national policy than pushing federal spending suddenly upward when deflation threatens and pushing it suddenly downward when inflation threatens. For that idea borders upon the notion that we should indulge in boondoggling to meet deflation and ignore even the most vital national needs to meet inflation. After all, the fundamental purpose of federal spending is not to iron out the business cycle, but rather to do those things which the nation needs and which nobody else can or will do effectively. We certainly do not have this kind of federal spending policy now. Whether spending is too high or too low, it frequently borders on the irrational.

To help combat inflation and deflation, a more suitable weapon is the national tax policy. Tax policy should be adjusted to an economic-growth course, steering between inflation and deflation. We need to abandon the process of tax making by special interest pressures and substitute tax policy geared to the well-tempered growth of investment and consumption. This applies at all levels of government.

Another example of the need for more enterprise in our thinking is monetary policy. The conventional use of monetary policy to regulate the aggregate money supply has proved to be too blunderbuss a weapon, in terms of the selective adjustments which our economy requires. As it has been used, monetary policy has frequently tended to deter growth rather than to curb inflation. Even while we maintain the established independence of the Federal Reserve System, I believe that we must move much further in the direction of co-ordinating monetary and fiscal policy by gearing both to defined objectives of balanced economic development.

There are many other policies of the federal government which need to be brought within this same framework. For instance:

1. Social security should be expanded, but it is essential to determine in what directions and how much at what time.

2. The minimum-wage question should be subjected to the same type of criteria.

3. Our agricultural problems are not being handled wisely. Yet we cannot achieve a sound national farm policy until we look at the farm economy in terms of the entire economy. As people move off the farms, what jobs are available elsewhere? If the federal taxing power is to be used to supplement farm income in the interest of farmers and the whole economy, what is the best balance that can be obtained?

To conclude, I am convinced that the major stimuli to investment and productivity will come from an over-all economic environment in which private enterprise and government work together toward sustained economic growth. I am confident that no group of reflective businessmen will permit their thinking on this whole subject to be muddied with vague epithets about "central planning" and "too much government."

The role of modern government is inescapably large and complex. We cannot avoid the need to impose upon our public business the mandate of self-discipline, intelligent coordination, and the adjustment of means to ends. This process would immensely enlarge the opportunities for true economy in government. Rational policies of spending and taxation and monetary management, geared to stimulate rather than to retard the private economy, would certainly add hundreds of billions of dollars to the national wealth. The weeding out of duplication and cross-purposes in public programs would certainly save billions of dollars in administrative costs.

Even more significant is the fact that better public management, with the concomitant clearly defined national objectives, will enable us to meet more successfully, under the methods of freedom, the monolithic power of the totalitarian regimes. With a mutually satisfactory and workable relationship between business and government, we can move forward with confidence toward a future of unlimited promise in a more secure world. For this kind of economic progress also ensures the strengthening of our traditional freedoms.

ECONOMIC GROWTH AND THE BUSINESSMAN

Frank Pace, Jr.

IN THIS VOLUME one may find many incisive analyses of the American economic situation and the role the American business manager plays in it. In particular, the emphasis has been on economic growth—what it requires, where it needs to go, how it should be directed. We also have been presented with exciting and new approaches to related issues of our day, such as inflation, unemployment, and the maintenance of national productivity. In order to ensure our national strength, it is clear that the business community must devote itself wholeheartedly to the problem of sustaining economic growth. It is to this question that I would like to address this brief chapter: why the businessman must be deeply concerned with the vast economic, political, and social problems besetting the nation today.

Note: Mr. Pace is Chairman, General Dynamics Corporation.

This is a direct and extemporaneous personal appeal and, as such, differs somewhat from the other contributions to this book. I wish to speak as a businessman to you as businessmen, and the only justification for this personal approach is the urgency of the problems before us and the vital need for business leaders to participate fully in helping to solve them. It is a time to speak out, to appeal directly and dramatically to the men the nation must have in order to grow and survive.

In the twenty-five years since my graduation from law school, I have been a member of the business community as well as the governmental and have come to know both sets of problems from the inside. I can say with certainty that the complexities involved in the day-to-day running of a business are more complicated than they have ever been before. There are not enough hours in the day, and the instances are rare when the businessman goes home unladen with a brief case full of more work to be done. In spite of this, however, there is more work to do, and it involves the frightening question of national survival. True, we must be concerned with the total growth of the business community, but the business of survival must concern us first. Without survival there is no business.

Let me emphasize that I am not here speaking of what a man must do as an individual to share in the social responsibility. Each man knows in himself what he is charged to do. Rather I am addressing these words to businessmen strictly in their function as businessmen. If it is agreed—and I think there can be no serious disagreement—that the business community is, by the very structure of American institutions, intrinsically involved in this nation's survival, then I would like to suggest a few ways in which business leaders might begin to think about fulfilling this broader function.

First, it is important for a man to see beyond himself to his part in the larger complexes: in history and in the society and time in which he happens to live. Arnold Toynbee, in a short essay entitled

"Mankind—The Invincible Mule,"[1] points out that we have now come to an era in which it is much more important than ever before for a man to envision all the "technology" of which he is a part, to move with and fit into the technology and the organization built up around it. In a sense, Toynbee goes on, there is no place today for an Alexander the Great. This does not mean the end of individualism; man will always be an "invincible mule." Yet it has always been important to the question of general survival that a man communicate with his times, that he be in tune with them. Great civilizations have fallen when their leaders stopped feeling the pulse of people, events, and history—when, in fact, the leaders stopped leading.

There is a strange continuity in history. In the beginning years of our country individual men were addressing themselves primarily to gaining a livelihood for themselves and their families. As the country became a nation, Americans became concerned with survival and prosperity as a nation. We had entered into the era of greater solidarity, with continental friends and neighbors to the north, a weaker neighbor to the south, two great oceans for protection, and a superabundance of rich land. We chose the free-enterprise system and brought good into the land. It is to our eternal credit that we turned the good in private enterprise into a way of life, not for the few, but for all, and achieved the highest standard of living ever known.

Yet this comfortable scene has changed; a new sense of nation is required. For before us we see the looming figures of the Soviet Union and Red China. These are societies dedicated to attaining a way of life equal to ours, and dedicated also to our destruction. With the development of the ICBM (thirty minutes from the launching pad in Russia to this country) and the thermonuclear warhead (more potential destruction than all the bombs dropped on Germany

[1] London *Times Literary Supplement,* May 13, 1960.

in the last war), the oceans become small and no longer afford us protection. With the tides of nationalism flooding the world, we are no longer the masters of our fate as we were. We must be in tune with the world, and part of that world would like to destroy us. Time, therefore, gets shorter and survival is the principal issue.

Let me point out here an important consideration in this effort to make the business function part of the function of survival: government, which is already a 52% partner in most of our businesses, is going to become an even greater partner in the future. It would be interesting to know what kind of chart would have been drawn by a businessman in 1920 as to what the degree of government participation in business sectors would be by 1960. I dare say it would have missed the percentage by a wide mark; today's estimated chart for, say, year 2000 would be far more accurate, for we know that government will grow. As the power of the dictatorships in Russia and China pushes against us, we will undoubtedly see increased pressure for greater government participation in the total operation of the nation's economy. It is of no value to weep and say this is unwise and unsound if it is inevitably to happen.

The problem is how this can be done wisely and sensibly. The solution can be provided only by people who have lived by business, who know the nuances of business and what is important and what is unimportant. In the next forty years it lies in the hands of business to see that the partnership that exists with government is a wise one, to see that the best relationship between the two is established and that the best elements are developed to the highest degree.

Only if this is done will we have the base on which great economic growth can be sensibly predicated.

But why, to be more specific, are businessmen particularly suited to meet the problems that are going to rise over the next forty years? If I had to oversimplify the problem of American survival, I think

I would probably say that it depends upon the intelligent and wise marshaling of our resources against the competition of the dictatorships.

The Russians hope to pass us in military power by the middle of this decade. They intend to equal us in productivity by the middle of the seventies, and we know that they hope to bring the whole of Africa and Asia together into a world Communist commonwealth. The Chinese are going through a tremendous industrial revolution, unparalleled in the history of man; their population will number a billion by the year 2000. You entrepreneurs know the competition we face. You know that the dictatorships will marshal resources effectively, marshal hours equally effectively. This is what the businessman is trained for—to know how to meet competition through long-range planning.

He is also trained and paid well for his managerial talents. But you all know as you move up to the top in an organization that the major rewards are no longer monetary. The managerial function is seen as a responsibility; there is a sense of value in the very commitment to leading the two- or three-hundred thousand people who participate in the affairs of economy. Thus businessmen have learned to accept responsibility for its own sake; they have developed the capacity to make decisions on a broad plane; and, inevitably, they have moved toward greater personal involvement in the community of which they are a part.

But businessmen can do more than lead the economy to a full utilization of our resources. They can also, in my judgment, recapture for America a belief in her destiny, an atmosphere of greatness, a sense of hot-war unity and cohesion in a period of intangible cold war.

The business leader is, after all, one of the end products of the American dream, the man who succeeded in the field America set as the basis of success. He is something of an ideal in this country.

If, then, he is capable of broadening his base of interests, if he recognizes this as an integral part of national survival, if he achieves the breadth required to justify himself as the proper end product of the American dream, he will have helped to restore that atmosphere of greatness which has drifted away. He will also have pointed out —especially to the young—that material success alone is insufficient and inadequate in the kind of world in which we live.

Now, when we think back to the early days of the United States, we remember that here was a country of some three million people, less than the population of Los Angeles, with no intercommunication in the sophisticated modern sense of the word. Yet out of this group came Washington, Jefferson, Adams, Hamilton. There had to be a reason for this phenomenon. These men did not just happen. In communities that love and enjoy music, there the great musician arises; in communities that love and enjoy art, there the great artist arises. So, too, in the community that admires and appreciates statesmen, great statesmen will arise. We always tend to think that American history automatically produces a great man who will somehow in the magnificence of his mind generate the solution to all our problems. That simply does not happen.

Thomas Jefferson once said in defense of plagiarism by a great artist: "he reached out in the sense of destiny," and out of that came greatness. So too with our country. There was a reaching out in a sense of destiny and from that came the quality of mind that gave us our governmental functions over the years. If that quality of statesmanship exists, and if the businessman assumes broader leadership responsibilities, then again there can be created in this nation a sense of destiny, a sense that we do and can lead. And out of that will come the leaders who have the capabilities of taking the people where they need to go.

Now, what does it require? Again, I am one of the brief-case-carrying boys, and by the time I get through the requirements of the tremendously complicated business of which I am a part, it is the long end of the evening. But I still say that there are more things we all must do.

We must improve our quest for knowledge. We cannot stop learning because we have stopped school. Businessmen have to do this, for they are basically leaders of America, not only in the business sense but in the broad sense, and therefore must have knowledge not only of business but of many things. Such a pursuit of excellence will have the added virtue of being an example for the whole community.

If these efforts can be made, our destiny is still before us, not behind us. This is no time for the dissenter. This is the time for the believer. Jefferson said hope had to be at the wheel of the craft.

Perhaps these strictures seem too burdensome or impossible for anyone to fulfill in this day and age. But are we to have greatness in this country? If so, then I say that there is not one American citizen, not a single American businessman, who cannot do more than he is doing now. A great nation is great in purpose, as well as in economy, and in spiritual striving, in moral understanding. These aspects of greatness so desperately needed can come only from the will and hearts of the people, and you are their leaders. It is a great responsibility.

ECONOMIC GROWTH FOR WHAT?

Erwin D. Canham

IT IS MOST important for us to define the purposes of economic growth. Undefined, the whole subject takes on a kind of gross, materialistic aspect, generally associated with chambers of commerce and madison avenues. We would seem to seek to pour more riches into our overflowing cornucopia of abundance—it is almost indecently greedy.

The fact of the matter is that we need a larger rate of economic growth for at least four stark and urgent reasons:

1. To meet the vast human needs of the nation: especially to provide jobs for the enormous throng of young people who will begin knocking on the doors of the labor market in the latter years of this decade and thereafter as far as we can see.

2. To compete with totalitarian and to cooperate with free economies in the world, to help protect and preserve freedom, to maintain our status as a great and responsible world power.

Note: Mr. Canham is Editor, *The Christian Science Monitor.*

3. To help in financing and implementing the development of the vast majority of the human race: the part of society where population growth outstrips economic development and where the fact, not of rising expectations, but of new starvation threatens to produce chaos.

4. To provide, by paradox if you please, the kind of society we would like: a society with increment enough to create and support the schools, the cities, the public and private institutions which will help to carry us through our present growing pains of materialism into a genuine, spiritually fulfilled society.

There is nothing exaggerated or lush about our need for economic growth. Like so much else in the modern world, it is surely a matter of survival. And the question is not simply that we need growth, but how we get it.

I believe our gravest internal economic problem in the decade ahead will be that of jobs. We have not yet begun to realize the consequences of population growth. So far, the growth in our people has been largely composed of those who were consuming rather than producing. It has been among the children, too young to go to work, and among the elderly, whose life expectancy has been lengthened. But by 1965 the numbers of producers in relation to the total population will begin to grow. The children who mark the first wave of the birth tide—the children born in and after 1945—will be appearing in the labor market ready to go to work. As the decade advances, we will need to create something like 25,000 brand new jobs every week just to take care of this flow of youthful workers. Also, a substantial number of new jobs must be created to give employment to those put out of work by technological change.

There can be enough jobs for this tide of workers. But they will not be created at our present rate of economic growth. I am sure that the Rockefeller Report is correct when it estimates that we will need a growth rate more than the present 3% annually, perhaps of 4% or 5%.

How will we get such a growth rate? How will we create new jobs at the rate of 25,000 a week and more? Partly by the expansion of industry—for the provision of goods and services. To create new jobs requires capital. And so the private sector of our economy must be able to accumulate capital and must be encouraged to risk it. To create one single new job in industry calls for the investment of something like $15,000. Thus we will need to accumulate capital at a very substantial rate if our economy is to generate the necessary jobs. We will need new annual investment of more than $15 billion to prevent unemployment.

An increased flow of capital will be needed for several other reasons. Much of our industrial plant is obsolete and must be replaced. Factories and equipment badly need modernization to keep up with retooled competitors overseas. Generalizing for industry as a whole, depreciation charges have been inadequate. Costs of replacement are much increased. A mere maintenance of present productive capacity will require much outside financing for many companies. In addition, the new technology—with all its advantages—generally requires new and more expensive tools and equipment. All along the line, the call is for more capital, and capital is generated by incentive—the chance of making a profit and keeping a fair portion of it. The flow of new equity capital must of course be supported by reasonable tax incentives. Galbraith and others are talking largely of taxes which will prevent people from buying what they apparently want in order to spend the money in the public domain. This is all very well, but it does not help in the accumulation of capital in the private domain—and that is where most of the jobs will be created. Merely to tax white (or red) the private sector of the economy in order to support public projects would be to deprive our economy of its most generative and growthful forces.

The accumulation of private capital at such a rate will require tax reform. Rates of taxes on profits and incomes must permit and encourage the saving and risking of capital. Depreciation allowances must be larger. We can safely say that nothing is more concretely urgent in the decade ahead than tax reform.

A question which is not yet fully resolved, it appears to me, is whether the expansion of industry should be financed by the investor or the consumer. Increasingly, the consumer is paying higher prices—and supporting inflation—just so the corporation will be able to store up reserves for expansion. Somehow that does not seem quite right to me. I would rather see the conscious investment of capital by the saver and risker, rather than the compulsory and often unconscious investment by the consumer in the higher prices he is required to pay. Perhaps our tax laws can do something about this.

But expansion only in the private sector of our economy will not give us all the growth we need, nor the goods and services which it may be most valuable for us to have. A great deal of our growth must come in what is called the public sector but which is in fact interrelated with and carried out by the private sector. Thus, for instance, among our great needs are the rebuilding of our cities, the continuation of our highway program, the construction of more schools and hospitals and institutions of many kinds. These elements may seem largely in the public domain, but they are usually built by private contractors, utilizing the basic industrial, professional, and mercantile resources of the nation. They are based not on governmental appropriation of money but on private industrial, constructive, and professional work. They are public in that they serve everyone—they are institutions for the benefit of the people—but they are not essentially socialistic, and they are created through the generative power of the profit motive.

We will need to evolve forms of taxation to service borrowings which will permit a large-scale expansion of the so-called public domain. In terms of consumer goods, many Americans are getting about as much as they need. Probably we do not need many more automobiles than the present rate of production, rising with our increasing population, and there are those who believe automobiles could be designed and built to last for fifteen years instead of five years. We do not need more agricultural productive capacity, at least not in the near future. We do not need more productive capacity in oil, aluminum, textiles, steel, and in various other products for strictly private consumption, except to keep up with population growth and a steadily rising standard of living.

But there are other things which we need very badly and are not getting fast enough. Stand on the highest building in any American city and look about you. You will see not only some shining new examples of growth but an even more impressive array of buildings that will need to be replaced as soon as possible. You will also see the dire necessity of creating more open spaces and of recasting the city to meet the needs of man. The city must not be an ant-hill, but a place where productive working and thinking and living can take place. There is enough work to be done in recreating our cities to provide employment for all who will need jobs in the decade ahead, and to produce a growth rate in our economy sufficient to sustain a rising standard of living.

Much of this work in rebuilding our cities can be accomplished through the impetus of the private-enterprise system in alliance with entirely proper social planning. We need to debunk the word and idea "planning." It need not be socialism, any more than it is socialism for a great corporation to study its market and strive to foresee and provide for its future.

Take another instance of cooperative planning. Real-estate taxation in our great cities must be moderate enough to permit the vigorous inflow of private capital to meet glaring economic needs. A large part of the rebuilding and retooling of our cities must take place in the field of private enterprise. In Boston, to speak only of needs with which I am directly familiar, an easing of real-estate tax burdens would free private capital to build many needed public institutions: a graphic-arts center, a decorating-arts center, and several others. At this very moment, by a happy alliance, Massachusetts Institute of Technology, urban-renewal authorities, and private developers are engaged in a $15 million industrial-research center in Cambridge. It shows how private and public forces can work together, and must work together, utilizing the best growth elements in our communities.

Another case in point is zoning. Just as we have zoned residential neighborhoods, and some industrial and commercial areas as well, so we will have to zone downtowns and entire metropolitan areas in the interest of the good of all. Our present beginnings at planned land use, the creation of open space, and the integration of our communities must simply be made deeper and more thoughtful and responsible.

Rebuilding of cities is only one of our great economic, social, and aesthetic needs. There are vast shortages of skilled personnel in many of our most important professions. We do not have enough engineers, nurses, doctors, and really competent school teachers. The bottleneck begins in the educational system, where we do not pay high enough salaries to attract the best people and, hence, do not educate enough specialists to meet our rapidly expanding needs. Except for engineers and other such scarce specialists, we simply do not pay enough for the people we most urgently require in a well-run society. Even in our society where higher education seems so accessible, no less than 53% of the top fifth of our graduating high school classes do not go to college. Such a waste of talent is unthinkable at a time when trained services are badly lacking in many vital areas.

If we are to have stable growth in our economy, we must have a better balance of economic power. The wise political scientists who devised our frame of government based freedom on balanced power.

They divided power between the federal government and the states and localities, and they split federal power into three balanced parts. They did not curb economic power in the same way, but we have tried to do so since. We have restricted sheer economic power in various ways. Government has acquired vast authority over the economy through widespread regulation, universal taxation, production and distribution controls and stimuli, farm price supports, and so on. The Federal Reserve System regulates the money supply, the control and cost of credit, which is a fundamental economic power. Transportation is rigidly controlled. Oil production, sugar production, rural electricity, federal housing, and of course the vast influence of the defense industry, all guide, channel, promote, and curb the economy. Through corporate income taxes, the government is a partner from 52% upward in the net earnings of all free enterprise in the nation. Some run to 75%, including excise, state, and local sales.

Organized labor is also a powerful controlling force on the economy. No monopoly is so strong today in this sphere as that of the nation-wide unions. No single repository of private economic power is so great as the AFL-CIO. Controls on this kind of economic power are still relatively few, but they will inevitably grow, for uncurbed power cannot exist in a free community without generating countervailing forces. Money and industrial power produced reaction and controls at earlier times, and labor power is beginning to do so now. Unfortunately, in the generally burgeoning economy of the past fifteen years, increasing union power has tended to join with management power to the detriment of the consumer and to the damage of price stability of the nation. The wage-cost push has been one of the mightiest causes of inflation, and it has helped put the nation in severe difficulties as it strives to remain competitive in world trade. There is no need here to do more than mention the fact that we need economic growth in order to help finance the desperately required growth of the lesser-developed parts of the world.

Nor do I need to expand on the need for economic growth in order to retain our place as a world power. The beginning competitive challenge of the Soviet economy is self-evident. The rifle power of state trading, when the Soviet government acquires enough increment to expend more in its world economic program, will be a formidable weapon indeed. And there is the ultimate challenge, of course, of the Communist countries surpassing ours in sheer economic power. Were that day to come, all free societies would stand in peril. Economic power is decisive.

Let me turn now to my last point: the need for economic growth in order to achieve, ultimately, hopefully, a spiritually fulfilled society. Here I know I am in deep water, wading in the tides of paradox. Abundance and affluence can certainly be spiritual handicaps. They are, at least, when the goals of society are materialistic. My point is that we need economic strength in order to make a spiritually better nation and world society. But first, we must re-evaluate our goals. We must decide on the things we want in an acceptable society.

We are at a crucial point in our social evolution. We have achieved a great deal: widespread education, of a sort; universal communication; a high standard of living; abundant possibility of leisure—and so on. And yet a good deal of this apparent fulfillment is turning to ashes in our grasp. People are literate in order to read silly things. We waste a good deal of our leisure. Education has not brought us wisdom. Our society ought to be exuberant, dedicated, fruitful. Instead it is depressed, cynical, profoundly self-critical.

Let us hope that we are in a transitional stage, feeling the growing pains of adolescent fulfillment. Certainly there is a considerable striving to define and refine our goals. We are painfully conscious of the doom of many earlier civilizations which lost purpose and morale. What are the larger goals of our present society, then, and how can they be served by economic growth?

The first purpose, the first need, is obviously to prevent nuclear war. I do not have to belabor the transcendence of this need. We prevent war initially by deterrent power, and to maintain deterrent power requires great economic strength. Our insurance policy is cruelly expensive, in both monetary and social terms.

The second need, closely related, is to prevent the suicidal consequences of war by controlling disarmament. I am convinced that to bring armaments down will require an even greater input of thought, technical skill, planning, and patient negotiation than was required to produce the atomic bomb.

The third purpose, on which no doubt the second depends, is to negotiate the fundamental terms of coexistence. If the free societies of the world, led by the United States, are strong, confident, and healthy, they will be able to negotiate coexistence in which first Moscow and later Peking—though the latter is a problem of different magnitude—can gradually be brought back into the orbit of world society. The few contacts we have had with Soviet people and leaders during the Khrushchev thaw show a yearning to return to world society and to re-establish an open society in the Soviet Union.

I have mentioned Communist China, so perhaps I had better say that I believe the power of our ultimate ideas and the strength and stability of our society are the only factors which will also in the long run modify the regime in Peking. I think there is also a yearning toward universality in the Chinese which will help bring them back into the world order, if we do our part.

And our part, in this as in other respects, is to make our own society sound and strong. Therefore, what we do within the framework of our society becomes of first importance. Our seeming internal goals become our total goals. The basic goal is to turn the dross of a merely comfortable consumer's society into the gold of a commonwealth where the development of individual lives rises higher in the scale of true values. One approach to these challenges, to repeat, is for us to awaken from the dream of false security or mere heedlessness to a grave awareness of the peril in which we all stand. We must rouse from the lethargy of sense-satisfaction and plunge anew into the adventures of the mind and the spirit.

In the face of danger, and with the infinite promise which modern technology makes possible, we should be an enormously alert people. We live in fact in one of the most revolutionary periods in history. But the great revolution is not the Communist revolution; it is the power of the free democratic system to liberate human life. We need to become very much more aware of the spiritual power we have inherited—and which we can and must implement by alert action.

Our nation still has deep goals and principles, even if we do not always live up to them, and they are meaningful and potent in the world. We ourselves need to understand more adequately the spiritual significance of a free society. We need to see that the meaning of human needs in a material way is in fact a spiritual triumph, an illustration of man's dominion over his material environment. It is perhaps the very grandeur of the time in which we live which has overawed and confused man—has seemed to reduce him in stature. The times are grand in every way: danger is greater than ever before; chance of fulfillment of aspirations is greater than ever before. We are reaching out toward the stars as we have never done. Men's minds and hearts—their fancies and dreams—have always soared out toward the stars, and today they lift their bodies toward space. And that epitomizes the nature of our time. We are turning dreams into physical experience. Naturally, it is an upsetting, challenging, confusing time.

Yet we do not need to be confused. To face understandingly the questions that have to be solved is half the problem. We have very powerful elements with which to work. One of the greatest of these forces—and one of the greatest of the dangers—is the advance of physical science and technology. Men have amassed power resources, physical resources in undreamt magnitude, and the power of the atomic nucleus is not yet fully tamed. Men have shrunk the globe already so that they can travel to any corner of it in relatively few hours. Men have learned communications techniques by which one man's voice can be heard in every corner of the globe at once.

These are only very partial references to the things we have learned and implemented in our time. Indeed, in the lifetime of every adult, men have learned more about the physical universe than in all the years of human history before. Best of all, however, we all know today that there is a great deal more to learn.

And, concurrently, we are all poignantly aware that knowledge is not enough. This vast stockpile of information which we have piled up will not save us. The central problem on which men must work is not the relation of man to his physical universe, but the relation of man to man. You have heard this so often that it must have become a cliché. But it is true nevertheless, and it is important to remember that we have made progress in improving relations among men.

In our time, men everywhere have accepted social responsibilities unimaginable a generation ago. Even though the American contribution to the needs of developing nations and peoples elsewhere may not have been as wise, as practical, or as extensive as the situations demanded, the fact that we have given so much would have been inconceivable even in 1940. On the issue of race relations, immense progress has been made in nearly all parts of the world. In the United States, though painfully and ambiguously at times, we have steadily achieved better basic human rights. As with the newly independent nations of the world, this freedom often brings new problems sometimes more acute for a time than the old ones were. But growing pains do imply growth.

American society has moved into a new period of massiveness. We live in a time of mass production, mass communication, mass education, mass distribution. What used to be called the "masses" are now offered opportunities which only the privileged few had a generation or two ago. Yet this vast potential improvement for the many has not brought the millennium some supposed it would. Fulfillment, in short, has left us about where it found us spiritually. The heart of man does not change automatically with the improvement of his standard of living, or even of his education. Sometimes adversity and challenge stir man deeper and lead him higher than comfort and ease.

The problems we face, surely, can be the spiritual equivalent of adversity. There is plenty of work to do. We must not be a satiated generation, or a rudderless generation, or a purposeless generation. Our society, in the fullest and deepest sense, is unfulfilled. It must keep the human race from suicide—that is job enough for any generation. It must also help the vast majority of the human race learn how to create a stable policy and a productive economy for itself, area by area. It must seek with new earnestness the better ways by which men can live together. It must learn to control the magnificent forces that have been seized as if by magic from the very atmosphere around us.

It is a world of fierce, remorseless, exultant change. We are fortunate, for these are great days.

We need economic growth in order to convert the gains we have already made—gains which are still largely materialistic—into protection first and then into progress in the growth of man's deepest spiritual resources.

THE PROBLEMS OF INFLATION AND PRODUCTIVITY IN THE UNITED STATES

Walt W. Rostow

TODAY'S BUSSINESSMEN are not in a complacent mood. Upon this assumption I base this essay, for I believe that American managers are conscious of and concerned with certain problems in our economic life which the cheerful notion of the Sizzling Sixties does not wholly illuminate. Specifically, I sense that there are four major issues on the minds of businessmen, which I would define as follows:

1. Inflation—and particularly the continued upward creep of prices at a time when farm and raw-material prices have been fall-

Note: Mr. Rostow is Professor of Economics, Massachusetts Institute of Technology.

ing and the economy experiencing fairly high levels of unemployment.

2. Unemployment and idle industrial capacity, which recently has taken the form of a somewhat disappointing boom—that is, a boom which has not moved rapidly to full employment. In the mid-1960s we face a situation where it is hard to see precisely which sectors of the economy are likely to achieve the momentum necessary to replace the waning impulses from the automobile industry and from housing construction, which saw us through the 1920s and the first postwar decade as the pillars of prosperity.

3. Foreign competition and our weakened balance of payments. In one field after another, we can observe Western Europe and Japan catching up with the United States in technology at a rate faster than labor costs are rising in those areas.

4. A sluggish rate of American growth which, in recent years, has fallen below our historical 3% average. This sluggishness sets a limit not merely on the increase in American private consumption but also on the resources which can be raised from existing tax schedules to support the nation's military and foreign policy and our tasks of government at home. If, as I happen to believe, our position abroad as well as at home requires an increase in such outlays, the effect on tax receipts of a sluggish rate of growth must be judged a serious matter.

I am aware that a great deal of constructive as well as troubled thought is being given by the business community to these four issues. It is my purpose now to contribute to this dialogue from the perspective of an economic historian and economist.

We must of course begin by establishing certain definitions. I take it that our common objective is an American policy which would solve the problem of inflation while permitting higher levels of employment than at present and a higher rate of growth. We would also undoubtedly agree that the fundamental answer to the problem of our balance-of-payments difficulties, as well as to the requirement of a higher growth rate, lies in an accelerated increase in productivity, which, if achieved, would also ease inflationary pressures.

These are not issues which are much advanced by vague generalizations or by old slogans. Nevertheless, let me say straightaway that what I am trying to present is a possible new approach to this mixture of problems—not a set of dogmatic answers. I would not pretend to have all the answers; but it may be useful to pose my questions in the form of a set of proposals.

First, let us look at inflation. What is the heart of the problem?

To start with, businessmen assume that money wages will tend steadily to rise and hence they believe that they cannot afford to lower prices, as productivity increases, without endangering the profits it is their legal duty to protect. Price competition—the heart of a vital capitalism—has radically decreased in American industry.

Second, labor leaders, assuming that prices will rise, and under heavy competitive pressure among themselves, strain for extreme money-wage bargains—beyond the nation's average increase in productivity—which will guarantee a steady increase in real wages in the face of an inflationary creep of prices.

Third, as a society, we have no agreed norm for wage and price policy. Thus, when the government finally intervenes, as it has done in one after another of the major wage negotiations of recent years, the government brings with it no criterion except to find a bargain which will get the negotiators out of the hotel room and the men back to work. Given the assumptions that businessmen and labor leaders bring to these negotiations, the net effect can only be government sanction of inflationary settlements.

As an economist I am, of course, aware of the supply-and-demand situations that frame the negotiation of particular wage rates and the setting of individual prices; and I am familiar with the general analysis of the level of effective demand in relation to capacity and employment that frames the whole process of wage and price setting.

But I am also stressing that a large component of the specific inflationary pressure we face lies outside these familiar terrains of formal economics. A part of our problem lies in attitudes and institutional arrangements which must be changed if we are to master inflation. And, quite specifically, my proposition is this: by assuming that inflation is the normal condition of our economy, business, labor, and government now act to perpetuate inflation, to the detriment of the national interest.

The object of the proposal I shall outline is to break this vicious circle. I believe it possible to do so by creating a new environment within the economy, but this will require a concerted effort in which government, industry, and labor each play a creative and cooperative role. There are six interrelated moves which I feel would achieve the common objective, with a high degree of flexibility for industry and labor and with minimum administrative intervention by the government.

1. The formulation by the government, after consultation with business, labor, and farm interests, of a statement of national policy which might be incorporated in a congressional resolution or act, along the lines of the Employment Act of 1946. Such a policy should state that the increase in the real wages of labor should approximate the average increase in labor productivity for the economy as a whole over some period which would iron out short-period variations; and that this goal should be achieved in an environment where the price level is stable or falling. The resolution should recognize that flexibility in wage levels among industries and within industries must be permitted as the structure and technology of the economy changes. There must be an agreed definition of an appropriate average labor-productivity index, much as a cost-of-living index was agreed on at an earlier time in our history; provision should be made for the regular publication of productivity data in terms of the agreed definition. The resolution should also provide for the possi-

bility of public surveillance of labor negotiations in terms of this policy and for the possibility of public arbitration (without, however, introducing compulsory arbitration).

2. There must be an initial wage-price treaty covering a limited time period in certain of the key industries. Perhaps automobiles and steel would suffice to set the new pattern in motion. The initial settlement should contain the mutual assurance that, if labor would accept the continuation of existing money-wage contracts, the industries concerned would undertake to pass along in lower prices the productivity increases achieved within the time period of the contract and within the limits required to provide reasonable profits and adequate plow-back capital for expansion and the introduction of new technology. Let me add here that the government, in encouraging such an initial treaty designed to set a new pattern for the economy, must make clear the full six-point framework outlined, for such a treaty is unlikely to be accepted unless confidence is felt about all six points.

3. The Department of Justice should be instructed to survey the economy, in its responsibility under the Sherman Act, with particular attention to price competition. Its job would be to assure that monopolistic arrangements do not prevent the passing along of price decreases initiated by the pattern-setting treaty.

4. The government should take such steps as may be necessary, through fiscal and monetary policy, to bring the level of unemployment back to a tolerable minimum; that is, to a situation approximating the frictional minimum of, say, two million unemployed.

5. Against the background of these moves, the government should undertake to introduce new farm legislation designed to afford equity to the farm population on a basis other than the present price supports. There are various ways in which this might be done. I would favor a system of direct subsidy to those whom we judge to deserve it, combined with arrangements providing transi-

tional support for farmers either to improve their productivity to a point where subsidy is no longer required or to find alternative economic employment. It is at least possible that the farming community would be prepared to accept some such revision in the present legislation if it were not confronted with the paradox of inflation in the industrial sector accompanied by falling farm prices and incomes.

6. The government should initiate a series of moves—in cooperation with industry and labor—designed to encourage an increase in productivity over a wide front. The specific measures I would tentatively suggest to increase productivity will be outlined in the second half of this essay. But it is clear that the possibility of making some such program viable largely hinges on an acceleration of productivity increase, partly passed along through price decreases.

Now stand back from these six measures and observe their purpose. They aim to produce a new environment that would not only provide the nation with a more wholesome internal economic setting—which would reconcile full employment and rapid growth with price stability—but would also have specific advantages for both business and labor.

For business this environment would remove the pressure for excessive money-wage increases which arises from the assumption of labor leaders that costs of living will steadily rise. It would provide a setting of diminished unemployment and of an evenhanded national productivity policy in which pressure could be legitimately exerted to diminish labor featherbedding. It would provide a national framework of price and wage policy which would ease the problem of foreign competition.

For labor the fact that the market process was yielding a part of the increase in real wages, through lower prices, would ease the burden on labor leaders which arises when formal wage negotiation is the only effective avenue for achieving a rise in real wages. It would provide a method for controlling inflation by means other than maintaining a chronic margin of unemployment. And, by relating the real wage level to the average increase in labor productivity, it would provide a legitimate incentive for labor to play an active part in the reduction of featherbedding. But it cannot be said too often that this incentive will not work unless labor is confident that the employment level will be kept high—higher than it has been in recent years.

As I have suggested, the over-all objective should be flexibly defined. There is no need to hold rigidly over a period of time to a standard of fixed money wages and falling prices. The six-point program might yield something like that result; but it might be that the necessary negotiating flexibility would, in fact, result in something closer to a stable price level with slowly rising money wages. What this program is designed to do is to alter sharply the wage-price pattern in the industries which have set the pace and to lift from the economy the heavy burden of built-in inflation.

Now let us consider the problem of productivity, for an accelerated increase in productivity, passed along substantially through the price system, is the key to the success of this approach to our problem.

As one examines the story of economic growth in the past, it is possible to identify for each economy, over each substantial period of time, the sectors whose disproportionately rapid growth made it possible for the economy as a whole to continue to grow. These leading sectors have, historically, been connected with new forms of technology in the relatively early stage of their introduction: modern cotton textiles, the railroads, steel, electricity, chemicals, the automobile, electronics, and so on. The power of these sectors in affecting the over-all rate of growth derived from the fact that they directly and indirectly stimulated productivity in other sectors. They set up new direct demands, such as the railway demand for coal, iron, and engineering products. They also opened up, through what we call external economy effects, wholly new avenues of economic development.

Economic history also tells us that each cyclical expansion was dominated by a group of leading sectors, whose rapid increase provided the effective demand which brought the economy to full employment. But the leading sectors in a boom were not necessarily also leading growth sectors. For example, some booms have been based mainly on a rapid expansion in housing rather than on the rapid diffusion of new branches of technology. Housing, unfortunately, has not been subjected to a major technological revolution with strong secondary effects on productivity. An expansion in housing will certainly increase effective demand and employment, but it will not, in itself, bring about a strong stimulus to productivity.

This distinction between the effect of leading sectors on productivity and their consequences for effective demand becomes of peculiar importance to the United States at the present stage of our history. We are emerging from the process of diffusing throughout our society a new level and pattern of consumption based on the automobile, electric-powered gadgets, and such. While that process of diffusion proceeded, we collected powerful and general productivity benefits in a wide range of industries directly and indirectly connected with the new pattern of consumption: sheet steel, the machine-tool industry, petro-chemicals, plastics, electronics, and so on. As we look around the world, we can see that Western Europe and Japan, as well as Russia and Eastern Europe, are now enjoying or may shortly enjoy the productivity effects which stem from pressing consumption on into the new high ranges which the United States first explored.

As nearly as we can make out, Americans, as they have become richer, have tended to allocate their increase in income to larger families and more services, rather than to manufactured products. The expansion in population and the increased demand for services will help to maintain full employment in the United States. Despite the pace of automation, there is no shortage of over-all effective demand in prospect unless the government creates it by a dour and persistent deflationary policy. On the other hand, a lateral expansion of our facilities to accommodate a larger population and the increased outlays on education, urban reconstruction, travel, health, and so forth, are not likely to induce new technological revolutions with powerful and widespread secondary effects on the nation's productivity level. There are, surely, great increases in productivity in the service industries to be had, but they are unlikely to come about without a purposeful national effort.

In short, we cannot look to the leading sectors in the next wave of business expansion—the leading sectors in effective demand—also to yield automatically the rapid increases in productivity associated with leading growth sectors. Here, as I say, the American position differs radically from that of Western Europe, Japan, and the Soviet Union, where high-income elasticity of demand is still associated more largely with manufacturing sectors and where productivity gains are still easily to be had. Some such distinction in historical phase is now mainly responsible for the embarrassment of the American balance of payments: our competitors can now increasingly match our productivity in fields where we uniquely excelled in the period, say, from 1920 to 1950.

In facing this situation we are not, however, without resource. We all know that we live in a world where science and technology are expanding at an unprecedented rate. Research and development in industry is expanding at something like 10% per annum. Can we not count on these developments to outweigh the consequences of our high-income elasticity of demand for more babies and services?

I believe there is some reason for caution here. In both scale and apparent effectiveness, industrial research and development has been historically concentrated in a relatively few sectors, linked in their very origins to modern science—electricity, chemicals, and aeronautics. These sectors, as well as atomic energy and electronics, will certainly yield general productivity benefits to the economy over the next decade. But the concentration in both scale and quality of research and development in a relatively few fields may not yield us the national result we would like to see. We should beware of global statistics: the general lesson of research and development is that results are proportionate to quality rather than scale. Moreover, a great deal of contemporary research and development is directed to fields of military interest from which the civilian economy benefits only in indirect and uncertain ways.

In my view is is necessary, therefore, to place the issue of productivity high on the national agenda. It might be useful, for example, for task forces of private and public authorities jointly and systematically to examine the productivity potentials—including improved methods of industrial organization—in various major sectors of the American economy. In these enterprises, the President's Science Advisory Committee and the Department of Commerce might play important roles of leadership. Such a joint survey should have three objectives:

1. To see what can be done to maintain our productivity advantage in certain sectors directly related to our export markets. A part of the job is increased attention to productivity.

2. To see whether it might not be in the common interest to allocate increased research-and-development talent of the first order to those older and less glamorous fields where declereration or decline has long since set in, but where very substantial proportions of the nation's resources are still consumed—for example, housing construction, railroads, steel, automobiles, and the service industries. The objective would be to correct the tendency for the new, rapidly expanding fields to absorb a disproportionate percentage of first-class talent.

3. To examine the extent to which entrepreneurship in the vari-

ous sectors is or is not effectively bringing to bear the potentials which already exist for increased productivity; and we might then consider what incentives could be created to bring average levels of productivity closer to best-proved standards.

Let me state bluntly what lies behind these proposals: in my opinion, featherbedding is not confined to labor. Many American industries and firms do a bad or mediocre job of introducing new technology and other productivity-increasing measures into the production process. Further, I would emphasize that the answer lies not merely in new technology but also in improved methods of organization.

Does this mean that the government must radically increase its power to intervene in the production process? I think not. The government's role in the drive for higher productivity should be confined, I believe, to the following measures.

First, the President should dramatize to the nation the productivity problem: its importance in providing a noninflationary basis for the economy; its importance in dealing with balance-of-payments pressure; and its importance in providing us with a growth rate which would permit us to enjoy higher living standards while also providing for the community's protection and for adequate public services.

Second, the government might help organize—and if necessary help finance—certain expensive research-and-development efforts, designed to break major technological bottlenecks in our civilian economy. I have in mind here particularly the fields of housing construction and intrametropolitan-area transport, where we must seek a cheaper way of getting in and out of the suburbs. A limited extension of the methods now used in military research and development might be wholesome, for private industry cannot handle research-and-development costs above a certain level. It should be clear, for example, that our civilian jet aircraft would not exist—at least at the present time—if the government had not met a high proportion of their research-and-development cost.

Third, the Department of Commerce should collect and publish more detailed productivity data on specific industries than are now available and organize sessions with industry and labor to examine these data and their implications for the national interest.

Fourth, the government might envisage certain alterations in tax schedules, designed to encourage increased research and development in industry and the introduction of new productivity measures.

It may seem odd to commend productivity teams to a nation which still leads the world in productivity and which, for so long, has been able to count on high productivity as an almost automatic by-product of its evolution. But we must bear in mind that high productivity is not enough; it is the pace of increase that will help determine how easy or difficult it will be to meet our domestic and international challenges. And we should also bear in mind that the stage of growth which the United States has attained has altered the old tight connection between areas of high-income elasticity of demand and high technological momentum. History appears to have decreed that, in order to remain a front-runner, we shall have to continue to pioneer—in this case to pioneer in engineering productivity increases along a broad front. And in facing this challenge we should not complain. A front-runner's status is never automatically sustained; it must be constantly renewed.

I am aware that any such proposals for dealing consciously and purposefully with our domestic economy immediately raise a serious question: will the effort to come to grips with the problems of inflation and productivity result in political damage to our society which would outweigh the possible economic gain? Will we be encumbering ourselves and reducing our essential freedoms? Let me set down my own conclusions.

As far as inflation is concerned, I am not proposing new interferences in an otherwise free, competitive, capitalist situation. Price and wage policy are now certainly not determined by normal market mechanisms. The net effect of what I propose would widen, not narrow, the role of the free-market process in our economy.

As far as the government's role in the inflation problem is concerned, again what I propose is not governmental intervention in a process where the government is now inactive. The government —and public opinion—has been a key factor in the settlement of most of the great labor disputes which have set the wage pattern of the economy in recent years. What I am suggesting is that government intervention be made—when it is necessary—in the light of a clear, impartial policy, understood by the public and backed by congressional action.

With respect to productivity, I do, indeed, believe the government has a new, limited but essential, role of leadership to play. But I see no reason why that role—and particularly assistance in expensive civil research and development and the encouragement of research and development through tax policy—should do anything but strengthen the private sector of the economy.

And in general I would say this: modern American democracy is based on a mixture of private market activity, corporate responsibility (both industry and labor), self-discipline in the public interest, and government leadership. We are a complicated and interesting community, which works in ways we have not—and perhaps cannot—set down precisely in textbooks. It is clearly in the common interest to solve the inflation problem by some means other than damping the rate of growth. It is clearly in the common interest that we pioneer in the application of modern science and technology to a wider area than in the past.

If we set our hearts and our minds on these objectives, there is no reason why our mature and resilient society cannot achieve the result we want and need while strengthening the system to which we are all attached. Our system is strong—not fragile—but it must endlessly prove itself by solving new problems. The problems of inflation and of increasing productivity over a wide front are just such new problems, and a solution to them is urgent. They will not go away by pretending they are not there; if unresolved, they will continue to weaken our performance at home and abroad. It is time to look at them firmly and, with confidence, mutual trust, and imagination, fashion answers in harmony with the spirit of our democratic capitalist institutions.

INFLATION—HOW MUCH IS NECESSARY FOR GROWTH?

Leon H. Keyserling

WHEN I APPEARED at the Harvard Business School to give the talk on which this chapter is based, I immediately ran into a gentleman who said: "I'm going to disagree with everything you say."

Despite this explosive comment which may have reflected the views of others in the audience, I feel that the degree of agreement

Note: Mr. Keyserling, former Chairman of the Council of Economic Advisers, is a consulting economist and attorney, and President, Conference on Economic Progress. The panel discussion on which this chapter is based was led by Saville R. Davis, Managing Editor, *The Christian Science Monitor*. Other participants were: Alexander T. Daignault, Executive Vice President, W. R. Grace & Company; Charles L. Schultze, Lecturer in Economics, Indiana University; John Post, Director of Industrial and Personnel Relations, Continental Oil Company; and Dan T. Smith, Professor of Finance, Harvard Business School.

with what I had to say was much more substantial than these persons would have thought.

I raise this point because I think it is a matter of grave concern, especially in a time of change and uncertainty. The only reason for the incident to which I have referred lay in the fact that the audience, like most business groups to which I speak, had been very handicapped in its opportunities to learn what I really do think. Aside from some few extraordinary translators of opinion like *The Christian Science Monitor,* our news media draw pictures of some of us who have tried to render a public service which are so extraordinarily devoid of sense and sensibility that it is impossible for the reader to have any idea of what the person in question actually does believe. This is no joking matter in a free democracy, because these journals of opinion are very important. It is dangerous for all of us when they do not acknowledge their high responsibility to bring to the informed, intelligent, and important businessman a true picture rather than a caricature of what others are saying.

I am, however, going to start off with one comment with which I suspect many readers will disagree. I say that when we concentrate on inflation and allegedly low productivity, we are looking at the wrong problems. Because we are looking at the wrong problems, we are not getting the situation in focus and we are not finding the right answers even to these secondary questions, much less to the central issues.

Why don't I feel that inflation is the central problem now, despite all the popular and governmental attention that has been lavished on it recently? First of all, our economy simply is not prone to inflation; its price history actually has been surprisingly stable. We have had great periods of inflation during wars and reconversion, but aside from them the American economy has not traditionally demonstrated this particular kind of weakness.

I made some careful studies of this matter recently and found that if you take out the periods of war and reconversion and also, to be fair, the Great Depression with its declines in prices, there has actually been a small net average annual price inflation in the United States of less than 1% annually. Furthermore, this figure has actually fallen very much lower in the past three or four decades than it did in the previous three or four.

Secondly, there is no absolute connection between inflation and depression, or between inflation and economic stability. Between 1922 and 1929, aside from a collapse of farm prices, we had virtually the most stable price level on record. But we had a stock boom and a tremendous crash. Even at a stable price level, the relationships among the different kinds of incomes, the relationships among the price trends and technological trends and wage payments, did not build that balance of consumption and investment which avoids serious economic distortions and ultimate depression.

Finally, the major weakness in our economy today is the same one from which we have suffered throughout this century, except in wartime: too little consumption. It is not inflation or productivity or prices or wages; it is an inadequate level of demand. Let me spell out what I mean.

In the period since 1953 we have suffered from a rate of economic growth which is too low. We have been deprived of public and private services which could be served with growth. The simplest way to make the point is to note that from 1953 to the present day we have witnessed a chronically rising accumulation of idle plant and manpower, albeit with some ups and downs. Today we are in a boom period. Our employment of both plant and manpower is much higher than it was in 1953. But even so, unemployment of plant and manpower is now tremendously higher than in 1953.

Furthermore, in view of the new technology and of automation, this process is going to continue unless we make some very substantial changes in our economic policy. We are going to accumulate vast and rising unemployment and idle capacity over the years, which will mean lessened ability to meet our private and public priorities. In the early 1930s, some of us felt that our basic problem in the 1920s was that our consumption did not keep up with our advancing technology. At the time this thesis was considered very radical. But a few years ago *Fortune Magazine* ran a two-issue story, based on its own careful studies, declaring that we had the great crash because the buying power of the people, both individually and collectively through their government, was not keeping up with the technology.

Some observers claim that increased productivity in the face of this raging new technology and automation is going to be the key that will solve the ills of our economy. This worries me. Of course I am for increasing productivity further, and I think that it will be increased further. But the primary way to raise productivity in the American economy is through the reasonably full pressure on business enterprises which comes from the knowledge that markets are growing sufficiently to justify new tools, new equipment, new plants. If we have that in reasonably full measuure, we will continue to chalk up a high rate of technological progress.

A famous economist activated the attention of the American people, saying that we are affluent personally and starved in our public needs. He urged that we ought to shift to higher taxation on consumption as the way to direct more resources into public use. I submit that this approach is completely wrong, as one can readily see when he studies the economy in action. What sense is there in talking about cutting down on tail-fins when we have already cut down from more than 8 million in 1955 to 6 million in 1960? We have created hundreds of thousands of unemployed in Michigan, which makes it harder to build the schools we need.

So we come back to the same tremendous problem: how can we bring consumption and distribution into line with advancing productivity? I realize that some economists' theory is that the people may have the income but that they are not spending it. This is simply not true. The great missing market in the United States which we must advance at a tremendous rate if we are to keep up with technology and automation is the one quarter of the American people —some 40 million—who have incomes below the minimum levels for the American standard of living, as set by competent agencies in terms of our technology. Here is the great new frontier in the United States for our economic inventiveness and organizing skill.

All of this does not mean that the problem of inflation is of no significance. It does mean that a great disservice has been done to the understanding and the treatment of the problem by those who have screamed that we live in an age of inflation, and by those who, in their concentration on the problem, have relegated to a secondary or tertiary priority all the things we need to do as a great nation. It does mean that we have misunderstood inflation and looked on price stability as an end instead of a means.

Take the title of this chapter, for instance: how much inflation can we have, or how much are we willing to take, it asks. This assumes, first of all, that more growth means more inflation—a point with which I do not agree. But more important, it implies that inflation or rising prices and growth are comparable, whereas, in fact, the price level is only a means toward achieving certain other ends.

The one great need in our economic system and our national life today is a clear national purpose, a statement of our ends. To achieve such a statement, and to do so not in the totalitarian but in the democratic fashion, we must take the various segments of our economy and material, moral, and spiritual considerations and blend them together into a composite. A discussion that isolates inflation and productivity as such does not do this. It fragments the problem and leaves us no framework within which we can build a set of answers.

What are the purposes of our economy? I believe there are three of them:

> The first is to increase our production per capita. I agree entirely with Mr. Canham's broad definition of growth, as set out in his chapter; I do not mean GNP alone. I mean growth in all of the fields which are related to, and in some ways spring out of, our material performance: public services, private economic progress, living standards, the sense of accomplishment, the conquest of the environment, and so on.
>
> I put growth first because, while its mere existence does not necessarily mean that we will use what we produce wisely, it is the condition precedent to any use of any kind. If you have more, you have more to use wisely; if you do not have it, you can make only difficult decisions that do not meet your national purpose.
>
> I would put meeting the great priorities of our national needs as the second general objective. We might not all define them in the same way. Some might care more for public services such as education than for slum clearance. On the private side, some might care more for improved distribution of income, and others for better incentives.
>
> The third purpose of our economic society is the securing of social justice. I am not going to try to define that term because all the universities in the world have not been able to do it clearly in all the years since they were founded. But we, the American people, know what we mean by social justice in a general way. We know, for example, that there is none when the income of about 40 million farmers goes down constantly while the income of others is constantly going up.

Let me illustrate with the problem of inflation. If somebody says he is against inflation and you ask him why, he may point out that it interferes with social justice because those on fixed incomes get left behind. He may say that it upsets the priorities of our needs, or that it interferes with economic growth because it leads to economic instability. But in making any of these points he is recognizing that prices, wages, profits, taxes, monetary policy, and all of the elements that the segmental economists (those who have become so specialized that they do not look at the economy as a whole) talk about are not the whole issue. Rather, they are merely means to our national ends.

So we cannot understand what we want to do about prices, much less how we are going to do it, unless we hold the basic objectives of the nation clearly before us, unless we describe how our economy has been functioning in terms of these objectives. Then we can look at price or wage or profit trends in a pragmatic way to see whether they served or defeated these purposes.

Such a study, as I have already indicated, will inescapably lead us to the conclusion that our central unsolved problem is consumption. Within this framework, to reach our national goals we must set some specific targets and levels of performance. We must decide:

- What is our productive capacity, and how do we want it to grow?
- What is our labor force, and how do we want it to be fully employed?
- What balance do we want to strike between business investment, government outlays which are necessary to meet the priorities of our national needs, and private consumer spending?

And let us, for once, do the analysis that must precede answering the questions now—not twenty years from now.

My concern is that we be more contemporaneous. It is not going to do us any good in 1980 to know why we were not meeting our public and private needs as we wanted to meet them in the 1960s. By then it will be much too late—as it has always been in the past.

In tackling this popular problem of inflation within the framework of a thoughtful national economic perspective, how do you move? One way of making manifest the program you have defined is through the front door, by price and wage controls. I am against that, except in wartime.

Another way is through the back door: by kidding ourselves into believing that we can tell the labor union to rely on management to fix prices lower and not to ask for wage increases. This is obviously unrealistic, and I see no reason to think that this procedure would follow a pattern in the national interest.

The third way is this. Can we not continue the free process of collective bargaining and management decisions with some improved national perspectives and goals which the government has set forth, these goals not to be accomplished by the government, but merely brought before the American people for their guidance?

I suggest that this is the right way to deal with the problem of inflation.

I suggest that under the Employment Act we can set some over-all perspective goals for production. Indeed, that was agreed upon on a bipartisan basis many years ago.

I suggest that we should urge management and labor and business to sit down together and think and talk and work at what combinations of prices, wages, and profits will lead to an investment and spending pattern and a private-consumption and public-consumption pattern that will be in the best interests of the whole economy. Gradually, then, we can rely on the free forces of an educated people and on an educated functioning of private groups to help bring these goals into reality.

Until we do something like this, until we relate our wage and price thinking and our public policy to the fundamental goals of our society, we are consigning ourselves to battles between the Keyserling School, the Galbraith School, the Harvard Business School School, battles between private enterprise and the people who believe in government partnership. But these battles give us no adequate focus as a nation.

I firmly believe that unless we build the purposes of the nation into our economic thinking, we will not be able to compete with the totalitarian nations over the long sweep of time. It is fallacious to state that in doing this kind of planning we are taking on the cloak of the totalitarians, and therefore losing all that we cherish in our desire to compete with them. Business now determines its company goals and plans the steps necessary to reach them. As a nation, with all we have at stake, can we do less?

This is half way between what we are doing now and what is done in wartime. And I say that our greatest tragedy as a nation is that we are in a period half way between war and peace without recognizing it.

DISCUSSION

Dan T. Smith: Despite Mr. Keyserling's comments, potentially we do have a very serious inflation problem. The circumstances that have developed in the past few decades have certainly changed the context of our economy and the forces that bear upon the pattern of prices.

There has been an overemphasis upon the role of the federal budget in determining inflation in this country. Certainly the type of run-away inflations which took place in Europe after both wars and is taking place in some of the countries now could be called budgetary in nature. But we in this country should not assume that a budget balance will determine whether or not we will have an inflationary condition. We have a new force operating here which will be far more significant in deciding the matter: the expectations, attitudes, and powers of labor and business groups.

Unless there is a change in these attitudes as they exist at present, unless there is a redistribution of the balance of power, we may have a sequence extending over the decades of an appreciable amount of continuing inflation.

As to whether or not inflation would be serious, I am not one of those who believes in taking a 1%, 2%, or 3% increase, compounded year after year, in stride. I think this is a serious threat and one which should give us real concern.

I do not think that the forces we have operating now will necessarily turn into a *run-away* inflation. But even if we do not have such an uncontrolled explosion, there are important implications to any amount of inflation, in terms of our balance-of-payments problem which is just beginning to trouble us, and in terms of Treasury debt management.

As far as Mr. Keyserling's proposal is concerned, talking to it is rather like the proverbial situation of being for good and against sin. As far as I could make out, there was nothing specific in it. Surely there should be something of a general concept of where we are going and then we should proceed to get there—but the point is, what specifically do you do to accomplish this aim?

It seems to me important that we recognize that our society has reached the stage where we have a good many consumer goods and that this means there are inevitably going to be differences as to what we want. In some years, it is going to be housing; in others, clothing; in others, automobiles. Whether we like it or not, there are going to be shifts and changes in consumption patterns. There lies one of the benefits and one of the misfortunes of a reasonably free economic system. It means that there will be some structural changes, adjustments, and resulting dislocations within industry, because you cannot convert an assembly line for automobiles into an assembly line for clothing.

My second point is that there has been a substantial emphasis in this book and, in fact, through the nation upon the importance of magnitudes of growth. Mr. Canham, in his chapter, did a fine job of putting the topic in perspective by equating the material with the spiritual. I want to emphasize that strongly, and I want to emphasize it, also, in the public sector of the economy.

We may have self-defeating and destructive effects on our economy when too much of the wrong sort of activity goes on in the public sector. There is as much room for the frills on the schools as the proverbial tail-fins on automobiles. The problem in the schools today indicates clearly that our standards of education are not related to the amount of money spent; in fact, the limitless purchases that have been made in some aspects may well have actually slowed down the needed change of getting the emphasis placed upon quality.

This leads me to the question of the extent of production we should have at any given time. Some people feel that we should have all-out activity, under all circumstances. To do what must be done to accomplish this end may well be self-defeating. If we are inevitably going to have some fluctuations and changes in our kind of economy, and if we can damage our economy and our society by ill-considered spending in the public as well as the private sector, we have to beware of hitting the panic button when we run into a little turbulence. If we seize upon monetary and fiscal policies as the device with which to produce improvement every time there is a sloughing off of activity, we are going to be pumping more and more purchasing power and spending into the economy. That process, in turn, will lead to quite unnecessary and undesirable results over the years.

I agree with Mr. Keyserling that the important thing for us to do is to look at the basic issues and problems. To me, this means learning to live with an economic system that has some inevitable fluctuation in it because of shifts of consumption and other economic factors. Within that context, we can consider possible ways to limit the changes in the levels of activity, and ways of alleviating the very real human distress that arises in the short range because of these fluctuations. Monetary-fiscal policies are not alone the answer to these temporary ills.

Alexander T. Daignault: I agree with what Professor Smith has said about the balance-of-payments problem. Our company is ever more aware in Latin America of the competition; we see it not only in the fact that we handle many exports from this country, but also in that we carry many of the exports of other manufacturers on the Grace Line. The trend away from looking to the United States for supplies is a decided one. Even though these countries still prefer the goods of American manufacturers, they are beginning to turn to lower European and Japanese prices.

Another problem of inflation—perhaps minor, but still important to many of us—is this: if we had a compounded inflation at the rate of 2% or 3%, it would give us a serious problem in providing standards of measurement for the performance of business. You get to the point where your profit-and-loss statements become almost meaningless unless you subject them to adjustments, which are always highly questionable. So you find that much of the incentive of good management is lost, and much of the safety of the position that you are able to build for the future is hidden. Suddenly you find yourself in a very unhappy spot, long before any of your controls warned you of the trouble ahead.

Charles L. Schultze: Given the institutions in the economy, if you run an economy at full employment you are going to get some inflation. The real question is how to choose the appropriate combination from among several objectives. Can we have stable prices, reasonably full employment, and good growth rate simultaneously?

I do not think we can. In any dynamic economy some prices and wages are always going to rise; on the other hand, they seldom fall. Our price and wage system is slightly biased toward inflation. This inflationary activity works its way through the economy. With the normal, full use of our resources, we are going to be subject to some inflation, although not of a very alarming variety.

In this connection I think you will probably find that the nineteenth century was the one century in which prices generally fell. One of the major reasons that this no longer happens is not so much that business is different now, but rather that a tremendous proportion of our production was taken up by agriculture and primary raw materials in those days; and prices of such commodities tend to be rather flexible. If you have an economy in which the heart of the cost of living is farm prices, other prices will be sympathetic. But when the basic goods are steel and automobiles and services, it is much more difficult to have a flexible price system.

Incidentally, I should point out that we do not yet know exactly how much inflation we have had. There is something called the cost-of-living index, which includes over 300 commodities, weighted in a fairly complicated manner. Further, there are a number of imputations in the index; I would hate to make it a goal of national policy to keep that statistical complex absolutely steady. It would not bother me if such an index went up 1% or 2% a year on the average. The real danger is that a lot of people are overly bothered about a small jump in the index; the real tragedy is that we are trying desperately to stabilize this index. In so doing we may sacrifice many other goals which I feel are worthwhile, such as the full use of our resources.

Let me comment briefly on this matter of planning. In the first place, we have to distinguish between planning per se and the objectives of planning. Any government has to plan; any government the size of ours, spending $80 billion annually, has to do some thinking ahead, and there is no question about that. We have to plan expenditures and take into account the relationship between expenditures and taxes. So the only question is: are we doing this job as skillfully and effectively as it could be done?

Let us be sensible about this matter. I am for more and better government planning, but I always keep in mind a letter that John Keynes wrote to Friedrich von Hayek. Hayek had written a criticism of Keynes's *General Theory*. Keynes, in reply, said something like this: "You and I disagree on the amount of planning that should be done. I respect your disagreement. What I would like to have, if my plans were put into effect, is people like you to run the thing."

In other words, planning is fine, but let us put a whole shaker-full of salt on it and keep it flexible because we do not and cannot know precisely the effect of our actions. We are fallible human beings, dealing with exceedingly complicated problems. But this fact should not keep us from doing our best to plan well (whether as conservatives or liberals), just as a businessman must do in running his company.

John Post: I feel much more relaxed about the inflation problem than I did five years ago, simply because we have really done something about it. And I think that we moved against it over the protest of people like Mr. Keyserling. The reason the job got done is because we did not fall for the kind of smooth talk we find in Mr. Keyserling's section of this chapter.

Let me be explicit. I remember very vividly the price increase in wholesale industrial commodities, beginning in 1954 or 1955. It was quite evident that this was being offset by a decline in agricultural prices, so it looked as though we had a stable price level. It was at that time that businessmen began to realize that they were going to be pricing themselves out of the market. The government became concerned about it, too, as it recognized that these changes and increasing prices would work themselves through the economy. That is just what happened when we had an increase in the consumer price level two years later.

The point is that it takes four or five years to get the job done. If we relax today and say, "Oh, inflation is no problem," then next year when Walter Reuther comes back, he will say "You fellows are creating a phony issue" and people like Keyserling will tell us to go ahead and grant a big wage increase which we cannot absorb. Then, a few years later, the situation will catch up with us.

So inflation is not as serious as it was five years ago, and I am glad that we can turn our attention to something more fundamental. But let us not make that "something" growth under "planning." Some people are all too tempted to think that all we have to do is plan everything nicely and it will come out the way we want it to. My experience with people in government, as well as those in business, is that they are not immune from mistakes; they just cannot plan that well.

Furthermore, in this country we have constantly moving targets. People are simply not going to be satisfied long with whatever you work out as a plan. We live in a society of group pressures, and they are constantly going to be pushing us into compromises and changes as desires and interests shift.

I think the answer does not lie in some mythical "plan," but in letting the economy run itself, accommodating to the shifts and changes in a natural way. If we let business take more initiative, this is what will happen. Businessmen have shown they can do more here and abroad if they are not shackled, if they are permitted to act according to their best economic judgment rather than being subjected to some over-all plan.

Keyserling: A serious-minded American people should put the inflationary problem in its proper perspective—not ignore it. If you measure national achievements solely by price trends, some earlier periods were better than our era in some aspects. But if you measure the two by economic growth, human welfare, and social justice, we all know that we have done an immensely better job since the Great Depression than we did before. And we all know that the Great Depression, which hurt us all more than anything else in history aside from war, hurt us during a period when prices were falling rapidly and when the dollar was worth more and more.

The period from 1955 to 1957 gives us a vivid illustration of how the efforts to stop inflation were made at the expense of growth, national security, and domestic social needs. We ended up with more price inflation than we had had in preceding years (other than war time) when we were meeting our needs more fully. We have had an inflation produced by an economy that was going too slowly rather than too fast. We have had administered price and wage systems. We have had an effort to compensate for deficient volume by raising the prices and the wages per unit of output of goods faster than if there had been a higher level of output.

Without the establishment by the government of some basic perspectives for investment and consumption, you have a situation akin to a business that creates its own money supply, through some system of prices rather than taxes, and creates its own production schedule, and then says: "We are going to keep our money policy entirely independent from our fiscal policy. We are going to run the money problem and production policy in separate rooms."

I would not have government regulate the rate of private investment, but government should have a concept of fundamental economic objectives before deciding on a tax policy.

I would not have government regulate prices and wages, but I would have the government expand the social-security system more rapidly when we need more consumption.

ADDITIONAL COMMENTS: MANAGING AMERICA'S ECONOMIC GROWTH

Erwin D. Canham, Leon H. Keyserling, and Walt W. Rostow

GOVERNMENT LEADERSHIP*

IN MY EARLIER remarks in this volume, I dealt with two major problems our economy must face: inflation and productivity. These are not problems simply of business or of government—they are issues a whole nation must consider, because they have emerged from the nature of modern American society; and the way we handle them will affect our total performance, at home and abroad.

The United States is now entering a new pioneering era. We were the first society to achieve what I call the age of high mass consumption, that is, the age of the mass automobile, suburbia, and durable

* By Mr. Rostow.

consumer goods. We are now in the midst of a transition to something beyond. The transition is colored by the fact that it is taking place in a cold war which absorbs about 10% of our gross national product and a much higher proportion of our research and managerial talent; but the transition itself is there, cold war or no, and it has created a whole set of novel problems. Karl Marx, who first posed the question of the affluent society, did not define the range of difficulties and opportunities we face, as we move beyond the age of scarcity. This nineteenth-century romantic believed that, as scarcity became one of society's lesser concerns, the better elements in human nature would express themselves and all economic problems would be solved.

But in this country, where Marx's dreamed-of state has begun—at the margin—to come to pass, we are confronted not merely with the satisfactions of high income but also with balance-of-payments pressures, a rapidly growing population, rising rates of juvenile delinquency, an increasing work force with not enough jobs in sight, and a high incidence of mental illness. And all these phenomena relate, in one fashion or another, to the fairly secure high incomes we enjoy. Moreover, the state is not withering away; rather, it is needed more than ever to balance and to organize the groups, countergroups, cross-pressures, and cross-purposes which are so much a part of America today—and should be in every complex, mature free society.

So there are many new things for us to do and great problems for us to solve. No one basically disagrees over the nature of these tasks that face us, but we do disagree over who will carry out the work, and how. Here is where the debate comes in, and this book centers around one aspect of it. "Managing America's economic growth"—who and how?

Any set of proposals advanced today to meet our economic problems must be loyal to the most fundamental commitment that underlies our society: namely, that it solve whatever problems confront it by the techniques of consent and freedom. In my view, there is no doubt that the federal government must take a large role in the next decade, in many directions which include setting the guidelines for wage and price policy. But I do not believe this need involve greater government intervention, especially in the way most of us may think of it. If the market and the price system were put to work more competitively, the direct weight of government in economic affairs might, in fact, be reduced rather than increased. We should not deceive ourselves that we now operated a free competitive wage and price system without government intervention.

Take the last steel strike, for example. In that major upheaval, industry and labor were tied up in a situation in which power was the only effective criterion: power on each side combined with what each guessed the government would or would not do and what direction in which each guessed public opinion would swing. A situation like this is extremely threatening in a democracy. In the end, the government intervened with what was inevitably an opportunistic formula: lacking a clear national wage and price policy, the government could only seek a formula that would get the men back to work.

Of course there is no one ideal government action in any situation, emergency or not; but in my opinion our democracy must take counsel through its political institutions and decide what principles should guide wage and price policy. We need a norm which only the federal government and Congress can supply, around which our competitive system should work.

If rough but explicit norms were laid down by law and if the price system could be used more fully as a means of creating an annual increase in real wages—and this is what should happen under a healthy capitalist system—we would be freer to let fiscal and monetary policy relax its restraints on full employment and growth. We could concentrate on the problem of increasing productivity and provide all sectors, public and private, with a greater margin of resources. My proposal would use regular market procedures more than they are now being used—it involves *different* methods for setting wages and prices but not *more* government intervention.

The heart of my proposal to reverse the current built-in inflationary pattern is an initial commitment by labor and management in the steel and automobile industries—which have set the pace in wage and price policy—to hold money wages and lower prices in accordance with productivity increases. As I emphasize, this limited treaty would not suffice. Labor, management, and the public would have to be assured that this pattern would be extended across the board and not confined to these two industries. But translated across the board, the real wages of the automobile and steel workers would experience the same kind of rise they have regularly been given in good years—perhaps more, since this method of dealing with price policy would permit the government to relax fiscal and monetary policy and achieve higher levels of employment.

Such a proposal is not designed to shift the relative shares of income between capital and labor. If there is any alteration in the balance, it will arise from the downward trend of prices and the higher levels of employment and output the proposal would permit. A shift of this kind might occur, however. Historically, when prices fall, the relative shares of labor are improved, and tax policy might be used to equalize the trend—notably, tax adjustments designed to increase industrial productivity. But there is nothing in this scheme that defines or aims to achieve a deliberate shift. In fact, the new pattern simply would not work if labor and capital did not feel that each was getting its fair share from the very beginning.

ECONOMIC NORMS*

Wage-price policy is of high priority in the whole problem of promoting economic growth. What we lack now is what I should like

* By Mr. Keyserling.

to term a basic, national sense of wage-price policy. The government alone cannot create such a sense, but I do believe enough in our system of enterprise to feel that, under the government's leadership, we can gradually attain an improved understanding of the whole problem of growth. The government should help to define and readjust the general concept before there is an emergency—a situation which, as we have seen so often, generates nothing but heat and a comparable emergency decision by the government. As Mr. Rostow has stated so well, we need a positive underlying attitude, which is vastly more preferable to wage and price controls and to intervention after a particular crisis.

There is one aspect which I would like to discuss in more detail. We have always relied for the division of income between wages and prices, or between consumption and investment, upon the competitive pull between strong unions and strong management. But to depend on this kind of competition alone today leads us only to stalemate. In the kind of world we have now, with its new and more complex problems, it seems that we must have a government that moves halfway between direct controls and doing nothing. If the government is to take the desirable middle position between the two extremes, it must provide some general values, some general standards to guide the member groups of the economy, at the same time leaving the groups considerable freedom to act within the standards.

Let us look at Mr. Rostow's interesting suggestion that, according to a devised national formula stamped with public approval, labor would agree to stabilize its wages, at least for a while. Industry would still have the responsibility of reducing its prices. Faced with the beneficial consequences of a stable wage policy, how would a major corporation like General Motors, say, decide to reduce prices? How much it reduces prices determines how much profit will remain. So the first question is how the proper level of profit can be determined. The corporation has a general concept of how much profit it needs for capital promotion, but it needs more than this: it ought to have a general concept for industry as a whole to guide it. It does not seem unreasonable to ask government to provide industry with the necessary norms for determining the appropriate balance between wages and prices and, through this, fair profit levels. The government can best outline what is reasonable in the over-all picture and what the economy needs.

The point might be raised as to whether the United States could have done as well as it has over the last forty years if the government had decided such norms in 1920. I would say that from 1940 to 1960 we had a higher degree of planning, safeguards, intervention—call it what you will—than we had from 1920 to 1940, and I think it worked better. This does not mean that we should go all the way to a socialistic system; nor does it mean that we have the right balance now. There is much room for improvement and, quite frankly, in view of the present world situation, I feel the improvements we have to make are in the direction of more coordination on a nation-wide basis. We are too loose-jointed—we must be able to compete better in the world arena.

What I would like to see done is this: some general national goals set before us, printed up in the President's economic report, in words to this effect: "This is what we regard as a reasonable tolerance of national unemployment. Here is what we consider an adequate rate of growth for the next such-and-such months. With the consensus of the people expressed through congressional discussion and action, this is what the government thinks should be taken out of the economy for national priorities and needs. This is what we will invest...."

Concomitantly with such measures, the government must improve on its own procedures. Tax policy, for instance, should be guided by the kind of broad perspective sketched above. If the perspective guidelines show that we are tending toward too low a level of business investment, then some kind of tax adjustment would be valid. If, on the other hand, investment was shown to be too far under consumption, then some other kind of tax policy should be advanced. Similarly with social-security policy: if we found that the nation was suffering from a serious deficiency in consumption, we would expand the social-security system more rapidly than we would in a situation where we might have to hold down consumption to get a higher business-investment level.

At any rate, the government must decide every year how it is going to manage the tax system. The present methods seem haphazard: action and policy determination through inertia, hysteria, and pressure. What I am calling for is the injection of business-management principles into government. Government should not have the power to say, "this industry cannot make a profit above x dollars, or there can be no wage increase above 10%." But through economic study, education, and guidance it can gradually bring management and labor to improve wage and price policy according to the long-range perspective.

Why do we need this new kind of management in an economy based on price competition? Simply because, even with a stabilized wage level, industry would not automatically reduce prices. Even if it did, the economically workable relation between wages and prices would be unbalanced again in the future if labor decided to bargain for more. There has to be a stronger basis for rational price reduction, and there is no sense merely in saying that the public will determine this. There is certainly no public determination now.

Let us look at the facts. The basic industries have raised prices beyond the extent that wages required them to be raised. There is not much price competition among these industries; prices are often a great deal higher than they need to be—the break-even point is fantastically out of line with the American concept of price-setting policy. How to get price competition among the battling giants in steel and automobiles is a difficult unsolved problem. Who can guarantee that, again assuming a stabilized wage level, General

Motors, Ford, and Chrysler would not all simply reduce prices by the same amount? This does not provide the necessary price competition.

I am emphasizing prices in this discussion because I feel they are more of a problem than inflation (which is on everyone's minds these days). To say that inflation is the main issue implies that a stable price level automatically solves the price problem. It does not. In the twenties we had a stable price level but also a rising technology. We did not distribute the fruits of that rising technology to the consumer through lowering the price level or sufficiently increasing wages and other forms of income.

Secondly, I think our confusion about inflation results from the use of an incorrect analogy. During World War II we had a 9% average annual growth rate, a tremendous pressure on our resources, a budget that rose 50% each year, a 16% annual increase in the money supply, and a deficit of $60 billion a year. From all these factors in combination we reasoned that the economy was moving too fast. The truth of the matter is that war is inflationary and the things we did were inflationary. But it is not necessarily anti-inflationary to have a smaller money supply, budget surpluses, smaller expenditures, and a lower rate of growth. This becomes a fallacy once you reach the point where you are going too slow. If a car is going seventy miles an hour, you slow it down to burn less gas per mile. But if it is going thirty miles an hour, you do not.

These suggestions for government initiative are not based on negative reasoning, on the idea that our economy is not working as it should because there is no effective price competition within industry or because there is too much power concentrated in labor. I am not against bigness and have never been much taken with the traditional "antimonopoly approach." I may be wrong, but I have never felt it necessary to have legislation insisting that no company may have more than 30% of the market or to have legislation to fragmentize corporations. Some of these suits have resulted in nothing more than mumbo-jumbo.

Nor do I consider big labor a major problem. My firm belief is that both big labor and big management create the possibility for more stability, more growth, more human progress, and more application to the nongovernmental sphere of the kind of coordinating policy which seems to be essential in a modern economy. And what does the question of whether labor or industry has gained too much power actually mean? If our definition of "too much" is that one group or another has captured too large a share of the national income in relation to the well-being of the total economy, I do not see any conclusive evidence that one side has become stronger than the other.

We need a positive program which recognizes the facts of bigness. It is not a question of balancing one group against another, one sector against another, but one of combining forces in an effort to take our total economy to the top.

THE BALANCED SOCIETY*

To take up a major theme repeated throughout this chapter, I would like to say a few words about this concept of a balanced society. Is our aim largely to contain the vast forces at work today—is this why we believe in fragmentizing power, to use Mr. Keyserling's admirable phrase? Or are we content with the notion that big business has its proper rival in the form of big labor, or vice versa? If we cannot break up power blocs, we seem to be saying, at least one will serve to counterbalance the other.

My own feeling is that we must seek a more positive kind of internal balance in society instead of trying to set up a vast monolithic structure that will break the minute it gets kicked because it hangs together so precariously. Nor should we wantonly attempt to smash large concentrations of power. The only way to develop a truly well-balanced body is to see that all its component members are each well-balanced in themselves.

* By Mr. Canham.

There are many aspects to this problem, but certainly one of the most important involves the prevention of abuses to the freedoms of people. We do need some legislation in this area, but we should first start at the roots. Democratization is a good solution. Much has been done to democratize the exercise of power within the corporation, but business itself should seek to do more for itself. A great deal needs to be done toward democratizing power within the union structure. The rank-and-file union members must have the same opportunity of exercising their rule as do stockholders in a corporation.

I think we clearly need to enact more legislation to prevent abuses in union power. Personally, for example, I am against compulsory union membership, though I do believe the practice may well fall out of existence as the unions mature even without legislation. Compulsion in any form is, quite simply, wrong, and I would hope that some day the right to work—not in the legislative sense, but in a real and fundamental sense—will prevail. This is one way in which certain misuses of power will be curtailed. But no one should misunderstand me: there should and must be organization in American life. This is a vast nation of increasing population and ever more complex problems. People must work together on a voluntary basis to build up the required balance; only through this kind of collective action can we have an orderly and fruitful society. Elsewhere I have called this free collectivism, and it is a powerful weapon against Marxist collectivism. There are possibilities for collective organization on the part of employers, just as there are for unions of workers, with certain legitimate legislative safeguards and perhaps under the administrative guidance of the Department of Justice. This is one way in which business can set up its own safeguards, one way of achieving a healthy balance of power which is at once workable and dynamic.

Let me add one word of caution about what has been said on coordination, and, for that matter, on the government's role in achieving the balance of which I speak. It is all well and good for the government to state national goals, but we must not go from the statement of goals to the imposition of controls. Our economy can never work in total freedom—the market itself imposes certain limits. By the same token, it is generally recognized that the government must play a role in coordinating various economic activities. But there must be a reasoned balance in this sphere also.

This nation is particularly fortunate in being so constituted that it can achieve this desirable state of balance. There is a natural moderation within our institutions as well as between them. For instance, take voting behavior. Members of labor unions are not different from members of any other group—they do not vote on a monolithic basis, or for a single set of reasons, or for reasons of pure economic self-interest. They divide widely. The voting behavior of the members of Congress on the Landrum-Griffin Bill is a good illustration. Many unions made campaign contributions to legislators who, responding to other pressures and convictions, voted for the bill.

The workings of our political system seem always to produce that historic consensus which responds to the needs of the nation. With this in mind, we can look forward to a balanced and secure society, functioning smoothly, progressively, and democratically.

DISCUSSION

Question: Earlier, Mr. Keyserling, you took exception to J. K. Galbraith's theory of shifting expenditures from the private to the public sector of our economy. How would you increase consumption, particularly with relation to the private sector?

Keyserling: My objection to Professor Galbraith's theory centers on my belief that the contrast between private opulence and public poverty is fundamentally incorrect. Both sectors need improvement, not just one—they are much too interrelated for separate treatment. Is raising the salary of a public-school teacher more urgent than trying to remedy the situation of a manual laborer who has to support a family of four on one dollar an hour?

We do not need to shift our resources so much as to reactivate our unused resources by reducing unemployment of plant and manpower. I do not think we should set aside tax increases if we need them, but I do not think it follows that we ought to increase tax rates in a slack economy. This is equivalent to increasing the tax rate to get a spurious balance of the budget; it seems to create the impression that there is something heroic about paying the bills. You really pay the bills of a nation by application of manpower, brains, and resources. The only time you need to pay the bills by taxation is when, during reasonably full employment, taxes are falling so short that you have a classic inflationary period. If the economy grows as it should, you have a budget surplus. If it does not grow as it should, then you have increased unemployment and, hence, still more taxes on private consumption.

Question: I have a question on the European Common Market. To what do you give credit for their extraordinarily rapid rate of growth?

Rostow: I do not think it should be attributed to government controls or planning. Between the two world wars, the United States emerged into the age of automobiles, sheet steel, petrochemicals, and durable consumer goods. For a variety of reasons, Western Europe did not. A good part of our relative advantage in major export industries stemmed from the playback effect of our high consumptive levels on our industrial structure.

In the thirties Western Europe began to catch up relatively in automobiles and durable consumer goods; but there was a rearmament boom. In the fifties, finally, Europe began to go through its own version of our expansive twenties. What you see now is a repetition of our patterns of consumption, and a new virtuosity in sectors where we formerly led. They are catching up on our historical, technical, and productivity advantages.

Thus, to my way of thinking, the European expansion of the fifties is similar to the American expansion of the twenties. It is the breaking out into the age of high mass consumption which had sustained the momentum of the Western European economy.

All of this serves to underscore the question, where do we in the United States go from here? Europe has just started this adventure of giving everyone a car, a single-family house, and all the accompanying gadgets. But we are almost at the end of the production road. The automobile industry will remain big and so will housing. But our economy can no longer get its lift from the automobile and private construction industries. We are learning in this generation what it means to have the leading sectors fade; and, at this point, we need some fresh thought about the future of American growth.

Part Two

MANAGEMENT PROBLEMS IN AN EXPANDING ECONOMY

WHO WILL MANAGE OUR ECONOMIC GROWTH?

Kenneth R. Andrews

THE ECONOMIC growth about which this book talks requires managers, and ever better ones, to handle the mounting problems effectively and creatively. So one of the key questions in the management of our economic growth is how business can develop better managers.

Just as the nation is beginning to realize the importance of well-defined purposes, so are the businesses of the nation gradually coming to the idea that a company's own objectives must be more clearly formulated. This, in turn, throws new light on the relatively recent area of management development, which dates back only some ten years or so. For the growing emphasis on concrete definition of a

Note: Mr. Andrews is Professor of Business Administration, Harvard Business School. He led the discussion on which this chapter is based.

company's objectives has come about largely through the company's desire to produce better managers: in the framework of a business, a man can develop his own personal objectives as a manager only if he grasps the company's aims, if he learns the potentialities and limitations of effective operation within the organization. A man functions better if he knows where he's going; a businessman functions better if he knows where his company is going. And this is especially true in a world that is changing.

What seems to be happening in this area of executive development is that companies are devoting far less attention to the mechanics and apparatus of development, the appraisal forms, the in-company educational courses, and the dispatching of long lines of people to advanced-management programs in universities. After ten years of all these fashionable things, the fad seems to be maturing. More and more, companies are returning to the actual functioning of the business itself as the means by which development is accomplished—not through the work of schools, consultants, seminars, or similar off-the-job activities. This is no simple return to a purer past, however. For, as soon as you get into the work of the business, you have to define what the work of the business is. And this requires new steps and approaches.

Let me speak of one company's action to improve its managerial skills. Rather than first poring over its personnel lists to decide how many people to send away to school or how many different kinds of technical in-company courses it might inaugurate, this company's officials decided it would be more helpful to set forth company improvement goals. They decided that more competent performance was the goal, not preparing people for promotion. Because of this, it was clear that top management needed development as much as anybody else. The new goals had to be presented to all managers. Hence a discussion group was set up in which managers considered questions like these: Just what kind of company ought we to be?

How did we get where we are today? What are the opportunities for expansion of market and product line? How much money will it take to establish ourselves, if we wish to, in other markets? What size organization will we need? In other words, planning for the future involved establishment of objectives, and this became the subject matter of training. This, I feel, is a wise and healthy kind of thinking.

First, in terms of the organization, such measures are profitable. It is important for a company to know where it is going or where it hopes to go. This is not a frozen commitment to one course of action, but rather a guide to logical action (objectives can, of course, change).

Second, in terms of the individual, if executive development is self-development, a man has some jurisdiction over his own improvement. He will become able to know whether or not it is possible for him to develop in the way the company wants him to; he will define his own opportunity, needs, and wishes.

This, then, is what the promising new trend amounts to: a verbalization of both corporate and personal objectives within the company. It is certainly not too much to hope that many management-development headaches of the past will cure themselves under this new approach. If a man finds himself in accord with the company objectives, can see himself fitting happily into the scheme, knows his chances and opportunities for personal growth, then the company goal will be one toward which he too will move. And when a man has a definite goal, he will somehow prepare himself to progress toward it. To oversimplify the case, a manager will be his own best developer.

Let us turn now to more specific ways of implementing such a management-development program. First, what is involved in a company's effort to state its objectives?

Most companies have objectives of some kind, but it is the process of articulating them that serves a developmental purpose. Actually the majority of firms know their objectives only intuitively: leadership is, of course, being exercised, and someone has to know what he is doing. Unless aims are written down and clarified for *all* managers—especially as companies grow in size and complexity—weak spots begin to show. The idea of total growth is lost sight of, and careless policies creep into other areas. How can this lead to better managers?

The point might be raised that a company is in business to make money—this is its prime objective, and what more is there to state? But there is a good deal more; more specific guidelines are required. A man can be told that he will make x dollars in a nine-to-five day, but this tells him nothing about what constitutes superior merchandising skill. A company can say that it is shooting for so many millions in profits next year, but does this help a manager direct himself? In the meantime he may get bogged down in the daily scramble for increased production or promotion without ever thinking of real improvement, either for himself or his company.

The company has to make the forest visible from the trees, and particular decisions must be made in many specific areas. A basic company policy should be spelled out and passed on to management at all levels; this is the compass but we have to operate from finer points on the compass. For instance, you have to know what your policies and practices are going to be concerning product line. You need established pricing policies and techniques of marketing. What are top management's long-term profit goals? What is the company's idea on treatment of people—does it favor promotion from within, for instance? These are only a few examples of areas in which decisions must be made, understood, and circulated.

In the general statement of objectives and their subsequent application to more particularized areas, the company must also consider its obligations. There are responsibilities which must not be lost sight of: to satisfy stockholders, employees, customers, and the community at large. However, it is possible that the objectives of any one of these groups may conflict with those of the company, or the separate objectives may pose conflicts for the company. Once again, though, the basic problem may lie in communication—do any of the above groups really know what the company is up to? Of course it is generally known that the company must make money and that it is desirable for it to grow, but there is more to a company's growth than increasing size. And this is what must be clarified by the company itself.

The character of a company emerges visibly from its statement of basic aims. It is highly important, particularly in terms of management development, for an individual to know what kind of atmosphere he is working in. Is it research-oriented, sales-oriented, youth-movement-oriented? Does this company expect its old traditions to be conformed to, or does it welcome innovation? What exactly does the company expect of the young manager, and how does the company's character measure up to an individual's? An ambitious, quick-moving, and irrepressibly active man may not want to go into or stay with a hidebound conservative firm, and this is something that should be known from the beginning. A man must know how he is to be judged so he can make a choice of whether to meet the company's standards and expectations or whether it would be better to look for another kind of company.

To a large extent, the character of a company is consciously determined, depending not so much on how an outside observer may evaluate it as on the policies that management differentiates and emphasizes. Personality, in other words, is largely determined by decisions—whether at the outset, for instance, the company decides to be a consumer business rather than a producer business; whether, for instance, management decides to take on a diversification program and expand markets and facilities. This is all the substance of basic objectives, and the importance of having them clearly stated is pointed up when, as so often happens today, management decides to change company policy in an important way.

What kind of performance can be expected of a manager when

suddenly a vigorous new president takes over and decides to introduce fresh dynamic policies? If the manager knows what the top executive intends to do and how he plans to proceed, he can make the appropriate changes in his own approach to his job. If, on the other hand, the manager simply receives new orders on the altered aspects of his job, how can he meet the situation head-on and with fullest efficiency? He also needs the new objectives stated, the new direction in which he is expected to go. A simple "make more money" instruction gets little results, nor will a simple "improve." If a company wants change or improvement, it must be explicit.

We often encounter companies that want to grow just for the sake of growth—hence they decide to introduce new products, go into new markets, or seek out mergers. They grow but they do not make more money. This unfortunate phenomenon is certainly due to faulty forward planning, an incomplete or inadequate understanding of the company's basic purposes and capabilities. New business opportunities must fit into the company's over-all plan, not vice versa. There has to be some preparation for change. A way to help smooth transition is to tell the company's managers where the company might go in the future, how its objective might change. This, again, gives executives a notion of what to expect and how to function in terms of those expectations.

Part of a company's statement of objectives ought to include some presumptions or hopes of what the company might want to make five or ten years from now, say, and the kind of product it might take up which it is not making now. We may not normally think of measures like these as having relevance to the area of management development. But let us take just one example to indicate the significance:

> Company A is in textiles, let us say: the business of buying, converting, storing, and otherwise processing cotton and wool into cloth. Its management board decides that this is not dynamic

> enough for the future but that the electronics business is booming. It learns that it can buy a manufacturer of advanced electronic hardware, with good volume but little management, and it does so. The whole plan for the product line thus changes: Company A is still a textile manufacturer but it also is a manufacturer of electronic gear. What is there about textiles that prepares people to make and sell electronic equipment?

Company A has no objectives in even as basic an area as its product line, and, unless a company does, how can it plan the kind of executives it needs? How can the managers themselves cope with sudden changes like these?

Most companies wanting to expand or diversify, of course, will buy a self-contained organization already existing. This may take care of the immediate need. But there still remains the question of what kind of future the company will have. How does the new organization change the company's long-range plans? What more will it expect from its managers? There are many such questions to be asked —the point is that a company must know its goals and must make sure that everyone charged with the fulfillment of the goals knows where the company is heading.

We have been talking about the need for clearly stated company objectives. Now, what of the need for the articulation of *personal* objectives, the needs, goals, and aims of the managers we want to develop? What can the company do to help its managers think about their own needs with the idea of creating better managers? The first measure, of course, involves the company's expression of what it expects and the direction in which it plans to go. If a company is competence-oriented and goal-oriented, it will want to encourage its people to decide what to do for themselves in terms of progressing toward these goals and toward securing greater competence. Further, it will want to record the results.

This is a new development of recent years. Companies are asking young managers about their personal objectives. They are actively seeking to gather information on what their staffs think their own objectives as businessmen require and how these accord with the company's plans and opportunities. How is this information gathered?

Because this is such a new technique, there is always the chance that such information might be misleading or not properly handled. But it must be emphasized that managers are not judged or appraised according to what they tell the company about their personal goals and requirements. The purpose is to provide an individual with a chance to appraise his own opportunities in the company; and, by knowing what managers hope to obtain, the organization may well take steps toward providing it. There is profit for both sides.

The company must make a manager or a potential manager feel that he can be as candid as possible about stating his own aims. He should be enabled to be frank about what position he'd like to have some day, for instance. However, the company, to make this kind of development program a success, must not stress promotion as the reason for seeking information from individuals. The focus must be on higher competence on the job at every level; in this way the pitfall of promoting a man beyond his capacity can be avoided. And the individual will know that competence is rewarded—only by these means can he get ahead (not by taking some extra business-school seminars). As has often been said, a whole organization can become corroded at the core when its men are more concerned about moving on, getting promotions, than they are about doing well in the jobs they hold. Part of doing well naturally involves knowing what the job is all about; a man should not have to guess what the company, in the person of his immediate superior, wants from him. Without imposing stifling restrictions, the company should state what it requires from each job.

If a man does not seem to be developing on his job, once more we move into the area which Douglas MacGregor has called "management by objectives." Instead of calling a man in and discussing or directly coaching him on how to cure his weakenesses, this question is asked: What, in light of the company's general purposes, are your own objectives for the coming year; what are you going to get done? The man is coached on the quality of the objectives he may express—he must be encouraged to set worthwhile goals—but the burden for defining those objectives should be placed squarely on his shoulders. And if the top executive has certain goals in mind that he would like his subordinate to meet—a certain quantity and quality of work—the subordinate must fully accept these goals as something personally desirable as well.

After objectives are clarified, there should be subsequent periodic discussions and reviews of progress—again, the work accomplished is evaluated, not a particular man's weaknesses. In the course of a natural conversation, it is more likely than not that the reason for the failure to attain a particular objective will come up. This is certainly a far more effective way of airing difficulties than is a session starting off with, "The trouble with you is...."

If a company feels that management development is one of the most pressing problems it has to face—and few people would deny that it is—then we need to assign a value to it, to put it high on the list of stated objectives. Now, how much time can the executive devote to the problem of developing managers? We often hear of cases of men who are so busy developing others that they sacrifice their own advancement. This is always disturbing, even if the tale is undocumented. Yet this should be considered one of the basic duties of the professional manager—considered basic enough, that is, to be rewarded.

A man who has special skills in helping others to develop may not qualify for promotion because he is deficient in other areas. But if a company wants to give impetus to the process of development, it must reward those people who contribute most to it. This development is not something an executive must "take time out for"—it is a basic objective of the company and is done right on the job as part of the job. All managers should be encouraged to pass on whatever they can to their subordinates and, if direct promotion is unfeasible for any reason, the developers should be rewarded in another way—a bonus, perhaps. At any rate, let the company mindful of the need for better managers do all that it can to bring the need to the attention of all managers.

To conclude, I have been sketching out a management activity which embraces both the progress of a company and the progress of individuals. A man's progress is best measured, not in terms of promotion per se, but of promotion as a by-product of self-development; mobility becomes a by-product of increasing competence. It seems to me that this method will accomplish more to produce better managers for this highly challenging era than can be accomplished by trying specifically to train people to be better managers, as such.

The kind of academic training the companies go into in their own educational programs and their participation in university programs may, in large part, be directed toward helping managers learn about their own situations, their industries, and the opportunities that exist for their companies. They can perhaps gain a better perspective on the strengths and resources of the company.

Now, schools can help in this kind of training; but the actual decision and actual development takes place in the company. It is there that the understanding of company objectives comes about and, through such understanding, better performance. Formal education is always secondary to actual experience. This is not to say that formal instruction has no value. The point is that academic objectives and company objectives must and can be brought together. It may be easy to teach people to understand a company's objectives; but it is not easy for the company to determine its objectives, and that has to be done before anybody can understand them.

We cannot keep turning our eyes away from the company itself by telling the business schools to train our people for us. Such an idea is premised on the notion that a good manager is a man with certain qualities, each of which can be taught to him separately. But we have found out that we do not know what a manager is—in the abstract. Until we finish our studies on what makes a good executive, we had better pay attention to the work a manager does rather than to certain vaguely defined qualities he may or may not have. I hope that we are beginning to realize this now and, consequently, that the management-development programs we undertake in the future will truly be up to the great needs which face us.

PROBLEMS OF PRODUCT-LINE PLANNING

Neil H. Borden

THERE HAS been a tremendous change in our teaching of marketing over the last thirty or forty years. In the more stable world of the twenties and thirties, we could, and did, assume that you could develop a good product, brand it, and develop a good market position which would persist. You could coast toward sure profits if you did a suitable job of watching the elements of your marketing mix. But today, and especially tomorrow, we can no longer trust to such a simple approach.

I am going to pass over rather quickly the background of what has come about to change all this, but I would like to point out what seems to be the major factor: the increased speed of change. We have

Note: Mr. Borden is Professor of Advertising, Harvard Business School.

always had a dynamic economy, but the acceleration has become greater and greater. No longer can we sit back and take it easy as far as our product line is concerned. The research that has been devoted to new products has been growing from year to year. Industrial research was once devoted primarily to processes, to cost reductions, but now it is used to a far greater extent for the development of new products and for improvements in the old products.

Another important change, particularly since the war, has been the speed-up in technology. This again has given us a push; it has kept new materials and new processes coming in all the time and has contributed to the concept of a shortened life and profit cycle of products.

Along with the growth of our large retail distributors' organizations, the private brand has stimulated more and more competition for a manufacturer to face. Nowadays he not only has the competition from other manufacturers' brands with their constant efforts to improve their products; he also finds the private branders coming into a product field and pushing prices down just as soon as there is an established demand. The phenomenon has also contributed to a shortened life and profit cycle for branded products.

Thus we find that the period available to produce good profits from a differentiated product and from building a market position has become shortened. It varies with different industries. In some, like heavy machinery, you can have a life and profit cycle that might be twenty-five or thirty years; in the drugs or grocery-products fields, often the period of profits is a matter of only four or five years.

The shortened cycle, then, means that a company has more competition than ever before. Future growth and profit success tends to turn on whether or not management constantly introduces new products with a profit margin that lives up to the hopes and expectations of stockholders and management.

In a recent article,[1] C. Wilson Randle gives a graphic picture of the concept of this life cycle or, as I have termed it, the profit cycle of a product. Ordinarily there is a rather slow period of development in sales following introduction of a new product. The period of sales accumulation is faster, of course, with less complex, low-priced products than for high-ticket items. The amount of money that has to be laid out by the consumer for package items is fairly small and, accordingly, consumers are more willing to take a chance on a new item. But even here you may run into consumer resistances and the development of a full market may take a considerable period of time.

In the case of high-ticket items, such as major household appliances, it may take years to attain a saturated market. For instance, electric refrigerators were introduced to consumers in 1915; by 1920 only 10,000 had been taken by the market. There was a slow development all through the 1920s, and it was not until 1928 that a big buying spurt in demand arose. In the appliance industry, the graph of sales growth of such products gives what is commonly called the "S curve." After introduction of a product you gradually get more customers. What I call emulative consumption sets in, a phenomenon after a fashion. Moreover, people become aware of the satisfactions the new product can give. The bugs in the product have been ironed out. Companies by this time are getting enough sales volume to permit lower costs, so prices begin to come down. Firms can now afford to throw money into advertising in order further to increase sales.[2] At this point industry sales take a rapid spurt, before finally leveling off as the product approaches market saturation. Profits can be very good dur-

[1] "Selecting the Research Program, II," *California Management Review,* Winter 1960, Chart.

[2] For a more complete history of the growth of refrigerator demand, see Neil H. Borden, *The Economic Effects of Advertising* (Richard O. Irwin, Inc., Chicago, 1942), p. 396ff.

ing these years of sales growth. When near-saturation level is reached in the market, however, there is generally overcapacity in the industry and price competition becomes keen. Profit opportunities tend to decline even though sales may still be expanding.

When the profit margin declines even though sales volume increases, a company does what it can to maintain profit margins by introducing product improvements. But management, in order to insure profit stability, may find it advisable to introduce new products. Theoretically, introduction should be timed to fit with the probable profit cycle of product lines.

We have already noted that the length of life cycles varies with different types of products. But I have found executives expressing the view that life cycles of products generally are becoming shorter under the stress of the forces I have recounted.

The uncertain life of products leads us into another area—namely, product diversification. If there is instability in any one product or line of products, companies reason, attempts should be made to create a broader product base. Thus, when profits go down in one area or when one product line tends to lose out, there are other lines to support the enterprise.

We have seen many products with a long-standing good position in sales and profits suddenly lose that position because a competitor has introduced something new and better. Today's firm is always under pressure to have its lines of intelligence out so that it can keep an eye on what is happening in new-product development among competitors. It must build on its research-and-development program in such a way that it not only maintains the competitive quality of the products in its lines but also develops new profit-promising products. We are all well aware of reports that a large percentage of the sales of many companies are due to products not on the market five or ten years ago. Fantastic figures of this kind come to us from the pharmaceutical industry and from other highly dynamic fields such as electronics. Here, particularly, product-line planning becomes very significant.

Now let us turn to an actual case (disguised) that will illustrate some of the problems; we call it the Hadley Company case. Hadley is actually a division of a large company and this fact simplifies the problem somewhat because the division is operating under a charter which restricts the products it can offer the market. The management does not have to think of diversification much outside its major product area.

Hadley's product line is cooling and heating equipment. In 1954 the company decided that it was important to create a department of product-line planning. The idea came partly because management saw some of its competitors setting up such departments. But, beyond this, they recognized the need for maintaining products that would fully meet customer desires in a constantly changing market. They also saw the need for simplification of product lines. As so often happens in a sales organization, the salesmen had been inclined to give the customer whatever he wanted. The company had done a good deal of special manufacturing to meet customer wants and specifications; costs had risen. In the face of an industry trend toward standardized units that could be put together to meet customer needs at lower costs, Hadley was suffering from the price standpoint.

Moreover, no one person or department had the responsibility for the introduction of new products. Different people in the organization would get an idea for an innovation which would be incorporated, or some product that had been developed for a particular customer would get into the regular line. Many of these items were not producing profitable volume.

Then, of course, the company saw the need for a responsible department which we have stressed more and more: any firm operating in this kind of dynamic world must plan to keep up with trends in the industry and with trends of consumer living which evolve.

The company also had a problem that I find to be not too uncommon: it had a research-and-development department which was likely to go off on its own. The research men would operate according to their inclinations and what they felt would be desirable from an engineering-scientific standpoint, without too much consideration of what the market would take. Here is one example of this uncoordinated planning: the design department (equivalent to a research-and-development department) decided it would be a good idea to develop a bituminous-coal stoker for households. After the engineers had worked on the project for a while, they found that they could get better results if anthracite coal were used in the unit instead of bituminous. They next found it advisable to incorporate the stoker in a furnace. Finally they came out with a very fine furnace that used anthracite. In the meantime, the trend in coal use was more and more toward bituminous. Even beyond this, in large segments of the market, oil and gas had come into dominant use. The end result was a good furnace in which the market was not at all interested. Needless to say, the Hadley management wanted to avoid this kind of error in the future.

What we come down to is the need for centering responsibility for product development, partly to take care of the old items in the line but, more important, to look well toward the future. In these dynamic times, the success of a company five and ten years from now turns upon what is put into research and development today, in what product ideas are accepted and developed to give a profitable product line five or ten years hence. Long-range planning becomes all-important, particularly in dynamic product fields.

Let us see what Hadley did to set up its new product-planning department.

One of the problems that always arises in these cases is organizational structure. Where you put people in an organization and what people you use, of course, is going to be different in each company. Organizational structure depends on the kind of men already available and the company's existing setup. From the accompanying chart (see Exhibit I) we can see that the Hadley organization is an engineering firm; it has its vice-presidents of sales, manufacturing, engineering, and finance and it is in the design-engineering department where the research and development are located. The management picked a young man named Holden to

Exhibit I. Hadley Organization

- PRESIDENT
  - EXECUTIVE VICE-PRESIDENT
    - VICE-PRESIDENT SALES
      - PRODUCT-LINE PLANNING AND CONTROL
      - SALES
      - ADVERTISING AND SALES PROMOTION
      - PRODUCT SERVICE
    - VICE-PRESIDENT MANUFACTURING
      - PRODUCTION
      - PRODUCTION PLANNING
      - INSPECTION
      - FACILITIES PLANNING
    - VICE-PRESIDENT ENGINEERING
      - PRODUCTION ENGINEERING
      - ADVANCE ENGINEERING
      - DESIGN ENGINEERING
      - QUALITY STANDARDS
    - VICE-PRESIDENT FINANCE
      - GENERAL ACCOUNTING
      - BUDGETING
      - COST ANALYSIS
      - CREDITS AND COLLECTION
      - ACCOUNTS RECEIVABLE

head the new department; he had been a marketing-research man in the commercial-engineering department for some time and had gone through the usual training program characteristic of engineering companies. He had also had company sales experience and graduate study in business administration. After some consideration, top management decided to put Holden under the sales vice-president.

In my opinion, the Hadley Company would have been better off from an organizational standpoint if it had placed him in a staff position reporting to the executive vice-president, instead of under the vice-president of sales. He was given a great deal of responsibility, but his position gave him authority only as he received it from his immediate superior. As product-line manager, he has to work with every department represented on the line of vice-presidents. Accordingly, if he is to get results, he should be placed where he will have the full authority of top management behind him—in this case the authority of the executive vice-president.

I can illustrate the need for this arrangement by pointing out what happened to Holden when he was made a subordinate of the sales vice-president. He started developing some new product ideas and carried development of these through the working-model stage, but he ran into trouble. The manufacturing department was inclined to establish priority for manufacture in compliance with the pressures of the everyday jobs of producing products for sales orders, so Holden's timetable was always being upset. After he got his working models out and wanted to run market tests or iron out a few kinks, his jobs were often shoved aside for current pressing production demands, or he could not get the field service he desired. The engineering vice-president continued to take product ideas into top councils without putting them through the new product-line planning department.

Let us take another look at why the product planner should be under the executive vice-president. The one important fact that we have to recognize is that new-product development, keeping the line up to date, has become one of top management's most important responsibilities. The top executives have to be the ones who finally decide what products are to be developed and the direction in which the company will go. They are the ones who must lay out the whole broad plan of future company objectives. But before they can act, they need facts. They need somebody who is well equipped to gather them, to develop ideas on what consumer, technological, and industry trends are going to be important, and to seek out the product lines which promise future sales and profit opportunities. Hence, the executive vice-president and president should have close association with the product-line manager.

This carries us over into another problem area—the kind of man that should be put at the head of product planning. Holden was a good choice for Hadley. He had engineering training; he had been in production; he had had several years of sales and of marketing research. Of highest importance, he was market-oriented; a man with market orientation prevents the kind of monstrous blunder Hadley committed with its unwanted furnace.

What are the responsibilities of a product-planning manager? The list is long:

- He has to direct the operation of a department of specialists, as well as coordinate projects involving many departments.
- He must keep appraising existing company products in relation to competing products.
- He is the one to watch product and industry trends. He must have enough knowledge of technology to be able to see threats, both those coming from his direct competitors and those coming from other industries, which may upset a company's market position.
- He has to analyze consumer needs and habits, not only in existing markets, but in contemplated markets as well.
- He must recommend prices, suggest the channels of trade, and see that a good marketing plan is devised.
- He must solicit and screen all new-product ideas and be able to suggest changes in accordance with what he knows about the market.
- He must be broad enough in background and training to deal effectively with all types of line executives.
- In addition to all the above, he must be a wizard in human relations because he has to work with all kinds of people in every department, sales, finance, and production.

If the company's product-planning department is not meeting expectations, it may well be that the head of the department is not well equipped in vital areas.

Now let us look at some of the work that the new department has to do. First of all, it must collect a kit of promising product ideas. Where do the ideas for new products come from? A great many of them, of course, are going to grow out of the company's own research department; some are going to come from the salesmen; others will crop up from outside the organization. They can come from any place.

But one must always solicit and encourage new-product ideas. A passive attitude is not enough: you need to have a place to which ideas can be sent, and you need plenty of them. The people who submit ideas must get recognition, which often calls for a great deal of skill in human relations because most of these new ideas will be turned down. To relieve this situation, it is extremely important to indicate explicitly what sort of ideas the company is interested in. The area of company interest must be defined. Does management want to look at new fields? What segments of the market does it want to maintain?

In this basic definition of product interest, a company must consider its own strength and weaknesses; the skills that it has; the assets it might have in its established brands; advantages of market know-how and of market entry to trade; and so forth. Decisions can be planned only after realistic consideration. If you look at some of the mergers that have been taking place, you can easily observe the type of problem that arises from the fact that businessmen are often inadequate in what they do in this appraisal area. Executives generally list what is needed for success in new product lines, but they do not dig deeply enough to determine what management requirements are demanded to bring success in the new fields and then make sure that they have provided for these requirements.

Let me give you an example. The watch industry is highly competitive in terms of both foreign and domestic challenges. American watch companies have sought product diversification, one instance being through costume jewelry. The Elgin Company felt it was skillful in miniaturization and decided to go into miniature electronics. But evidently there was no one in the business with enough experience and ability in electronics, and there was not enough money available to buy the good brains that are required in this field. Consequently, annual reports reveal that the new-product policies of this company to date have not been very successful. I think lack of success turns largely on the fact that although management wrote out what sounded like a good diversification program, it did not study deeply enough to determine what makes businesses successful in the field it entered.

One duty of the new-product department, after ideas have been collected, is to screen them in terms of development feasibility and profit potential. This must be done fairly quickly. What is needed is a quick estimate as to whether there is enough sales and profit volume in the project to make it worthwhile and whether development is technologically promising. Holden, in making these first appraisals, went to the several functional departments of the Hadley Company, asking for estimates and any information on the potential value of the idea. Ideas that were clearly inappropriate were abandoned.

The next task is to subject ideas surviving the initial screening process to more intensive study to make sure that they are worthy of research-and-development expenditure. At this point, intensive study is required, real market study and extensive inquiry regarding technology. Holden had some marketing-research people on his staff, as well as a competent technical man. These men worked on each product proposal and went to men in the operating departments for their opinions. Holden then had to prepare a preliminary report for top management. Only projects promising enough to get the signatures of all the functional vice-presidents were carried finally to a top-management new-product committee for discussion and approval. Only approved projects went to research and development.

At this point it is important to emphasize the need for periodic reviews once research on an idea is actually under way. If a project is not going well, management must decide whether or not to shelve it. Research costs money, and management has to keep setting up research priorities. Accordingly, a product-planning department must keep refining its estimates of future profitability of projects. Research budgets should be directed to promising projects only. Thus, in any product-planning program it is highly important to have provision for periodic review and interim reports on what is happening during the research-and-development stages.

Here is another case which illustrates the kind of problem that may arise in product-line planning: what should be done in a company that has product managers? Product managers are usually responsible for keeping the quality of a particular line up to competitive standards. Moreover, it is very common for companies with brand or product managers to place the responsibility for new-product development on them. In such companies, when management gets an idea that looks good, a young man who has product-management experience will be selected to carry the product project through all the trials and tribulations involved in developing a new product. He will work under the direction of a product-manager supervisor. There is a very interesting case coming out of the Bristol-Myers organization which illustrates the kinds of problems that develop. Exhibit II (p. 100) shows the company organization in 1957.

In 1957 and before, the director of product planning, who in fact was the technical man in charge of research and development, was responsible for calling a meeting every so often of various key people to consider new-product ideas. This group would agree on an idea and it would then go to the advertising manager, who was the most important marketing executive and to whom a number of supervisory brand managers reported. Each supervisor, in turn, had a number of brand managers reporting to him. The advertising manager and the supervisor into whose product stable the new product would go would assign the task of product development to a brand manager. This chap had to get the necessary research done, arrange for production and finances, develop a marketing plan, and generally take charge of carrying the product idea through to final

Exhibit II. Bristol-Myers Inc. (A) Organization—1957

PRESIDENT

EXECUTIVE VICE-PRESIDENT

DIRECTOR OF SALES | DIRECTOR OF ADVERTISING | DIRECTOR OF MARKET RESEARCH | DIRECTOR OF FINANCE | DIRECTOR OF PRODUCT PLANNING | DIRECTOR OF MANUFACTURING

LABORATORY

PILOT PLANT

ADVERTISING MANAGER | ADVERTISING MANAGER | ADVERTISING MANAGER

PRODUCTION MANAGER | PRODUCTION MANAGER | PRODUCTION MANAGER

PRODUCTION MANAGER | PRODUCTION MANAGER | PRODUCTION MANAGER

PRODUCTION MANAGER | PRODUCTION MANAGER | PRODUCTION MANAGER

PRODUCTION MANAGER | PRODUCTION MANAGER | PRODUCTION MANAGER

PRODUCTION MANAGER | PRODUCTION MANAGER | PRODUCTION MANAGER

Source: Company Records.

marketing. This procedure worked fairly well when the company was smaller, but tended to break down as more divisions and products emerged.

To try to avoid the confusion and uncertainty that had arisen in product-line development, the company made an organizational change in 1958 which centered final authority for product plans in a planning committee (see Exhibit III). The new scheme provided for a product-group supervisor under whom new-product managers would carry product ideas through all stages to final marketing. The thought behind the change was that new products could best be handled by product supervisors and managers who were not under

Exhibit III. Bristol-Myers Inc. (A) Organization—1958

- PRESIDENT
  - EXECUTIVE VICE-PRESIDENT
    - PRODUCT PLANNING COMMITTEE*
    - DIRECTOR OF MARKETING*
      - DIRECTOR OF ADVERTISING
      - DIRECTOR OF SALES
      - PRODUCT GROUP SUPERVISOR
        - PRODUCTION MANAGER
        - PRODUCTION MANAGER
        - PRODUCTION MANAGER
        - PRODUCTION MANAGER
        - PRODUCTION MANAGER
      - PRODUCT GROUP SUPERVISOR
        - PRODUCTION MANAGER
        - PRODUCTION MANAGER
        - PRODUCTION MANAGER
        - PRODUCTION MANAGER
        - PRODUCTION MANAGER
      - NEW PRODUCT GROUP* 1 SUPERVISOR
        - PRODUCTION MANAGER
        - PRODUCTION MANAGER
        - PRODUCTION MANAGER
        - PRODUCTION MANAGER
        - PRODUCTION MANAGER
    - DIRECTOR OF MARKETING RESEARCH*
    - DIRECTOR OF PRODUCT PLANNING* 2
      - LABORATORY
      - PILOT PLANT
    - DIRECTOR OF MANUFACTURING
    - DIRECTOR OF FINANCE

* MEMBERS OF THE PRODUCT PLANNING COMMITTEE

1. THE NEW PRODUCT GROUP SUPERVISOR WAS CONCERNED WITH NEW PRODUCTS ONLY. AFTER A PRODUCT WAS INTRODUCED, THE PRODUCT MANAGER WOULD BE TRANSFERRED TO ONE OF THE OTHER TWO PRODUCT GROUPS.
2. THIS DIVISION WAS CONCERNED WITH DEVELOPING PRODUCTS FROM A TECHNICAL VIEWPOINT. ITS WORK WAS OF AN ENGINEERING NATURE.

Source: Company Records.

the stress of current product marketing. The new setup has reportedly worked out well.

But here is still another problem: should these product-group supervisors be responsible for the improvement of old products as well? One large concern uses this procedure: whenever a product manager feels that one of his products needs improvement, he has it put into R & D, and it thereby automatically comes under the direction of the product-planning manager. In this way the company provides for improvement of old products all the benefits of the procedures which have been set up for product development under the company's planning department.

In its program this firm has adopted a good rule: some executive who is really enthusiastic about a product idea must be included on a "sponsor committee." Other companies have similar arrangements. These managements reportedly believe that all too many excellent ideas have gone down the drain for lack of some person enough interested in them to push for their successful development.

There are a few other problems I might mention in connection with new-product planning. One of the most difficult involves questions of carrying a product clear through to final marketing. Generally, product-planning departments, as they are now set up, supervise product development and market planning all the way through to its launching on the market, and in many instances this means supervising test marketing. One of the difficulties encountered is that, while test markets in theory have a scientific objective of finding the sales and profit potentials of a marketing program for a new product, in practice test markets are also an entry into the market. If test marketing is made the responsibility of a line sales department, the enthusiasm of such departments for making sales may lead them to forget testing and to proceed rapidly to national marketing. The scientific objective—getting the bugs out of the product and testing the marketing program—may be left by the wayside.

We had a very good instance of this in the case of General Mills, when some years ago it put out a new product, "Apple Pyequick."

> General Mills had real know-how for the development of a flour mix for pie crust, but it did not know its apples so well. At first it was going to use culls, but R & D found this would leave hard bits of the core in the dried apples they were going to use. Betty Crocker could not have anything like that in her product. Then they found

when they were ready to market that apple costs were higher than they had anticipated because of a short apple crop. The new product had to be put on the market for 49 cents, 10 cents more than planned when they made their sales and profit calculations. Even so, the product in test markets sold like wild fire to the trade—the product introduction took place at the end of World War II when shortening was still being restricted by the government. The trade evidently was influenced by the fact that consumers would be attracted by a pie-crust mix containing shortening.

Under the stimulus of the ready trade acceptance, the sales department proceeded quickly to national distribution. Management did not wait to get full appraisal of test market sales to consumers.

In the meantime, controls on shortening had been removed, and suddenly the grocers found themselves with their shelves full of high-priced boxes of Apple Pyequick that were not selling. To reduce the price and move the product from trade shelves cost General Mills a great deal of money, and finally management dropped the product. The company had not spent enough time in providing a real test of the product and the marketing program that had been adopted.

This case indicates that a company's executives must decide in advance just how far its product-planning department should carry the new product. In general, a product should not be launched broadly until its potentialities are known. At least management should decide definitely whether the risks of early advent on the market are offset by advantages which make proceeding without market testing advisable.

A different kind of problem may arise in a multidivision company. An illustration comes from a large electronics company which has a product-line manager and an R & D department for each of its many divisions. Although the company has a central planning department, all the divisions are given opportunity to develop product ideas that fit into their own product areas.

One division in this particular case produced and sold audio and television parts and sets; another division handled magnetic materials. The central research department came up with a promising new concept for developing magnets and carried its development up to a point which implied important commercial application. The opportunity for research on the material's application to commercial uses was offered to the magnetic-materials division, but its director did not choose to accept it. At the time, he had other ideas for product development to which he gave priority in his R & D budget. The audio and television manager then accepted the idea when it was offered to him, spent about $500,000 over five years on research, and developed something that was of great promise to his division and to outside buyers of magnets. This all seemed fine and it was—until the enterprising manager of the audio-television division was advised by the magnetic-materials manager that, if the device was going to be sold by the company, it would have to be sold by magnetic materials. Since his charter covered the sale of this kind of product, he wished to take over manufacture and sale. It became necessary for the two managers to reach a compromise which was acceptable to the company as a whole and equitable to each division.

In brief, the problem of finding new-product ideas, of appraising them, getting the good ones developed, carrying them through to the market-launching stage, and then hoping that they work out is now a vitally important one for American business, and will become even more pressing in the days ahead. Under the circumstances that have developed—call it an "economic explosion" if you like—a good product-line planning department is vital in many businesses. Not only is research and development involved but, in addition, marketing, financing, production—in short, problems and decisions touching every department of a business. If responsibility is centered, and a good procedure established for managing new projects, the company's chances of long-range success are considerably improved.

DISCUSSION

Question: In many small companies you do not have individuals who are specialists for any function, not even market researchers, nor anyone assigned to the task of product planning. Do you have any examples of small businesses that have successfully approached this problem of new-product development?

Borden: You pose a difficult problem. In the bigger company there is a chance for a division of labor; the smaller company has to give each executive many responsibilities of an operating or staff character. On the other hand, in the small company as in the large, responsibility, I believe, should be centered; the task of getting new-product ideas, of appraising them and of carrying through to marketing, is essential. Obsolete products should be dropped. Some one must take on these responsibilities; many of the things to be done in the way of research and development may be done through outside organizations.

Question: In many product lines you see segmentation taking place, not just through technological advances but through developing new brands with distinctive images—the cigarette and soap fields are good examples. What is the long-term effect on the growth curve and, particularly, the profit picture of the company when it takes so much money these days for launching new products?

Borden: As we move into an era in which we are getting more and more consumer discretionary buying power, we are getting more segmentation of the market. The aim is to develop a product that will appeal not to the whole populace, but to some segment of it. Consumer product choices are increasing.

Now, as far as I can see, a company needs much the same kind of thorough investigation into volume potential for segmented markets as has always been required in any new-product market appraisal. Long-range budgets must be set up and these budgets must be realistic. The companies which have a high degree of brand differentiation, such as Proctor & Gamble, are not interested in a product unless their investigations indicate that there are enough sales—a thousand cases, a million cases, whatever the figure might be—with a margin of such and such, which will permit them to promote the product and attain desired profit objectives. I believe that a company must make similar volume and profit appraisals for a segmented market. If the desired volume is not present, seek another idea.

Question: Considerable thought has been given to an alternative method of development of new products; that is, first determining a market that offers an opportunity and then developing a product to fit this market. What do you think about this?

Borden: I think that the approach you suggest is the approach often taken by the idea man. Let me give you an example from one of the big companies in the diesel electric business. Traditionally they had sold their diesel electric drives to transportation enterprises like railroads. Then the company considered the possibility of supplying two new markets—diesel electrics for marine transportation and diesel electrics to drive oil wells.

Management asked itself these questions: can we develop a product that is an improvement over the other machines which these industries use? What is the potential volume here? Do we have something that will really meet a need, and can we see enough volume and enough profit in it to warrant developmental expense for such ventures? This is where market analysis and forecast come in. In the marine field, studies showed that the diesel electric was not good in boats except for those under a certain tonnage, and then good only for those vessels which required a great deal of maneuverability: tug boats. The company found out how many such boats were going to be built in a year, and it calculated industry volume and the probable share of the market it could get. The project did not seem worthwhile. The company then looked over the oil industry and saw a potential that had not been exploited yet. A product and marketing program was developed. The market was entered, and profits have been satisfactory. But both decisions were carefully studied by the product-line planning department.

Developing an established product to meet the needs of new markets is one way of going about expansion and diversification. A company should be ready to move wherever it sees a good profit opportunity. Take Minnesota Mining and Manufacturing Co.: it will look at any new-product idea; management is willing to go into diversification whenever the results are adequately profit-promising. And, by the way, I believe MMM has a central product-planning group working in some ways along the lines of the Bristol-Myers setup. An executive is selected to take charge of carrying through the development of the product for the market; when the product is developed and marketing plans are made, he is the man who handles the management of the enterprise.

Question: How do you run your research-and-development laboratory? Do you let these research fellows go off in all directions, or do you make them follow specific lines?

Borden: Many laboratories seem to be having success in splitting up their research effort—part applied and part basic research. The basic-research men are given more latitude to follow their interests than the men with applied assignments. The latter have specific assignments for a commercial development. But even the basic researchers generally are expected to follow avenues of investigation that hold promise of future application.

A good R & D lab is one of the best sources for new-product ideas. The leading technicians in the basic-research General Electric Laboratory in Schenectady, for instance, have freedom to work on all kinds of projects of interest to them; when something has been developed that looks promising for specific application, then applied research takes over. The same approach was true in the case of another electrical company which I referred to a few minutes ago. The central laboratory got the concept of a new magnetic material; the laboratory carried it far enough to see that technologically it had promising applications, and then tossed it over to a division to work out these applications.

Question: You mentioned earlier Elgin's problem with diversification when the company got into an unfamiliar field. How can a company that wants to spread out tackle this problem?

Borden: Generally, if you are going into a field that is new, you need people who have enough know-how in that field to make an enterprise go. You can get some of this know-how through hiring consultants, of course, but the whole area of know-how is so significant to the success of any business that sooner or later you have to make sure that the needed personnel get into your own organization. If you need to go out and hire your own specialists, that is the thing to do.

Joel Dean, in his *Managerial Economics,* has a chapter in which he points out the importance of a company's acquiring these new fields of knowledge. Many mergers do not work because of management's lack of know-how of the particular type of business it gets into. The same is true of product diversification through new-product research.

Question: In the question of product life cycles, you mentioned the fact that the cycle on any product group may vary but that in general the cycles are shortening. In the future, will companies have to get a higher return on investment to come out ahead because competition and product change are going to come so quickly?

Borden: You will naturally want to get as much profit as you can to meet a shorter life cycle, but this is something that no longer rests fully in your hands. You have to think of many factors.

If, for instance, you bring out a new product and put your price too high, you are merely inviting competitors to copy the product and sell it at a lower price. Clearly, with shortened cycles logic indicates that we may expect a venture to pay well for a shorter period of time than might have been the case before. It all seems to boil down to the fact that the business of management does not get any easier.

THE LINE EXECUTIVE AND LONG-RANGE PLANNING IN A NEW ECONOMY

H. Edward Wrapp,
Edward M. Scheu, Jr.,
and Sterling T. Tooker

INTRODUCTION*

FOR SEVERAL YEARS now we have been hearing more and more about "long-range planning." It has become increasingly clear that management in an era of change and uncertainty has to make a conscious effort to look ahead, to plan, and to establish goals. Without

* By Mr. Wrapp. *Note:* Mr. Wrapp is Professor of Business Administration, Harvard Business School. Mr. Scheu is Vice President in charge of Development, Thomas J. Lipton, Inc. Mr. Tooker is Vice President, The Travelers Insurance Companies.

such a program, a risky expediency is the rule; with it, changing circumstances can be met by rational and appropriate shifts and a business can negotiate its way through the rapids in some kind of an orderly fashion.

There are six distinct steps in long-range planning as it is developing in industry today. Though I am not necessarily listing them here in the order in which they should be accomplished, they are:

1. Setting broad company goals. These initial objectives may be quite general, such as a decision by top management that the company is going to grow at the rate of 20% a year. Or it could be a broadening of the product line, or an effort to meet foreign competition.

2. Collecting data and forecasting. This material might be cost or market information within the company, industry information, or facts on the total economy.

3. Development of alternatives. Under this heading comes the task of working up the various ways in which the company can meet its goals.

4. Selection of an alternative. That is simply a matter of deciding which one of the alternatives is most appropriate.

5. Implementation of the plans. By this we mean a timetable, worked out step by step from the present into the future, and the phasing of operating decisions into the program—an often-neglected part of the total planning process.

6. Updating of long-range plans. This process is a continuing one, designed to keep the blueprint current.

During recent months, it has become quite clear that most large companies have decided that long-range planning is an important function which needs to be formalized in some way. But, having reached this decision, they have still left wide open the question of who is going to do this long-range planning. Here, then, is one of the issues which has become crucial and, naturally, one that is precipitating a good deal of debate.

By and large, the contestants break into two camps. One group feels very strongly that the operating managers, or line managers, should be deeply involved in the process. They offer a number of arguments. They point out that you can make good long-range plans only if you have the operating point of view; that the decisions on operating problems are going to be better decisions if the operating people are involved in long-range planning. They emphasize that long-range planning is one of the most effective devices for developing operating managers so they can move on to top-management responsibilities.

Despite the cogency of these arguments, however, it is fair to say that most of the companies which have tried to involve their line managers in this process have run into real snags. The operating executives, even though they are given a fairly explicit kind of responsibility by top management, seem to be much more concerned with their immediate day-to-day problems. They are concentrating on making profits, rather than talking about what it will be like in 1970. So I do not think that too many companies have made much progress in this direction.

The other camp feels that operating managers should not be involved in long-range planning. All you are going to do is distract them, they argue. They know how to do the operating job, so keep the focus on this because, if you get them involved in long-range planning, they will do neither job well—or so the discussion runs.

Theodore Levitt, in an interesting article in the *Journal of Marketing*,[1] has this to say: "Salesmen are constantly told how wonderful they are, and their company. To allow them to question the superiority of the present setup invites them to lose confidence in the organization. A salesman without confidence is not a salesman. He has to think and continuously be told that the present arrangement is the best."

[1] "Growth and Profits Through Planned Marketing Innovation," *Journal of Marketing*, April 1960.

This position typifies the thinking of some of these people who want to keep the sales and production managers out of long-range planning. They do not want them to look too far ahead; they believe in keeping their eyes pretty close to this month's problem. And, I might add, many of them feel very strongly about it. Here is a transcript of part of an interview I had recently with one such executive.

"Don't get me wrong, I have great respect for our top management; they have done an excellent job of giving direction to the company's growth. It is this attempt to 'formalize' long-range planning which seems to be such a miscarriage. In my opinion there is a big difference between the planning job and the job of actually operating these divisions, and I don't think you can mix the two of them up.

"Now, for example, top management keeps saying to me, 'We want the division to develop itself on its own plans, and we want broad participation. We want all of your key people actively involved in the development of these plans.' Well, I for one don't think this will work. I know I don't want my subordinates involved in that kind of activity. You know, we have a first-rate division here, a division that really knows how to make profits. We can squeeze every last dollar out of the market in the product line that we have. My sales manager and my production manager are just about the best in the business, and I don't want these two men wasting their time on long-range activities. In fact, I am not at all sure they would be good at it even if I let them try. In my experience, people who are good at operations are not too good at the planning work and vice versa. However, I think I may be an exception in this. Don't write me off as just another peddler who doesn't want to do anything except sell goods. I came up from the financial side of the business and I know all about capital budgeting. Nevertheless, I am still convinced that my subordinates should not be working on long-range plans. As I see it, this is a job of the people at the corporate level. On the other hand, if at the start of each year they will just tell us what they want us to do, why then we can go ahead and do it.

"Naturally, as general manager, I think I should be consulted in advance before the goals of my division are finalized; but my people are better off when they do not have to look beyond the one-year horizon.

"Now, as to the effect that long-range planning has on our particular company, I can tell you one thing: it is slowing down the introduction of new products to such an extent that we are losing profits. In fact, I can cite you chapter and verse where some of our own forecasting experts recently became so involved in the act that, by the time we finally got the new product to market, it had already been taken over by our competitors and all our development expense went down the drain. In today's competition you have no choice but to keep really close tabs on the market so as to get every last dollar of profit out of your existing products over the short term. Those of us who are trying to do this job shouldn't have to be worried about where the company is going to be five years from now."

As we study these opposing lines of argument more closely, we immediately ask ourselves: just what kind of line executives are we discussing?

In one kind of organization we have a rather typical arrangement with a president sitting on top, a group of corporate-level vice-presidents who are mainly advisers to him, and several division general managers. Each of these general managers has sales, production, and control people reporting to him. Most of us would look on the division general manager and probably his sales and production chiefs as the line people in this system.

Incidentally, I should mention at this point that one company with which I am familiar says that sales and production are no longer the key line functions; that engineers and researchers have become the line personnel and that the others are beginning to slip into an advisory role. Be that as it may, most of us are not in situations of that kind.

In other cases, we have a more highly centralized organization. The president is on top, along with the vice-presidents of sales and production. Under them come various echelons of personnel. In such an organization, we might say that the line managers in sales go up through the vice-president of sales, and the line manager of the production side goes up through the vice-president of production.

THE ATTITUDE OF THE LINE EXECUTIVE*

It is clear from Professor Wrapp's introduction to this chapter that we are discussing *formalized* long-range planning on a corporate level rather than the sort of departmental forecasting in which the line executive frequently indulges. While the line officer's responsibilities may be limited as to time and scope, he is frequently concerned with the future of his operation based on estimates of his market, his production, his territory, his plant, or even his own career. Very often, his success as a line officer depends on his accuracy in making projections of this sort. It is when he is forced to participate in formulating the corporate big picture, in setting objectives and goals, that he most often feels unhappy and out of his element. This kind of long-range planning tends to demand a sacrifice of individual objectives and a diffusion of the line executive's sense of purpose and direction. Because of his intimate understanding of current operating problems, and his unique facilities for forecasting, he should be a valuable member of any long-range planning group. But how to engage him in this activity willingly without undermining his effectiveness as a line officer is a difficult and somewhat subtle process.

To put the problem in perspective, until the fairly recent past the

* By Mr. Tooker.

concept of formalized long-range planning was relatively foreign to most business organizations. The typical executive was a line officer by training and temperament, even when he carried the title of president or chairman of the board. Very often he had built the organization from scratch, started it from his own idea and shaped it in his own image. His job as he saw it was to manufacture a product or produce a service at the lowest possible cost and sell it on the marketplace at the highest possible profit. If he was successful in this, he grew and prospered. If he was not, he turned his hand to something else; or he kept going at a slow but steady pace, and perhaps that suited him fine. The businessman generally viewed with suspicion and alarm the big thinker, the long-range planner, the starry-eyed dreamer. He flew his company by the seat of his pants, by hunch and intuition, and by that indefinable American something called "know-how." He prided himself that in *his* organization the impossible took only a little longer to accomplish than the difficult. For the most part, however, he solved his problems as they arose and did not spare the time or have the inclination to bother mapping the future.

In the years following World War II, long-range planning became legitimatized as a business function. The development of new techniques of economic forecasting, statistical analysis, and operations and market research made this transition possible. The business executive in our new economy cannot very well ignore these tools which science has placed in his hands. But it must be admitted that he is still uncomfortable using them and very often reluctant to admit they work.

As Professor Wrapp has pointed out, an increasing number of business organizations are presently restructuring themselves in an attempt to formalize long-range planning. They have been persuaded that the old organization chart, with its almost autonomous operating departments and separate financial, legal, and administrative staff functions, is not feasible for this purpose. The size and complexity of most modern corporations demands a greater degree of control and a far more effective use of the new business techniques.

So the line officer responsible for bringing home the bacon, turning a profit, developing a market, organizing a sales force, or manufacturing a competitive product has gradually found himself surrounded by an increasingly large number of staff officers. His traditional freedom to pilot his own ship is hampered, he often feels, by staff decisions in such areas as expense control, methods and planning, and research and development. No longer is he flying by the seat of his own pants. He is sitting instead before a complex instrument panel and often has the justifiable sensation that someone else is at the controls.

These are perhaps oversimplifications, but they provide a recognizable frame of reference for our problem. The line executive is convinced that *he* has a "responsibility" while the staff officer merely has a "function." One has to pay off directly and measurably. The other's impact may be felt only over the long pull. Thus, while it is apparently a staff function to develop company-wide plans for the future, the line officer must make the achievement of these plans possible every step of the way. And he believes he works best when he can keep his eye on the ball and not on the flag in the distant cup.

In the insurance business, we have traditionally been involved with long-range planning of a sort. Our product is a legal obligation to take effect at some definite future date, or upon the occurrence of a named contingency. In The Travelers, our price for the most long-range promises we make—our life-insurance contracts—is guaranteed over the lifetime of the policy, which may be generations. It must be based, therefore, on long-range projections of interest rates, mortality, and probable expense costs, all of which requires planning of the highest order.

The line officer, however, responsible for the sale, service, or underwriting of these contracts has traditionally divorced himself from this planning function. He has relied upon a staff of actuaries to develop his product and its price. This has, especially in a competitive marketing situation, made him impatient and at times dissatisfied. He, after all, knows *today's* market and *today's* competition and the kind of product that will be most attractive to his salesmen and their customers. He is frustrated by actuarial arguments as to why he cannot have precisely what he wants now. However, it often seems that he would rather use his creative skill in promoting the product as given than be involved with the long-range considerations so indispensable to the actuary. So strongly does he feel this way, and so uncertain is he of the "new techniques," that some firms purposely steer clear of the term "long-range planning."

The Travelers Insurance Companies have been pioneers in multiple-line insurance, underwriting, and sales—and this has been our broad plan for 35 years. We produce all major forms of insurance: life, casualty, group, property, liability. We sell them through independent contractors. This multiple-line concept was conceived years ago as our unique long-range plan of operation. For decades, however, our line responsibilities were rigidly departmentalized. Strong operating executives developed independent organizations and methods. The life department and its agency force was almost as distinct an entity from the casualty operation as if it belonged to a separate company. And this was true right down the line from the department head to the new trainee. As long as the line officer was producing, he saw no need to alter his course. And no nonproductive staff executive had the right or the reason to tell him to do so.

Faced with a completely new marketing situation after World War II, with heightened public demand for all forms of insurance, some Travelers executives saw the need for a more cohesive view of our product and its sale. The burgeoning middle-income, suburban, family-centered, property-owning, and mortgaged-to-the-hilt market needed our product by the package, not by the policy. It needed protection for family, home, car, life, and health *all at once* and needed some way of paying for it as it did for every other major purchase it made, by the month, in easy installments.

Needless to say, these were revolutionary concepts for a business which had never considered itself a factor in the rapidly changing mass market. To meet this situation, as we could project it into the future, line executives were asked to create new products and new marketing approaches. Committees were formed; surveys were made; interdepartmental groups held meetings. But for months nothing happened because each line executive was too much concerned with his present responsibility to take seriously a long-range activity which might change the whole method and philosophy of his operation. He was unwilling to jeopardize his ability to meet department goals by directing his energies and efforts toward an uncertain future.

What did we do about it? Essentially this: new staff positions were created to coordinate the sales and underwriting functions along the lines of our multiple-line, mass-marketing blueprint. These staff officers were charged with developing products and methods that would conform to this corporate thinking. Line officers were encouraged to contribute to broad planning either directly or through the services of selected junior staff members. Sales promotion, merchandising, advertising, and training were geared increasingly to this new marketing approach, and ultimately some line departments were actually merged.

Ours has not been a revolutionary approach. Line officers were not handed ultimatums to abandon their immediate responsibilities for the development of future programs. Instruments-in-being were created, both individuals and groups, to generate an atmosphere of change and to stimulate line officers to keep moving toward newly redefined corporate goals. The line executives, for their part, are not forced to dilute their energies or blunt their thrust. They can, however, feel the constant pressure of a prevailing wind and find it far easier to move with it than against it. The fact that our long-range, multiple-line plan is now proving its value for *other* insurance companies has given the entire concept a new respectability among formerly hostile or indifferent line officers.

We believe that merely to present the line executive with a fully developed program and say, "go to it," is to invite disaster because he will do just that and no more. He will go to it and not one step further. If it is a program that runs contrary to his training or his ingrained business experience, he may answer, "it is going to lose money," and lose money it will. If, however, he is permitted to operate in a total environment of directed change in which he is provided with constant opportunities for adaptation, he becomes a partner in planning, not an unwilling hostage to it. Most important, he perceives that all other operating departments are moving with him, in the same direction and at the same pace.

At The Travelers, it became increasingly apparent in the booming postwar years that we must make more efficient use of the masses of data being processed continuously—and that we must integrate the *methods* of processing as well. This could be accomplished only through increased mechanization and the centralization of procedures which were formally handled separately and departmentally.

The line executives involved were not prepared to give up their departmental prerogatives or to admit that present methods of operation could be improved in kind as well as degree. And so, after a period of trial and error, they simply were not forced to make this decision. Instead, key members of operating staffs were detached and placed on teams comprising an amalgamation of disciplines and skills. These teams were given the responsibility of redesigning the whole company's approach to data processing. Their work has not been joyfully accepted by all operating executives. However, as they resolve a problem, this solution becomes part of an integrated program. Their conviction that the ultimate goal *can* be reached becomes a pervasive atmosphere; and the line executive absorbs this change almost by osmosis.

In the area of new-product development, we soon found it impossible for line officers to agree on what they should develop and how best to accomplish radical changes in policies and programs. By creating a staff specifically charged with formulating plans for new products, we produced a brisk, energizing climate which the line officer soon found stimulating and challenging. Old prejudices and the natural desire to preserve a reasonably successful status quo are far more difficult to maintain in the presence of people actually working to alter this status quo. Rather than diverting the line executive from his primary responsibility, we have given him and his staff the opportunity to join in a general activity of product planning. As this work has gone on around him, his imagination has been stimulated and we have found him increasingly willing to devote part of his efforts to planning for markets beyond the present.

In our experience, then, the line executive is usually unwilling to change by directive an operation for which he is responsible, and in which he believes, simply because of someone else's long-range planning. Very often, abrupt shifts in method or direction can be destructive of his energy and his operational value. But as long as movement and direction are taking place around him, and as long as he is given a sense of participation, the line executive cannot help but make corporate planning a part of his own. Indeed, he will more willingly contribute to it when he sees it can enhance rather than undermine his basic responsibility. As each plan unfolds, as it is updated and altered to conform to changing events, his insights, data, and ability to forecast become an integral part of long-range planning. Of equal value, the planning itself gives an added significance to the objectives for which he is responsible.

Now we are undertaking a broad program to give *upcoming* management a larger perspective of the place of our company in the economy of our nation and of the world. Rather than remake the valued operating executive of today, we are enlarging the horizons of those to come. Ultimately, we hope, the distinction between planning and performance, function and responsibility, line and staff, will be less apparent. A new kind of executive, the corporate management man, will combine the skills of line operations with the techniques of long-range planning; he will be a participant in the future as well as a shaper of the present.

THE MANAGEMENT OF PLANNING*

In pulling together my thinking about long-range planning I have come to two rather simple and very obvious conclusions:

1. Every businessman does long-range planning of sorts.
2. Long-range planning is not an easy task. There are no quick ways to establish it as an effective function.

Though these two conclusions may look simple and obvious, I would like to elaborate on them briefly because they are so often overlooked.

In the first place, I say everyone is doing long-range planning. It is true, of course, that many of the good operators I know claim that long-range planning should be left to the so-called long-hairs on the corporate staff. These managers say that they cannot do their job of making daily profits if they have to be concerned with problems five years from now. Though these gentlemen are not being purposely facetious, they are in fact kidding themselves. Even if you are just operating a division, you have to be thinking five years in advance or you are going to find that the daily problems ultimately overwhelm you because you had not thought about them far enough ahead.

* By Mr. Scheu.

Why do these people feel as they do? First of all, most of these line operators are frankly a little hard-pressed to take the time to do the job of long-range planning. It is a hard job—no question about that; it calls for the burning of much midnight oil. It is no easy task to get a line sales manager who has been doing nothing but selling to sit down and formalize his thinking on product lines or future markets.

Secondly, I suppose the operator is a little worried, maybe subconsciously, that he will be putting something into the files which may finally prove that his thinking is somewhat erroneous. This familiar fear of error is a big stumbling block to planning. It should not be an obstacle, of course, because we should not be concerned if events do not work out completely according to plan. One of the great benefits of the process is that you get a good plan which allows you to make changes, even radical changes, as you go along instead of endlessly drifting with no chart at all.

Finally, the planning operator does not want to go ahead with serious formal planning because he already has quite a bit of confidence in himself as an operator. He thinks he can and should keep himself flexible; he does not want a formal plan. He does not feel any necessity for setting his thinking or that of his top-management people down in writing. He will look back at the last five years and say: "Look, we have grown: our sales are up; our profits are up; what good would a five-year plan be?" More power to him; probably he has done a good job. But I am convinced that he would do a better job if he actually had a formal plan.

Secondly, this is no simple business. In itself, it must be planned, and not the least of the problems is the selection of the personnel to do the job.

My own first experience with formal planning was in a centralized organization. The company was a very fine one, one of the best on the industrial scene. Although we derived much good from the efforts of the so-called planning committee, of which I was a member, I feel that we failed to accomplish our mission—and for just one or two important reasons. One was the leadership of the actual planning function which was assigned to a man who had been kicked upstairs from a top line job. This executive was a very fine person, and top management hoped that this would be his opportunity to put himself back in as a strong member of the key group. But all they succeeded in doing was putting him in an almost impossible situation because when you do embark on planning it has to have the fullest support of the whole top-management team. They all have to be dedicated to the conviction that they are going to do this job. By appointing a man who has somewhat lost the respect of the management group, those responsible did a great deal to erode the effectiveness of the planning committee.

Then, instead of having the committee made up of top-management men, it was made up of the secondary people at the department-head or assistant-vice-president level rather than the vice-presidential. These men were really not in touch with all the information they needed to make up an intelligent plan; there was a good deal of material they simply did not have, or have ready access to. Furthermore, the top men—the vice presidents—somewhat resented the fact that this planning function had been delegated to their subordinates. Although I do not think they openly sabotaged the efforts of this planning committee, they did not openly support it either. They rather looked down their noses at the whole operation. They seemed to say: "Well, you boys do all this fancy planning; then we will go out and buy another mill and that will destroy all your plans."

Some good did come out of these early efforts. We developed a great deal of interesting historical data, and I think we further stimulated an awareness of the importance of better planning.

Having chosen the right people, the first step in long-range planning is to develop an effective short-term plan. Too many companies launched into a long-term plan without a really effective blueprint for the immediate future. They are not really clear on where they have been or where they are going in the short run.

I do not mean simply looking at the last year's sales results or the sales results over the last five years or the production results. A company needs to study its last ten years of experience in terms of all the phases of its own operations and its competitors' as well. By putting all this down in readable and concise form, one places the past in better perspective so he can sail forth into the future.

To be a little more specific: when I moved into the job as manager of a medium-sized division of a large business, it was suffering as a result of a declining market. But it was suffering even more because of a complete lack of communication between the line organization at the division level and the corporate group. I am sure there was some planning going on, but it was of limited scope in the line organization; probably only a little more formal planning was being carried on in the corporate group. I soon found that once I had demonstrated to my staff that I was willing to revitalize the business, I was besieged with ideas of how to get this business off the ground.

I became convinced very soon that, rather than take the ideas and start to build, we should find out where we had been in the past. I asked all my department heads to give me a detailed analysis of where we had come from in the last five years. This was not only very interesting for me, being somewhat an outsider; it was twice as educational for my department heads. Most of them had been in the company for twenty years and they learned much they had never known.

Once we had a reasonably clear picture of past performance, I asked each area to draw plans for the coming year. Generally speaking, this started off with a realistic appraisal of our financial budgets. Then we established production levels which were realistic with past sales patterns, not with the hopes and aspirations of the sales department. We also set up sales budgets that were consistent with production capacities. In looking at prior budgets, I found an amazing lack of coordination in this area. Also, there was very little knowledge of the price and cost trends which had put a lot of past planning out of whack. I found that many of the service groups were riding dead horses as far as their efforts went.

We had a mechanical development group working on a sizable project to automate a particular phase of our operation. But after a scanning of the sales projections, I was convinced we were going to be out of the business within about three years. It was just money going down the drain as far as our needs were concerned. All in all, from these studies we found we had a lot of problems. Unfortunately many of them were too complex for an early solution. But the important point is that I felt that every person in my staff or in my organization, either line or staff or the top people, knew what our problems were; they knew the priority we had established for trying to solve them and to reach various goals that we had established over a short period.

I will be the first to agree that this is not really what I call long-range planning. But I was convinced that we were at a point where we were finally ready for long-range planning. First, we had collected a backlog of historical information, which I think is the foundation of any project. Then, I am convinced that we developed an attitude in our top-management group which was conducive to long-range planning. For example, when we developed a rather detailed marketing projection going off into two and three years, our sales manager, who was a hard-driving line man, saw the benefits that came from the struggle he had had for three months in trying to pull this thing together and put it down on paper.

This experience has convinced me of several points:

> Do not leave the line people out of long-range planning. You can do a great deal to relieve them of the leg-work involved, but I am convinced that you cannot leave them out of the basic decisions.
>
> Do not let yourself or your staff believe that your plan eliminates the need for future hunches or intuition or whatever you want to call it. I still feel this is what we all get paid for as managers; it is our ability to roll with the punches and not make a plan inflexible. For it is clear that long-range plans will fluctuate considerably.
>
> When you do make hunches that go into long-range plans, do not let yourself or your organization be afraid to prove your hunches wrong. I found that a good and loyal organization will do some amazing things sometimes to prove that the boss—either the top boss or the boss down the line—is right.

I had a recent experience that illustrates my third "do not." We were forced to shut down a rather obsolete plant in one area of the country. It did not take any crystal ball to see that the plant would have to be shut down, but I was convinced that we were going to have to be back in that area with a new and modern plant within the next two years. I announced this not only internally, but externally to the general public in that area.

As a part of our two-year plan, I had a group specifically working on this problem and charged it with the responsibility of justifying my hunch. But for some reason I could not seem to get anything out of the group; it was dragging its feet terribly. I finally found out that my hunch was so completely erroneous that we had no business whatsoever building a plant in that area; and that the group was embarrassed to bring all this information to light because I had so foolishly publicly announced that we were going to be back in there soon.

When this group did present the report to me, albeit somewhat reluctantly, I think I surprised them a little by thanking them for saving me the future embarrassment of explaining the misappropriation of about $2 million.

In conclusion, planning is like any other area of the business which requires real management. I do not think you can put it up in some "ivory tower"; you have to bring it down to earth and make it a part of your daily operations. It has to stay flexible. Finally, a few top people have to be in the act.

DISCUSSION

From the floor: This all seems pretty much geared to a high level of operation in the company. In other senses, however, it goes down quite low. As a plant manager, I disagree that there is a lack of interest in long-range planning at my level. In fact, I think most of us want to participate in some form of long-range planning. This self-exercise works well in shaking up your own thinking and might be useful in developing better medium-range plans.

Wrapp: I talked to a man in one company who says that the only time operating managers really take to long-range planning is in companies where they do not have adequate measures of current performance. He said he is convinced that if you have not really tied these people down in terms of measuring the current performance, they will gobble up long-range plans and spend a good deal of time on them.

From the floor: I worked in a company where the planning is on three levels: every three months, every year, and every five years. It got to the point where everybody was neglecting their normal duties because they were working on the plans all the time; nothing was happening in the company. It was very dangerous.

From the floor: I am in pharmaceuticals, a fast-moving business, and if we knew where we were going to be in *two* years, that would be wonderful. Furthermore, I am a line supervisor and I can't do long-range planning because I don't know what the top managers are going to come up with next.

Wrapp: Are you suggesting that the faster the rate of change you might expect in a given company, the more likely you are to control the long-range planning at a very high level and not really disclose very much of it down the line?

From the floor: I say this is true in a fast-moving business like electronics. Much of this growth is in the acquisitions and mergers and consolidations. How can they fit in with the long-range corporate policy?

Wrapp: We found differences of opinion on this point. One company that comes to mind has taken a reverse position. It says that the simple fact that we know there is going to be very rapid change argues for having more people informed; it also argues for taking into account a good deal more know-how from the operating level. This particular company has moved planning down so that the people at this level in their various divisions, and some of their divisions are rather small, the people in sales, production, and engineering research, are very actively involved in making long-term plans.

From the floor: I would like to make a distinction here. Mr. Tooker is discussing really long-range-planning ways in which we can expand the market of the company, develop a different product, and so on.

Mr. Scheu is thinking about planning from year to year. I am inclined to put myself in his corner, when you consider planning in that sense. The line people very definitely should be informed on long-range planning as much as it is practicable to do so.

Tooker: Yes, but the first time you hammer out a plan you should not expect to get everybody to agree to it, no matter how good your communications are. Others get a chance to think about it, and before you know it, you change and refine it.

Wrapp: We are really touching on the distinction between setting broad company goals and collecting data and forecasting. Some companies spend a good deal of time collecting information, analyzing that information, and developing their long-range plans out of it. Others have said that all they want is someone up on top who is very imaginative, has all kinds of ideas, and is not really controlled by the facts. In other words, they say that if you spend too much time collecting facts and analyzing them, you close off all the imagination that you have around the place and the plans tend to become pedestrian.

Still other companies are beginning to try to have both of these activities. They are collecting more and more information—whether it is on the industry, the economy, or the company itself—so they are in a better position to test some of the wild ideas which come from the "vice-president in charge of revolutions."

From the floor: As one who spent seven years in consulting on long-range plans, I believe that one of the most common problems companies get into is trying to become too sophisticated too fast.

AMERICAN MARKETERS ABROAD

James A. Hagler

DESPITE ALL that has been written and said about the opportunities for United States business abroad in these days of world-wide economic expansion, the flow of companies into the overseas market has been something less than a rush. Several years ago, when our experience as a nation was thin in this field and our sources of vital information were scanty, this reluctance might have been understandable. Now that the maps are more available, the excuses for hesitation are much less valid.

Furthermore, we are rapidly reaching the point where the national interest demands more and deeper American business activity overseas. With the cold war significantly warm in the area of economic

Note: Mr. Hagler is Lecturer on Business Administration, Harvard Business School, and Executive Director, International Marketing Institute. He led the discussion on which this chapter is based.

competition, and the importance of greater growth and higher standards of living established as extremely important in the attitudes of the middle-ground, uncommitted nations, our commercial enterprises can make a central contribution to the easing of age-old problems and the consequent strengthening of our position vis-à-vis the Soviets.

A more specific matter of public policy is now being called to our attention: the gold flow. In figures, the picture is of American exports running at the rate of about $5 billion, more or less. They are going up, and we have a favorable balance of trade to start with, so the situation by itself is all right. But we have $4 billion going out, of which about a billion is in military aid and about a billion in economic development. Add that to the $3 billion in foreign investment and $1.5 billion in tourist travel, and you have an unfavorable balance to the tune of about $3.5 or $4 billion.

There are many ways for us to close this gap. I suppose, for instance, that we can cut out foreign travel and economic development. But this negative approach would have serious repercussions on the cold war. Or we could start increasing exports, and make a real effort to meet our current goal of $7 billion by 1965.

Companies are devising a number of ways to encourage an increase in exports. Some are developing foreign deals of various kinds even while they are maintaining their existing trade. Leaving aside the matter of public policy, why should a firm want to get into this business? For many companies, I really believe it comes down to a question of survival. We all know that forward-looking companies are now thinking in global terms.

For there is a major market developing here, being generated by a number of forces, including the European Common Market. The increased competition from foreign goods at home, the increased availability of dollars abroad, changing tastes and growing economic well-being in other countries—all are building up substantial opportunities.

General Foods, where a decision has been made to make foreign business a larger proportion of its sales, is a good example. It is convinced that it can do this and get as good a return on its money or better than it can by increasing its investment on the domestic front. Suddenly the company has discovered how profitable foreign business can be, so it has determined to go after it.

Why then do companies insist on keeping aloof? There are two reasons: the parochial, unadventurous attitude of the management, which is content with life as it is, and the lack of personnel. The former approach is clearly outdated; the latter argument is clearly spurious. Actually, there are thousands of people ready to work for you if you just ask them to. In fact, these fellows will start looking for you rather than you looking for them in the next six months or so. Soon enough there will be plenty of them knocking on your doors.

Furthermore, many of the people available are not as naive as you would believe from *The Ugly American,* or some of the other fiction we read. There is a whole crop of people who have been in the foreign field for some time, working for companies like GE, Westinghouse, the oil industry, National Cash Register, and General Foods. In addition, there are small companies, down to five-man shops, who have become expert after a number of years of experience.

But I must add a word of caution to go along with my enthusiasm: you will not find it easy to get into this field. It is no get-rich-quick scheme. George Bryson, until recently vice-president of international operations at General Foods, says that getting into it is like building a skyscraper in New York. You spend three years on the drawing board, one year in the hole, and suddenly in one year the skyscraper goes up. Everybody sees this great speed of construction and is amazed, never suspecting the work that went into the project. But it is worth the effort.

Because of the experience which has been accumulated by a number of companies, we can now begin to pull together some of the booby-traps to be avoided. Let me run through some of them quickly. The first, and a significant one, is the failure to adapt the product to the market. For example, one American firm wanted to take cook stoves to the Far East. But the company found that the Indians did not like ranges designed for the American consumer and could not afford them. So it came out with a tin stove and the customers went crazy over them.

Similarly, I recall a firm making turbines. It is currently working to see what it can do toward producing a turbine that will be low in cost and that will meet the standards of foreign demand but not necessarily the standards of domestic demand, which are higher. Reliability and outage rate is not as important abroad as it is at home. In Argentina, for example, they frequently turn off the power or lower it without causing any great repercussions. If you did that in this country there would be the devil to pay. The new design the company is working on is aimed at providing the qualities which really count abroad—like low cost—and leaving off some of the aspects that are considered necessities only here.

Another pitfall is the failure to grasp the attitude of consumers to price and quality; in other words, to understand and weigh correctly the type of export marketing that has to be done. You cannot simply ship it abroad; this is old-style dumping rather than really working into the market to determine how your product should be sold and, importantly, how it should be advertised.

A third may sound ridiculous, but it is a real factor: the failure to enter potentially profitable markets because of personal or political dislikes on the part of managers. I know people who do not like to do business in Egypt because they dislike Nasser, or in Turkey because of the high degree of government ownership of business. Yet both offer great profit opportunities. I heard about a fellow who was sitting in a restaurant in France once and was insulted by a waiter; so he refuses to market his products in France.

It works the other way, too: one man does business in a country because his wife spent her junior year of college there and likes to go back there now and again.

Too many companies fail to go in for the long pull. This is no quick operation, and you have to be prepared to take the thin with the lush. I know one firm that sells cool TV tubes in Europe. They are in there to stay, even though they recognize that the market for this particular product is a temporary one. In due course, the Europeans will catch up technologically and find out how to build these tubes themselves. Maybe it is a matter of only a year, or a couple of years, but in the meantime the Americans are making a very profitable business. When they run out of possibilities in that field, they plan to go to a higher-temperature tube and see if they cannot better the Europeans again and keep going.

The point is that they have learned that, if they are quick enough on their feet and flexible enough, they can make a lot of money in one field this year and in another field the next year. But they are committed to stay in operation there, on one product or another, just as firmly as they are in the United States.

Another typical mistake is the failure to identify oneself and one's company with the country in which he is operating. One of the principal ways of doing this satisfactorily is by taking the country's own men into key executive posts. Experience has shown over and over again that they can be trained to be top-notch administrators, and the gain in local standing for the American company in the process is considerable.

Finally, I should mention the failure to provide for an adequate flow of information to and from the parent company. The first man out in the field selling your product always has a hard time. He is not understood by the company and the chances are he will be fired in a couple of years. Then a man goes out for one or two weeks and comes home, not knowing the real proposition, but full of hot recommendations. The company follows them and promptly gets shot down.

In short, I am saying that you use the essential tools of marketing whether you are selling at home or abroad—and if you do not, you will be in trouble.

The next obvious question here is: how do you get the kind of information you need? There are many sources, as a matter of fact. I will list only a few.

First of all, I would suggest the bulletin from the Select Committee on Small Business, House of Representatives, 86th Congress, First Session, drawn from hearings held on July 14 and 15, 1959. This document tells how in the Small Business Administration one can find some answers and suggestions. For example, there are pooling arrangements which make money available to you. I know about the difficulty of doing business with the government—it takes so much time, and so on—but if we are really in this for the long pull we can accept the difficulties.

Secondly, a company needs material on the Webb-Pomerene Act. Kingman Brewster's book, *Anti-Trust and Business Abroad,* costs $12 and should be in everybody's library who is in this field.

The field offices of the Bureau of Foreign Commerce are invaluable. The sooner a manager goes to them, the sooner he will get the answers to the questions he is running into all the time. Here he has literally thousands of people working for him in foreign markets all over the world. If he is not using them, that is his own fault rather than the government's.

I wonder how many managers subscribe to the *Foreign Commerce Weekly?* A check for $6 brings it every week, and it is loaded with trade opportunities. In fact, trade opportunities are coming in so fast down in Washington that they do not have the people to get out the information to those of us in the field.

Still another good source is the Business and Defense Services

Administration of the Department of Commerce. The information that is fed in there is available to you and constitutes a form of market service. They also put out industry studies, country by country, and yearly, quarterly, and monthly economic reports of countries where we have missions.

In conclusion, I want to refer to what Malcolm McNair says in his chapter of this book. He sets forth the proposition that we are rapidly moving into a time when the marketing manager in the United States is the key man in the company—if that moment is not already upon us.

I submit that precisely the same comment could be made about the expanding opportunities abroad. If American business wants to capitalize, serve, and stimulate the world-wide economic explosion which bears so much relation to our national cold-war problems and the issues of lasting peace and prosperity, it should concentrate hard on the marketing factor of its overseas operation. We are now beginning to assemble the necessary facts and experience to make this possible—it is up to us to use these tools and do the job.

PRODUCT PLANNING AND THE IMPACT OF FOREIGN COMPETITION

E. Raymond Corey

FOR MANY AMERICAN companies foreign competition means not simply price competition but product competition as well. What can we do to meet the challenge of the growing European and Far Eastern goods in the world market—well-designed products of high quality at low prices? Let us start by examining a few facts in connection with the impact of competition from abroad:

1. United States imports in 1959 were $15.2 billion. This was up from $10.9 billion in 1953, which is a sharp rise over a six-year period. Of the 1959 amount, 35% was in manufactured goods.
2. The effect of imports on domestic manufacturers has been

Note: Mr. Corey is Associate Professor of Business Administration, Harvard Business School. He led the group on whose discussion this chapter is based.

spotty: it has greatly affected a number of industries without touching a good many others. For example, imports accounted for over 25% of the United States markets for bicycles, typewriters, steel flatware, nails, and plywood; imports accounted for over 50% of our markets for transistor radios, sewing machines, and jeweled watches.[1]

3. Turning to the industrial-goods segment, there are some striking examples of the impact of foreign competition. In 1959, for example, two large orders for turbines for electrical utilities went to foreign manufacturers. One of these was a 500,000 KW unit that was sold to TVA for $12.9 million by C. A. Parsons, Ltd., of England, and this was some $5 million under the lowest domestic bid. Two 200,000 KW units were bought by Los Angeles from Brown-Boveri for $9.1 million; and again this was about $5 million below the lowest domestic bid.

It is arresting to note that these two orders combined represented 45% of the total amount of such turbines sold by American manufacturers in 1958.

Here is an even more striking example. Last fall the Panama Canal opened the bidding to both domestic and foreign manufacturers for about thirty tow locomotives to carry ships through the canal. The lowest domestic bid was $5.6 million, and a Japanese manufacturer came in for $2.5 million.

But this is not a one-way street. United States businessmen are doing quite a bit abroad in their own right:

1. Direct and indirect investment for United States manufacturers abroad is now over $40 billion, and combined sales from exports and overseas operations in 1959 was over $50 billion. Some experts predict the figure will double by 1970. This is big business —over 3000 American firms now have a significant portion of their sales abroad.

2. McKinsey & Company made a recent study of some forty firms doing business abroad. In all forty cases, survey reports showed, these manufacturers were realizing rates of return on their

[1] See Clee and di Scipio, "Creating a World Enterprise," *Harvard Business Review,* November–December 1959.

> foreign investments at least equal to those from their domestic business; and in over 30% of these cases the returns coming from abroad were more than double the return on investments from domestic operations.[2]

What, then, is the nature of this new facet of competition, and what kind of special problems does it pose for United States businessmen? Let us seek to answer these questions with reference to a specific case. In this way we can formulate more concrete solutions and then see how the ideas we develop can be applied to other situations.

The company in this case needs no introduction: it is General Electric. Its problem in this instance was Japan, a nation from which we now import some $1 billion a year, or an increase of 500% over the last decade. In the same period, United States sales to Japan doubled, increasing from $4.5 million to $9 million. Here, then, are the facts with which we are concerned.[3]

The General Electric Company is a large manufacturer of electrical and electronic equipment for consumer, industrial, and defense markets. Approximately 90% of its output is sold in the United States, and the remainder is marketed in many countries in the free world. All products made by the company carry the internationally recognized GE monogram.

The company is decentralized. Its business is carried on by more than a hundred different product departments, each one relatively autonomous and having profit responsibility to GE's top management. In its International Division there are eight wholly owned

[2] Clee and di Scipio, *op. cit.*

[3] This case is based on studies prepared by P. S. Coomes, H. R. Cunning, Jr., K. C. Frankenberry, and C. K. Moses, General Electric Company. Case material of the Harvard Graduate School of Business Administration is prepared as a basis for class discussion. Cases are not designed to present illustrations of either correct or incorrect handling of administrative problems. Copyright 1960 by the President and Fellows of Harvard College.

affiliated manufacturing companies (mostly in Latin America and South America) and affiliated marketing companies in nine countries. Independent distributors (more than two hundred) were established in virtually all of the remaining countries. The affiliated marketing companies sell GE-manufactured products abroad both direct to dealers and users and through distributors. Like the domestic product departments, the overseas units have independent profit-centered responsibility.

Up until about 1950 American exporters had strong demand abroad for the surplus output of their domestic plants. Foreign countries had dollars to spend and needed goods, while manufacturing facilities in many of these countries were still being rebuilt following the war. After that year, however, the position of American companies in world trade changed markedly. Large and modern plants had been completed in Western Europe and Japan. Dollar reserves had been depleted and the governments of these countries placed pressure on manufacturers to regain prewar market positions in other countries. Foreign markets demanded products designed differently in many instances from goods sold in the United States. But American manufacturers found it uneconomical to produce short runs of products specifically designed for foreign markets because of rising labor costs and increased automation.

In the meantime, with the combination of efficient new plants and low labor costs, many foreign manufacturers led from a position of great strength in moving into world markets. One member of GE's management, traveling abroad, had this to report on a Japanese transistor plant:

> Toshiba is a full-line local manufacturer with a product scope similar to the General Electric Company's. Only one phase of their operations will be covered, transistor production. Last year Toshiba completed its new transistor factory which is located in Tokyo. This building is windowless, and in assembly areas temperature is

maintained at plus or minus one degree and relative humidity at plus or minus 3%. This is an extremely fine facility. Production is slightly over 3 million units per month. Toshiba is rapidly increasing production. This is a highly mechanized plant. For example, transistor washing and sealing is mechanized and new machines have been developed to automatically insert transistor leads into bases.

Commenting on Japanese labor this same observer noted:

> Perhaps the greatest single key to Japan's commercial success in the electronics export business lies in its labor force. Virtually all factory workers are women or girls who appear to be in their late teens or early twenties. Minimum starting age for girls is sixteen years. Their average salary is $39 per month. These workers work at a high rate of speed with machinelike movements and seem unusually well suited to miniature work. This is probably due to natural dexterity developed through certain manual training courses taught in school.
>
> A pay scale of $39 per month should not be taken as an indication of low-class labor. Most of the girls are high-school graduates and the balance are elementary-school graduates. The employer (if the company is large enough) can be extremely selective in choosing his employees. All are given mental and physical examinations, including tests for manual dexterity. Toshiba, for example, employs about four of each one hundred applicants for tube or transistor manufacture.
>
> Engineers are paid $100 to $150 per month and tool and die workers average $85 to $90 per month. Salaries are based on age and education. It is not uncommon to find college graduates working in the factories in inspection and quality-control work. All workers observed were very diligent and appear to be devoted to their jobs.

The strong growth in world markets of such companies as Toshiba is suggested in these statistics on United States exports of radio receivers and household refrigerators as compared with total free-world production of these products outside the United States and Canada.

Radio receivers

Year	*World production (Estimated)*	*U.S. exports*
1949	6,000,000	421,000
1953	10,640,000	218,000
1954	12,140,000	205,000
1955	13,120,000	224,000
1956	14,050,000	172,000
1957	15,970,000	234,000
1958	17,000,000	153,000
1959	—	133,000

Household refrigerators

Year	*World production* * *(Estimated)*	*U.S. exports*
1950	925,000	187,000
1952	1,390,000	216,000
1954	1,870,000	212,000
1956	2,550,000	256,000
1958	3,965,000	234,000

* Excludes United States, Canada, and Communist bloc countries. World production is not an indicator of world export market since much of production indicated exists for local consumption in countries which forbid importation of radios or refrigerators.

In the case of radios, it was an important consideration that strong demand existed in foreign markets for short-wave sets. Short-wave radios were considered standard by foreign firms, while they were special for United States manufacturers. By 1954 United States short-wave radios were noncompetitive in world markets.

As for refrigerators, the problem again stemmed from differences between habits of use in domestic and foreign markets. To meet domestic needs, American manufacturers turned out increasingly larger refrigerators after the war. Europeans, who purchased food daily, wanted smaller, less expensive models. Units of four to six cubic feet in size sold more readily abroad than ones with an eight to twelve cubic foot capacity.

In 1957 Japanese pocket radios began to appear both in the United States market and abroad. An important factor in the development of these small sets had been the development two years before of moderate-cost entertainment transistors. Transistors replaced tubes, thus permitting the design of miniature units since transistors were considerably smaller than tubes. Moreover, transistors required less power than tubes and relatively small batteries could be used, therefore, in transistorized sets. Japanese firms had moved quickly into making and supplying these transistors.

Early Japanese pocket radio sets were not of high quality and were not attractively designed. By 1958, however, these sets had been considerably improved; even smaller "subminiature" models had been introduced, and the American public purchased them in large quantities. American manufacturers did not make models as small as the Japanese subminiature sets and so could not compete with these units. By 1959 foreign manufacturers accounted for 29% of the United States market for radio receivers (see figures below).

U.S. consumption of radio receivers

Year	*Total units*	*Total units supplied by foreign manufacturers*
1953	13,300,000	.5%
1954	11,100,000	1
1955	13,500,000	1
1956	14,200,000	4
1957	15,500,000	5
1958	16,056,000	17.2
1959	21,963,000	29

With its loss of market share abroad to manufacturers of short-wave radios and with its loss of share domestically to Japanese subminiature sets, GE faced foreign-product competition both in the United States and in foreign markets. The alternative approaches suggested within the company to meet this competition are discussed below. GE's top management faced the question of which of these several alternatives to elect and whether to apply similar policies both in the United States and abroad.

Domestic market position. Engineers and marketing personnel in GE's radio receiver department had studied the market for compact portable radios as early as 1956. Marketers had favored the addition of small sets to the company's line but believed that performance standards in such sets should be good. Engineering personnel did not believe that it was possible to have good performance in small radios. Because of the tiny speakers and cabinets that would be used, good tone would be impossible to achieve. Furthermore, such sets would have to have small antennas and their receiving sensitivity would necessarily be limited. Finally, small batteries could last only fifteen to twenty hours as compared to seventy-five to one hundred hours for batteries in conventional portable radios.

The rapid acceptance of Japanese radios, however, had indicated the strong demand existing in the United States for subminiature sets, in spite of the fact that by GE standards these sets did not have good performance. It became apparent, then, to the management of the radio receiver department that GE should be represented in this new segment of the radio market.

Cost studies indicated, however, that GE would not be able to market a subminiature radio for less than a list price of $34.95, while an approximately equivalent Japanese product could be sold profitably for $29.95. Under these circumstances, the department's management gave consideration to the possibility of importing Japanese radios for sale through its distribution system. Alternatively, the department could import all or some of the components from Japan and assemble these radios in the United States. As a third possibility, the department's management could elect to design, manufacture, and promote a set, somewhat larger than Japanese models, which would have better tone, greater reception sensitivity, and longer battery life.

It was an important consideration that GE policy normally prohibited the use of the GE trademark on products not actually manufactured by the company. According to policy, therefore, sets imported from Japan or made from Japanese parts could not bear the GE trademark and, by FTC rules, would have to be labeled, "Made in Japan." Several of GE's major competitors did not follow this branding policy. They were contracting abroad for subminiature radios and were selling these sets under their company brand names.

Position in foreign markets. Because GE's top management had indicated a strong interest in expanding the company's activities in world markets, it was important to strengthen distribution channels abroad. International GE executives, therefore, believed that they should adopt a "serve the market" concept with regard to products moved through these channels. Logically, then, if GE-manufactured radios were not designed to meet the needs of foreign markets, it would be advisable to contract with foreign firms to make competitive sets. Thereby International GE could serve as a full-line supplier to its customers abroad.

After serious study, International GE took the position that its primary objective, which was the profitable export in maximum volume of GE proprietary products, would be furthered if it were "to arrange to purchase products from sources other than GE–USA where necessary to establish, maintain, and augment a position of market leadership and to support a distribution system profitable to GE–USA . . . since not all export markets can be served adequately by GE-branded products of US manufacture."

Having taken this position, International GE executives considered with interest the proposal of one large Japanese manufacturer to supply specially designed sets to International GE. This company's prices were extremely favorable and payment would be accepted in nine different currencies. Its product-development schedules were about half of those of United States manufacturers.

Moreover, International GE could buy as few as 5000 units of a given model. Finally, International GE representatives would have the right to inspect quality-control procedures in the Japanese supplier's factories.

International GE's management recognized that company branding policy applied abroad as it did in the United States. It did not wish to request a waiver of this policy so that the GE trademark could be used on products manufactured for the company by outside firms.

DISCUSSION*

The question seems to separate into two parts: one is whether you are after the foreign market and the other is whether you are trying to save the domestic market which has been invaded by foreign products. But this is not an either-or proposition; any action that is taken must cover both spheres, both markets. Let us look more closely at the possible courses of action.

How important is trade-name reputation as compared with the desirability of a complete product line? This is a top-priority decision for a company. Will the American consumer pay more for the well-tested brand name? Brand names seem to be important, as well as the service—such as rapid and sure replacement or repair of parts—that goes along with them. Yet this would also seem to be only a temporary security, based on the premise that Americans are not concerned with price—or at least that they are more concerned with service and parts than with price.

The primary invasion is a price invasion, for even if the Japanese, say, are coming out with better designs, there is no reason why we cannot also progress in developing design. The point is obviously that lower prices have appealed to the consumer: the Japanese have

* What follows is a summary of the seminar participants' comments on the case problem.

been able to sell. At this time we cannot compete in terms of cheaper manufacturing, and American consumers seem to want to pay less. This leaves us with one immediate possibility: to concentrate on those radios which are better in quality, possibly of a different type (emphasizing high fidelity or better tone, for instance), and not try to compete in the compact set. This means giving up the small radio, but at least this would give the company breathing space and a chance to do more technical development in the hope of eventually recapturing this segment of the market.

But why should a company like GE take a defeatist attitude and give up what could be a profitable piece of business? Realistically, no such company today can afford to have an incomplete product line; un-diversifying is no way to meet expanding foreign competition. Even if the American company gave up manufacturing the radios, it would not want to abandon selling them. Converting plant and facilities—if GE were to change its huge Utica radio-manufacturing plant over into the booming defense segment of its business, for instance—does not answer the problem of how to keep a foothold in this market, or how to maintain a complete product line.

Thus, we would not want to vacate this segment of the market. But any company should want to protect its own trade name. One way is, of course, to get back to our case problem, for GE to import components from Japan and build them into its sets here, making an effort to keep its own brand on them. There might be broad enough implications in this for a company to try to get a change in FTC trademark policy, and this is something to keep in mind. (This is not the same as seeking changes in tariff levels to protect the domestic market from foreign imports.)

If GE wants to stay in the market and continue to use its brand name, one alternative would be to instruct the foreign division to set up a manufacturing facility in Japan, if that is the best location, and compete by using Japanese labor. GE, then, would not buy from Toshiba—it would do its own manufacturing and then ship back to the United States. This is similar to what one of the watch companies has done with both Swiss and Japanese watches.

A GE outfit in Japan, however, would probably have to pay higher wages than a comparable Japanese plant—there are always these "nationalistic" intangibles to consider. Also, if many American companies did this, what would the effect be on our own economy? Who would have the money with which to buy radios? The man working in GE's Utica plant is also buying GE washing machines and television sets. By abandoning the manufacturing setup here, you are throwing him out of work. Magnify this situation many times and it could lead to a substantial general trend toward unemployment.

Another approach to the whole foreign-competition problem is one which many companies are following today; again, it has to do with trading on a quality name. Probably the biggest advantage a company like GE has is its tremendous organization for distribution, mass production of products for distribution, and such. Why not use its great marketing ability, its brand name and capability of giving product service, as the major weapon in meeting competitors' lower prices?

Under this scheme a company would concentrate its own manufacturing facilities on the higher-quality products in its line and contract abroad for cheaper products. General sales volume could thus be built up and there would be some competition against the cheaper price coming in.

But this is balancing a better product against a poorer one—using the poorer one to fill out the product line while counting on the better one to bring in the profits. Should a major company even consider putting its name on a product it knows is not all that good? In ten years' time, perhaps, the dependable company would not represent what it does now; the all-important general impression of quality would be cut into.

This leads us into one of the advantages of Toshiba's offer to

GE: a guarantee of quality through factory-inspection rights. There has been a good deal of shoddy merchandise brought into this country by American firms—a short-range (and short-sighted) desperation measure in many cases. If GE could bring in the Japanese-made radio and market it under its own brand, or import components to assemble into GE sets here, there is a strong selling point involved. The company could say that it made a careful search of all foreign manufactures and that it had Toshiba make the sets or parts to its own specific standards.

What role does automation play in this story? If a company automates, it does not make very much difference what its labor costs are, and it is felt in many quarters that the United States' great advantage lies in this—its highly developed degree of automation and mass production. The Japanese, for instance, are thought to be particularly effective in fields where hand labor is involved and at a disadvantage where machinery is involved. This is something of a fallacy and becomes more of one every day; no country in the process of building up its industry will ignore automation.

Toshiba provides a striking example of the high degree of automation the Japanese have achieved—it is a modern plant in our sense of the term. The same is true in Europe. In many instances in the plywood industry, for one, European firms have better equipment than firms here, and their productivity per manhour exceeds ours. Ten years ago they had almost no equipment; today they can undersell us even when wage rates are almost equal to ours.

The same is not true in all industries, of course. But the point is that we must not rely too heavily on a supposed automation advantage. In general, we may have it now, but we cannot afford to sit back and count on this forever. Progress is not exclusively American.

Let us look at the picture from another angle—that of a foreign firm faced with competition from world markets. The Netherlands exports some 80% of its national production; the country is naturally much smaller but it is also at the stage of having to face a briskly growing international competition. The Dutch Philips Company is a good competitor of General Electric and has a name in Holland comparable to GE's here. Philips is meeting the competition challenge in a flexible way—it is not insisting stubbornly on using only Dutch-made parts in a product made only for the Dutch. For instance, some of its electric shavers are made in Japan, and parts of the shavers are made in Japan, Holland, and the United States. The Philips name itself puts a certain quality on the product. Could not GE do the same? This is cashing in on brand name in the most imaginative way.

Nor is the picture all that bleak for the American economy as a whole. We often get too industry-minded. Why not have free trade on a world scale? There are many industries where we have our place—we still make cars more cheaply here than they do in Europe, despite all the hubbub—and many where the Japanese or Dutch or Germans have a place. These developments are something we have to live with and meet—as both Philips and GE recognized —or else close our plants.

Such problems will not disappear by our efforts to pretend that they do not exist. There are innumerable products manufactured abroad of exceedingly high quality, such as the transistor radios we are talking about here. Many industries are almost out of business in some of their lines. The decision a company must make is not whether it must take measures to meet this new competition; the question is the extent to which a company can afford to reorganize by moving its shops and manufacturing facilities and how it can best set up subsidiaries overseas.

No one is saying that we should pack up the whole United States industrial plant and put it in Japan. There certainly is something of a transitional period to take into account; labor rates are bound to rise in many countries. Toshiba, for instance, is beginning to feel a labor shortage; there is not the same labor selectivity that there was a few years ago. However, to round out the picture, there are many other Japanese industries which still have their pick of workers. There are many areas which have not even begun to develop industrially, and what has happened in Japan could also happen there. Once again, we cannot count too much on hopes—the fact that we are going through some kind of transition does not mean the dissolution of the problem in the next stage.

We have been talking essentially of the domestic market in our case problem—how the company can adapt itself to new conditions without great sacrifices in market position, product quality, and organizational changeovers. But what of the international aspect of the GE case? It is quite different because there are no commitments abroad in terms of organization, plant, manufacturing facilities, employees, and such.

Looking at this particular situation, there are several courses of action from which the head of International GE could select.

First, he could forget the whole thing. Why, he may reason, does the company need a full product line? Second, of course, he could take the Japanese transistor radios. The third choice would be to go back to the United States and point a finger at the home office, saying, "You've got to come up with something that is reasonably competitive, at least in the quality line, so that I can put a GE label on it and sell it abroad."

Now, you would not take the first alternative because you want to sell radios; you have a full-grown organization going. You would not pick the third because you have already admitted the Japanese can do it in half the time you can. Yet you can sell. If you can buy Japanese sets, sell them, and make some money, why not?

For if you give up an item as important to GE as a transistor radio, then you run the great risk of losing other electrical items that the company can sell at a profit. In other words, isn't the transistor radio to GE something like sugar is to a grocery store? If you give that up, don't you take the dangerous chance of losing other markets? If you take the position that this radio is needed for a full line and it becomes part of a market basket, then you have only one alternative here.

Should the international division set up its own manufacturing facilities abroad? This would tie in the GE name by setting up a subsidiary—but is it worth an investment of millions of dollars just to keep the GE name on products? Toshiba already has a fine plant, excellently organized, good workers—why not use it? In addition, could the American plant in Japan produce as cheaply as Toshiba can produce for it? Among other things, Japanese might prefer to work for a Japanese firm.

But let us look at the kind of arrangement which the Philips Company has made. It has exchanged its technical know-how with one of the largest Japanese electrical manufacturers and has received, for no money at all, half interest in this and other electrical companies. When you buy Philips products anywhere throughout the world, you really do not know whether they were made in Japan, Germany, or Holland because the brand-name identification has been made so strong and the quality so good. This is because Philips was able to control the whole manufacturing process from beginning to end. Profits have been great because of cheaper labor rates, particularly in Japan.

The point here, though, about taking on a partnership with a firm already established in the country is that the American company can bring in its knowledge and technical ability. We are still as capable in the long run as any other country in technical ability, and, with an associate overseas, a company is acquiring an existing organization into which can be fed confidential innovations. There is more involved than simply radios or refrigerators—it is the world-wide functioning and growth of a business.

But is this only a temporary situation? As the labor market does get sapped up, your organization and equipment are going to be the same in both cases. As far as better technology or better equipment is concerned, you would be using the same labor, so doubtless you will be coming out with the same-priced product. But if, on the other hand, they do incur a labor shortage, and their costs start going up, would the manufacturing-cost advantage be a transitory one?

Again, this question takes on broader overtones. Even if the foreign and home costs get to be on an even par, there can be a new advantage in market opportunities. The American firm would be closer to its overseas market. If labor rates are going to rise, millions of people are going to have more purchasing power. And your products will be there.

CONCLUSION

Let us see what General Electric actually did in this case.

On the domestic side of the question, it elected to compete with the Japanese with sets manufactured in the United States. In order to produce the very small radios, it was necessary to use a few miniature Japanese components, since components of comparable size were not available from United States sources. My understanding is that the sets are being sold under the General Electric brand name because Japanese components still do not represent a major part of the total manufacturing cost. Even though not fully price-competitive with Japanese sets, the GE sets have been well received because of good performance and strong distribution. There has not been any problem of unemployment in the Utica manufacturing plant where the sets are assembled.

On the foreign side, International GE took up the Toshiba offer. Toshiba designed several models that International GE is now selling abroad under the trade name, "Igetric."

While this case concerns only one product and two companies, it is a product the history of which can be repeated many times over in a company like GE. And the situation can be repeated many times over in other companies in this country. What lessons are there to be learned?

One of the major problems involves the transition stage. We know we are not going to stay where we are and always do what we are now doing. We can already see ourselves moving toward business on an international scale from a position as essentially domestic manufacturers and marketers. From this discussion and this case situation we can begin to see some of the implications of running a multination business.

In the first place, it is likely to mean locating manufacturing facilities with the primary objective of being cost-competitive. We do it here in this country, but we will probably find ourselves soon, if not now, doing it throughout the world. When we talk about being cost-competitive, we will find ourselves analyzing products with regard to what the major cost element is and making a location decision accordingly. If the major cost element is hand labor, a firm might find itself producing in Japan. If the major cost element is raw materials, a firm might locate in Africa. If the major cost element is technical research, a firm might set up in Germany where technical research reportedly is far less expensive than in this country.

Another important implication is that there will have to be more effective integration of operating units within a company. Should, for example, International General Electric go off by itself and do what is best for its own profit picture? Any international unit must have some responsibility for trying to make the *whole company* competitive in world markets. International GE is not just another department and should not be regarded as such. It is an organization within the company that might well have responsibilities not only for selling, not only for manufacturing, but for product planning and plant location in world markets. The international division needs to play a very important part in guiding the rest of the company in its product-planning activities.

What will this company's organization chart look like ten years from now? It will undoubtedly be quite different. Suppose that the General Electric Company had consumer goods, producer goods, defense and utilities, and then the California division. This makes little sense. But this is what they have here in effect, consumer, producer, defense, and international. It is quite conceivable that this firm, as it becomes a world company, will have more of a geographic organization than it has now.

Let me offer one final thought. It was suggested in this discussion that we need to be asking ourselves what kind of a company we want to be. In other words, we are in the transition period, surely, but toward what are we moving? In this particular case some of the choices open to GE became apparent.

Does GE want to continue to stake its reputation on being a manufacturer? This it has done in the past, and this is where its skills lie. Or, as time goes on, does GE want to be essentially a marketer? Or, like Philips in Holland, does it want to mesh these two?

So as we make these decisions one by one in connection with single products such as transistor radios and television sets, we are also forging a general policy; we are likely to be changing what we are doing and affecting the whole scheme of things. For many companies the problem is to try to determine what they are good at, what their strengths are, what the world of tomorrow will look like, and where they want to move in terms of it.

MARKETING: APPRAISAL AND OUTLOOK

Malcolm P. McNair

THIS CHAPTER will present a general survey of today's marketing situation. I believe that we are in the process of getting a New Look in American marketing, that we are developing a system of concepts appropriate to the phase into which the American economy is now entering and which I believe can best be described as "the consumeristic economy."

What are the signs of this New Look? To begin with, I should like to cite the changing definition of marketing. At an earlier stage marketing was more or less synonymous with selling; it was the

Note: Mr. McNair is Lincoln Filene Professor of Retailing, Harvard Business School. In somewhat modified form this chapter was presented by the author as a speech at the Conference of the Green Meadow Foundation in Ruschlikon, Switzerland, July 18, 1960.

business of the sales department of the manufacturing concern under the direction of the sales manager, whose job was "the hard sell," and the business of the advertising department, whose job was to build consumer acceptance, preference, and, if possible, insistence for a particular brand of product. But this idea of marketing began to change some time ago. A signal instance of the new thinking was when Paul Mazur, a banker, defined marketing as "the delivery of a standard of living." Subsequently I ventured to try to improve this definition by defining marketing as "the creation and delivery of a standard of living." Then, about two years ago, Charles Mortimer, Chairman of the Board of General Foods Corporation, elaborated the definition by spelling out three major areas of creativeness in marketing, namely, creative pricing to broaden and deepen markets by creating more consumers, creating more and more convenience in products and services, and being creatively dissatisfied with what we know about markets and marketing and about the consumer's habits, ideas, and aspirations.

It is in keeping with this revised definition of marketing that we are currently beginning to hear more and more about the so-called "marketing concept." This concept is described as follows by John E. Wakefield of Barrington Associates:

> The marketing concept is a philosophy of business which is based on the belief that identification and satisfaction of customer needs, wants, and desires are vital to sucess—success being measured in terms of profitable sales and return on investment....
>
> The marketing concept starts with a company's chief executive. It is he who must recognize that, without markets for his company's products and services, there is no business.[1]

The same thought is expressed by Charles Percy, President of Bell and Howell, when he says:

[1] "The Ten Cogs in Marketing for Profit," *Sales Management,* October 16, 1959.

> Pointing your company toward the customer is one of the president's jobs, and he does it by working through his Marketing Division. The Marketing Division has the responsibility for moving the product and for helping other divisions of the company to plan and produce what the customer really wants and needs.[2]

Again, Ralph J. Cordiner, Chairman of the Board of General Electric Company, has this to say:

> Experience has taught General Electric people to see each product as a type of organism, with a life cycle of its own. There is the laborious process of bringing a new product to birth, from its abstract beginnings in scientific thought or in some salesman's perception of a customer need. Then the expensive period when this new product, like a child, is not fully developed and not able to support itself. As the Company is able to develop a market—and keep the product designed for the market—the product enters a growth period, when other companies are all too happy to join in the process of competing for a share of the new market. As the product becomes established, the Company must keep renewing it with fresh innovations and features. And finally, some totally new approach makes the product obsolete and it must be retired from the line while new products are brought on the market.[3]

To this question I would simply add that the essence of the marketing concept is that the function of marketing-minded top management is to infuse planning and coordinated operation into the whole process of organic change described by Cordiner.

As additional evidence of the changing concept of marketing in the United States I would cite the growing recognition that the consumer, or, more precisely, the desire of the consumer to better his position, is the motivating power in today's economy. It is consumer spending that takes 66 per cent of the gross national product in the United States; and it is consumer spending that has pulled us out

[2] *Ibid.*

[3] *New Frontiers for Professional Managers* (New York, McGraw-Hill Book Company, Inc., 1956), p. 30.

of all three of the postwar business readjustment periods which we have thus far experienced.

In his recent book, *The Powerful Consumer,*[4] Professor George Katona of the University of Michigan points to the fact that in 1957 over 38 per cent of the 53.5 million American families had annual income of over $6,000 and that the number of families with "supernumerary" incomes—that is, income available for spending on things other than necessities—was 20.5 million in 1957 as against 12 million in 1944. Under these conditions consumer spending is not merely a passive function of income; it is indeed an active determinant of the course of business activity. With such a degree of discretionary spending, the American economy is one in which marketing thrives.

But I would also say that, to a substantial extent, this is an economy which marketing has built. It is a want-creating, desire-creating economy, in which seemingly by some psychological law the luxuries of yesterday become the necessities of today; and there are no foreseeable limits to consumer demands. To be sure, there are those who look with disfavor and apprehension on this kind of economy, notably my Harvard colleague, J. K. Galbraith. But while recognizing the validity of some of the criticisms, few in America today are prepared to renounce the values of the democratic process or of the competitive free-market system which has nurtured this kind of consumeristic economy.

I have sought to indicate the changes which seem to be taking place in the concept of marketing in the United States. Let me next touch briefly on some of the changes in demand, which give evidence of our increasingly consumeristic economy.

The sheer *growth* of total personal income to a figure of $400 billion out of a gross national product of $500 billion is an important dimension, but even more important is the *shape* of the market which results from changed income distribution. Formerly we thought of the shape of the market as a pyramid, tapering sharply from a small

[4] New York, McGraw-Hill Book Company, Inc., 1960.

percentage of people with very high income at the top down to a great mass of people with low incomes at the bottom; and it was a market of this shape that we were thinking of when we developed the concept of mass distribution, namely, distribution adapted to meeting the demand of the low-income groups at the broad-base level of the pyramid. Because of the great change in income distribution over the past 25 years, the shape of the market is no longer to be thought of as a pyramid. Rather, it is something more nearly resembling a balloon, with the big part closer to the middle rather than to the bottom. Thus the significant group for American marketing today consists of those families with annual incomes between $6,000 and $10,000. Additional facets of the growth of American consumers' purchasing power, of course, are the substantial growth in the liquid assets of American families and the very large growth in the use of consumer credit.

More important from the standpoint of a marketer than the quantitative growth in demand are the qualitative changes which are taking place. With the increased discretionary spending, with the shorter work-week, with the spread of education and culture, consumer demand in the United States is becoming a far more complex phenomenon. Demand is segmented; for instance, there is no one single uncomplicated demand for automobiles, but rather there are a whole series of differentiated demands for different kinds of automotive transportation for different purposes. Similarly, the greater extent of leisure time, plus the greater purchasing power, opens up opportunities for the development of differentiated groups, for the expression of individuality, for the cultivation of hobbies or, more properly, advanced amateur activities, such as photography, hi-fi, boating, skin diving, and so on, all leading to an enormous proliferation of interests, multiplied by the ease of mobility resulting from personal automotive transportation as well as from ease of communication.

All this has brought about an increasingly complex demand for more and more kinds of goods and services and increased gratification of wants, desires, and whims, frequently of a psychological rather than a material character. Thus demand seems to multiply itself by a sort of "fission" process. With today's crowded life, stress on the value of time and stress on convenience become important ingredients of demand. Thus housewives are willing to pay higher prices for food products which they can take home and pop into the skillet for ten minutes, primarily because the pressure of activities puts a premium on time saving as an element in value. Other aspects of qualitative change in demand become evident as the forces of fashion extend their sway, aided rather than repressed by growth of education, spread of information, and improvement of taste.

A further qualitative change in demand is manifested by the increasing outlays for all kinds of services (household, medical, and health), personal care (cosmetics and such), recreation, travel, and education. Proportionate consumer expenditures in this category have been rising in the United States steadily for the entire postwar period.

Along with all these qualitative changes in demand, the consumer himself is also changing. Although willing to spend to gratify an enormous variety of wants and desires, today's American consumer is more sophisticated. The consumer figures the angles, looks for the advantageous price, has declining allegiance to brands or institutions, does not necessarily accept any one retailer as his purchasing agent. Nobody owns this 1961-model American consumer. And the degree of sophistication is highest among those consumers who control the major part of the discretionary purchasing power. The essence of sophistication is not only a greater willingness to accept and demand change, but also a greater readiness to reject that which does not please or that which has outstayed its welcome. Note, for instance, the American consumer's rejection of the sack dress in 1957, the rebellion against the 1958 Detroit automobiles, and the change in status symbols from automobiles to houses, cabin cruisers, swimming pools, and foreign travel.

And with all this, contrary to the apprehensions of some economists, there is considerable evidence that this sophisticated consumer makes a fairly wise use of consumer credit. To quote Professor Katona, "Installment buying, through which contractual obligations are increased and discretion for making less necessary expenditures is reduced, has become a budgetary device contributing to self regulation." [5] (Having thus alluded to economics, I might parenthetically voice a personal suspicion that perhaps this new consumeristic economy is one which the economists understand less well than do the marketers and the sociologists.)

I have dwelt at some length on changes in demand and changes in the consumer as evidence of the new stage into which the American economy seems to be entering. Next let me comment on some of the changes in retail distribution which seem to me to point in the same direction.

First, there is what we have sometimes referred to as the retailing revolution, meaning by that all the changes that took place when retailing followed the population to the suburbs and began to create *planned* rather than *unplanned* retailing facilities, based largely on the transportation pattern of the private automobile, and meaning also the more or less accidental juxtaposition in time of the almost universal consumer acceptance of the supermarket method of retail-store operation. Salient features of this retailing revolution are the planned shopping centers of all types, of which some 4500 now exist in the United States, automobile shopping, off-street parking facilities, evening hours, stress on convenience and speed of shopping, self-service and/or simplified selling, informal dress of customers, and stress on fixturing, display, and sales procedures designed to facilitate ease and speed of selection and to promote impulse purchasing.

[5] P. 241.

This retailing revolution in the United States also has a threatening side, namely, the fact that the future of major retailing enterprises, such as department stores in the downtown core areas, is becoming increasingly problematic. As the explosion of population to the suburban and exurban regions continues, and at the same time the concentration of population in areas contiguous to large cities goes on to the point where in such areas as the Atlantic seaboard the outskirts of one city begin to run into the outskirts of the next city, it seems clear that we shall have to rethink the economic functions of the central downtown cores. To what extent will the retail distribution of general merchandise continue to be an appropriate function of such downtown areas? Readjustments, possibly painful in character, may well be required.

The next feature of the American retailing scene on which I should like to comment, and which is also an aspect of the retailing revolution, is the role played by innovation. Perhaps the most conspicuous instance of innovation in marketing channels is to be found in the battle for the general merchandise dollar, the contest which extends over the whole broad category of apparel, soft goods, and general merchandise, where the conventional department stores, the specialty apparel stores, the apparel chains, the junior department store chains, the variety chains, and the so-called mail-order chains face new competition both from food chains invading the soft-goods field and from the various kinds of discount houses or supermarket department stores. Of the latter one may recognize at least three types. There is the older type of hard-goods discount house, which now frequently has added soft goods to its line—E. J. Korvette, for instance. Then there is the self-service soft-goods supermarket of the type which began a few years ago in New England and is spreading rapidly westward, such as Zayre and Atlantic Mills. Somewhat in contrast to this type is the closed-door, or membership, type of self-service, low-margin operation, such as GEM and Fedmart, which seemingly originated on the Pacific Coast and is moving eastward.

It is probable that these latter two types together comprise between 400 and 500 stores and probably accounted for sales volume approaching $1 billion in 1960. In contrast to the gross margins of conventional department stores, specialty apparel stores, and conventional variety chains, which normally are in the area of 34 per cent to 38 per cent of net sales, the gross margins of these newer types of retail enterprise, including the nonfood operations of the food supermarkets, apparently range from 23 per cent to 28 per cent. The wage costs in ratio to sales for some of the newer types of retailers, for instance, are probably less than half as great as the equivalent costs in department stores.

In the meantime, significant changes are occurring elsewhere in the general merchandise field. The traditional limited-price variety chain is rapidly evolving into something quite different; simultaneously these organizations have been moving into self-service and at the same time have abandoned their low, fixed-price limits, are stocking a much wider range of merchandise, and are beginning to offer consumer credit. Significant changes also are evident in the large mail-order companies. Their retail stores are increasing in size and are trading up in quality and range of merchandise as well as in decor and promotion. Although the retail stores account for the largest part of their total sales, the most rapidly growing sector of business for these companies is the catalogue order office, offering a type of convenience to the customer which embraces aspects both of the retail store and of the mail-order business, at the same time pricing its goods on the lower mail-order basis.

One is tempted to offer the generalization that today there are three significant institutional concepts in retailing in the United States, and that all three of them are drawing more closely together. The first of these is the department-store concept: most large-scale retail enterprises in America today are department stores in the sense of carrying a great variety of merchandise on a departmental basis under one roof; this is true of conventional department stores, chain variety stores, general merchandise chains, discount houses, soft-goods supermarkets, and even, to some degree, food supermarkets. The second concept is the chain store, or multiple-unit basis of operation: a majority of the large-scale retailers in the United States today are multistore operations; even the department stores are rapidly becoming regional chains of suburban branches. The third concept, newer than the other two but clearly well on its way to significance, is the self-service supermarket: the techniques of open selling, exposed merchandise, self-selection (with or without checkout), have spread well beyond the field of food distribution and are steadily gaining new adherents.

It would be a mistake, however, to assume that the present dominance of these three institutional concepts, and the fact that all three not infrequently are found in the same enterprise, connotes the emergence of any settled pattern of American retailing that will persist indefinitely. The one thing that we may infallibly expect is change. The free-market forces of innovation keep the wheel always revolving; sometimes it revolves slowly, sometimes more rapidly, but it does not stand still. The cycle frequently begins with a bold new concept, an innovation. Somebody gets a bright new idea. There is a John Wanamaker, a George Hartford, a Frank Woolworth, a W. T. Grant, a General Wood, a Michael Cullen, a Eugene Ferkauf, a Gottlieb Duttweiler.

Such an innovator has an idea for a new kind of distributive enterprise. At the outset he is in bad repute, ridiculed, scorned, condemned as "illegitimate." Bankers and investors are suspicious of him. But he attracts the public on the basis of the price appeal made possible by the low operating costs inherent in his innovation. As he goes along he trades up, improves the quality of his merchandise, improves the appearance and standing of his store, attains greater respectability. Then, if he is successful, there comes the period of growth, the period when he is taking business away from the established distribution channels that have clung to the old methods. Repeatedly something like this has happened in American distribution. The department stores took it away from the smaller merchants in the cities in the late nineteenth and early twentieth century; the original grocery chains took it away from the old wholesaler–small-retailer combination; the supermarkets then began taking it away from the original grocery chains to the extent that the latter had to climb on the supermarket bandwagon. And today the discount houses and the soft-goods supermarkets threaten to take it away from the conventional department stores and the conventional variety chains.

Characteristic of recent years is the squeeze on retail profits. Productivity of labor in distribution, particularly retail distribution, does not increase so rapidly as in manufacturing. Therefore, when wage rates rise more rapidly than do retail prices, as certainly has been the case since the early 1950s, the retailer's operating expense ratio tends to rise; and with the severe competition on margins previously noted, his profits are squeezed. This situation has been clearly evident in the department-store business and in the variety-chain business for the last several years. In principle, the remedy is clear: an increase in the productivity of these retailing organizations. And it is just possible that the prospects for a development of this kind are beginning to brighten. It has long been a commonplace observation that "goods are manufactured by horsepower and distributed by manpower"; and, while in the main the observation still holds good, signs of an approaching dawn of technology in retail distribution are not wholly lacking.

Vending machines are increasingly important in some lines, such as soft drinks and cigarettes; modern store buildings and their fixtures are increasingly becoming "machines for selling"; physical handling of goods is being substantially reduced by devices and systems for materials handling; warehouses are becoming automated; and automatic data processing promises not only economies in operation but, perhaps more important, vast improvement in speed, accuracy, and extent of information made available to management. Improvement of productivity may not come rapidly, but certainly the prospects for this kind of technical revolution in retailing have greatly brightened in the last decade.

Whatever form it may take and however uncomfortable it may be for established competitors, the innovation factor is vital in holding down the cost of distribution in today's marketing-oriented economy. There is much evidence that ordinary competition among retail distributors tends generally in the direction of higher costs (barring fluctuations related to the course of general business). As new types of distributive enterprise become well established, they trade up; their capital investment increases; they undertake greater promotional efforts; their costs of operation rise; and they find a need to increase their gross margins. Particularly when real wage rates are rising, they find that their productivity of employees does not keep pace with wage increases, and hence they encounter a squeeze on profits, especially if the rise in retail prices is not keeping pace with the advance in money wages. Therefore the status quo in retailing, even though vigorous competition is taking place among the established institutions, seems always to generate a tendency to higher retail distribution costs. The saving factor is the freedom to innovate, to start a new turn of the wheel, to develop a new concept, to fashion a new distributive institution on a low-cost basis, slipping in under the umbrella that the old-line institutions have hoisted.

Emphasis on marketing and distribution, indeed preoccupation with marketing and distribution, is a distinguishing feature of the consumeristic economy. I have sought to bring to your attention some of the signs of this consumeristic economy in the United States, including the changing definitions of marketing; the integrated marketing concept; the key position of the consumer and his desire to better his standard of living as the motivating power in today's economy; the qualitative as well as the quantitative changes in demand; the evolution of the sophisticated consumer; the retailing revolution of the past quarter century; the dynamics of change in distributive institutions and channels.

Now may I speculate a little on what may be ahead in the 1960s. Obviously some of these trends on which I have been commenting are strong and therefore may be expected to continue. Nevertheless I would remind you that these are mostly trends that have developed in a favorable economic climate, and it is conceivable that we may not have such a climate in the years ahead. I have never subscribed to the rosy picture of the "soaring sixties" which some commentators projected last December and January. It has seemed to me quite possible that the "fabulous fifties" might be succeeded by the "sober sixties." During the period of postwar boom we have been carried forward by momentum, and at the same time we have been sweeping a considerable number of problems under the rug—that is, evading significant issues by inflationary policies. But now our foreign-trade balances are against us, and our gold supply is dwindling. Therefore we must pay real attention to the job of increasing productivity and getting our costs down. This necessity can well be a sobering influence in the 1960s.

In this new decade without question we must pay more attention to the foreign scene in order to be able to live with the rest of the world. We will have to take substantially greater interest in foreign markets and develop methods of marketing effectively in foreign countries. At the same time, we shall witness a marked growth in the number of companies operating on a multinational basis, that is, shifting the scope of their marketing logistics to a global, as contrasted with a national, arena. The situation in the underdeveloped countries of the world is of the utmost urgency for the years ahead, and I believe that a marketing approach to some of the problems of these countries is not without merit. Conceivably there are situations in which it may in the first instance be better to build supermarkets than to build dams.

Finally, there is one questionmark which I should like to emphasize in regard to the direction in which marketing concepts ought to be moving. As I remarked earlier, Professor Galbraith and some others have deplored certain aspects of the consumeristic economy. They are unhappy because consumers seemingly are influenced by marketers to prefer gadgets and tail-fins, annual model changes dictated by fashion rather than utility, and shoddy entertainment on TV and radio, instead of devoting their purchasing power in greater proportion to such worthy objectives as education, health, culture, and national defense. It is true that there are some answers to such critics. First, as I have already suggested, and as Professor Katona's studies indicate, consumers are smarter and less subject to manipulation than the critics have supposed. Second, improvement in the cultural level is the product of many influences and is a slow-moving process, and any long-range perspective of the American scene cannot fail to discern progress toward desirable social goals. And, third, a fatal defect in the remedies proposed is that they point in the direction of transferring from the individual himself to vested authority the making of decisions with respect to what is good for the individual.

But it may be that such answers are not quite enough, especially in the kind of world in which we live today. In the 1960s may it not be necessary for us to shift our objectives somewhat, to change our way of life to a certain extent—may we not have to think more of survival than of self-gratification? And is there a danger that marketing has made us too soft by its emphasis on ease, convenience, and current enjoyment divorced from any necessity of immediate payment?

If these doubts have any substance, the question then becomes whether we can make the powerful force of marketing serve some new objectives in the 1960s. In addition to the more abundant life which marketing certainly has given us today, can marketing give us the better life? Can we use marketing to persuade people to insist on more spending for defense, for example? Can marketing channel our objectives toward liberty and freedom for the world as a whole and not merely to affluence for the United States?

COMPETING FOR THE CAPITAL TO FINANCE CORPORATE GROWTH

Charles M. Williams

MY JOB in this chapter is at once ambitious and modest. My aim is to stimulate thinking about likely developments in business financing in the decade ahead. I will sweep over a wide range of probable developments, then focus on certain key aspects of competition among business firms for the capital to grow. Depth of support for my forecasts of the shape of things to come will be deliberately limited, partly in recognition of the conjectural quality of any forecast, partly because my objective is to stimulate your thinking rather than to convince you of the merits of mine, and partly as a practical consequence of my choice of a wide, rather than tight, topical focus.

Note: Mr. Williams is Professor of Business Administration, Harvard Business School.

In looking ahead at business financing in the next ten years, for working purposes I should identify some postulates as to the kind of economy in which we will live.

First, I think we can expect substantial economic growth in the decade ahead, despite what the London *Economist* has called "the leaden beginning of the Golden Sixties."

Second, there will be active and vigorous competition for the funds generated by personal savings. Those of us interested particularly in the financing of business should keep it much in mind that business is only one and indeed, on balance, a minor claimant for the supply of funds in the marketplace. Business must compete with consumers whose desire for mortgage and other credit promises to remain voracious. Savings and loan associations alone extended net new mortgage credit last year in greater amount than the total of net new security issues by corporations. Last year state and local governments raised almost as much money through new security issues as did business. Of course, the United States government periodically is a net claimant of funds. So business must compete actively with other would-be users of the nation's savings and self-generated monies.

Third, there will be enough legitimate and justifiable concern over inflation so that public restraint on the creation of credit through the commercial banking system will continue to be exercised.

With these basic assumptions set, we can gain some perspective for our look at business financing in the ten years ahead by a look backward. By orienting ourselves to what has been happening, and by making some projections of the more striking developments, we can shape up major outlines of a picture of the future.

In Exhibit I we have a summary of the sources and uses of funds for all corporations in the United States, except banks and insurance companies, from 1946 to the middle of 1959. During this relatively homogeneous period of growth, what was the nature of the business demand for funds?

Especially striking is the huge outlay for plant and equipment accounting for roughly two thirds of the total business usage of funds during the postwar years. Increased receivables stemming largely from much higher levels of sales volume absorbed funds, and there was an important sponging up of funds in increased inventory levels.

Exhibit I. Sources and Uses of Funds
All U.S. Corporations Except Banks and Insurance Companies
January 1946 through June 1959
(in billions of dollars)

Uses

Increase in Cash and U.S. Bonds	11.8
Increase in Inventories	54.4
Increase in Receivables	73.4
Increase in Gross Plant and Equipment	297.9
Increase in Other Assets	7.6
	445.1

Sources

Increase in Trade Payables	32.7
Increase in U.S. Income Tax Liability	3.0
Increase in Bank and Mortgage Loans	26.2
Increase in Other Liabilities	20.2
Retained Earnings and Depletion	119.5
Depreciation	155.5
Net New Issues of Stocks and Bonds	87.7
Statistic Discrepancy	.3
	445.1

Reflecting the general profitability of business during the period and marked restraint in dividend payout, retained earnings have represented a very important source of funds for business expansion. But even more important has been the inflow of funds related to depreciation—not nearly enough to match the gross outlays on plant, but by far the most important category on the source side. And within the years summarized in the exhibit, depreciation has shown a rapid and continued rise. During the years 1946–1951, depreciation averaged about $6.6 billion a year; most recently it has been running almost $22.0 billion a year. The rise in the depreciation inflow is attributable both to the increasing volume of investment in plant and equipment and to the impact of tax legislation permitting faster write-off of fixed assets. As long as plant outlays continue to climb, the depreciation offset should mount.

Although the increases in trade, bank, and other debt are significant, the extent of reliance on external financing—that is, of new issues of stocks and bonds after deduction for retirements of bonds and stocks—is shown by the table to be modest: only about 32% of the amount provided by the internal sources, retained earnings, and depreciation. Worthy of particular note is the fact that business more and more is getting on a "do-it-yourself-financing" basis.

The fact that business generates most of its own funds has broad economic and social significance. Obviously a greater responsibility is placed on the management that does not have to go to outsiders or to the marketplace to justify its plans for capital investment.

The management that must issue securities in order to finance projected new investment is subject to at least a degree of objective check by the "outsiders" that facilitate or take up the security issues. Granted that the degree of depth and discernment in the outsiders' analysis of the economic validity of the demand for funds may in fact be modest. But the company management that can finance very large new investments from internal sources alone is subject to no outside check on these investments. To illustrate: I recently received an annual report of a successful uranium-mining company whose balance sheet showed increasingly heavy liquid assets as a result of retained earnings, fast depreciation, and depletion, and a contraction of mining operations. Significantly, all that management considered it necessary to report to shareholders about its plans for the ultimate use of these resources was that it hoped to find some way to enable the stockholders to continue to get dividends. The only clear conclusion investors can draw is that management will invest the funds in something, sometime, with the choice of form, time, and place its and its alone.

When business managers do turn to the capital market for external financing in the decade ahead, the odds are very heavy that they will draw their funds predominantly from financial institutions. Despite a rise in direct investment by individuals last year, particularly in the bond market, a very large portion (well over four fifths) of the financial savings of individuals now flows into use through financing intermediaries—mainly life insurance companies, banks, savings and loan associations, pension funds, and investment companies. Furthermore, a large amount of the one fifth of personal savings reported as invested directly is made upon the direction or recommendation of professionals, such as trust officers of banks.

There is no reason to believe that the long-term trend toward increasing institutionalization of savings—and their allocation to users by professional investors—will not go forward in the sixties. So the business management raising funds externally must appeal to institutional sources and be prepared to cope wtih the policies, legal limitations, conventions, prejudices, and idiosyncracies (even professional investors are not immune to these qualities) of those who control the employment of the billions pouring into the institutions.

Direct placement of corporate-debt issues with institutions, which has reached such volume in recent years, should continue to be of great importance. This is not to sound a death knell for investment banking. Rather, in an environment of keen competition for institutional funds, it suggests that business use of investment bankers on an advisory, fee basis to help in the search for the most suitable lender, and in negotiating the best terms of direct placements, will become even more common. For investment bankers what began as a minor, almost incidental, activity to help carry overhead will firm up as a major and continuing function.

Shifting topics, what can be projected as to business use of debt—particularly long-term debt?

The external financing by business in recent years has been predominantly through debt instruments. If the public utility concerns which have done considerable equity financing are set apart, the relatively great reliance on debt issues by industrial concerns is even more striking.

In my view there are good reasons to predict that business will continue to emphasize debt rather than equity issues. Indeed, greater use of long-term debt than in the past decade is likely. Why this prediction? First, debt money continues cheap, measured in either relative or absolute terms. Even if interest rates settle at levels of 5 or 6%, the after-tax cost to the corporate user of 2½ to 3% is low compared to the cost of equity money accumulated in the firm as retained earnings or raised through new equity issues. In academic and certain business circles, in recent years there has been much interest and debate about the best way to measure the "cost" of equity funds from retained earnings and new issues. Though no single "right" gauge of cost has emerged, the inquiry and discussion is serving to accentuate the general impression that debt money, within rather broad limits, is cheap capital.

Second, the self-imposed restraint by management in use of debt in a great many companies will be relaxed. Although a number of individual firms and indeed some industries (the airlines in order to finance their new jet fleets) have pushed their borrowing to the practical limits imposed by lenders, the use of debt by corporations generally has been restrained and moderate. Many growing corporations of quality have no long-term debt at all. That business generally has abundant unused debt capacity is evidenced in a number of ways. Perhaps one of the most meaningful measures is the ratio of current interest to pretax earnings. During the twenties, and indeed just prior to World War II, some 30% of earnings before interest and taxes was required to cover interest charges. By the early postwar period this percentage had fallen to 7%. In recent years the figure has risen to about 13%; and, of course, most companies enjoy large cash inflows from depreciation, which could ease the burden of carrying debt in years of depressed earnings.

Granting then that corporations could carry more debt, but will they? Management reluctance to assume substantial debt risks and burden cannot be explained in economic terms alone—psychological factors difficult to measure and predict are important. Yet the longer we go without a severe cyclical downturn which would revive memories of great depression bankruptcies or financial stringencies, the weaker will be the reluctance to assume the risks of debt. Barring a major depression in the sixties, it is quite unlikely that oncoming generations of top management will have the same attitude toward assuming debt as recent managers to whom the depression years are still vivid memories.

So I conclude that management attitudes in the next decade toward the use of debt will be relaxed; there will be pressure to use more debt in many companies that have not used much up to now. It should be noted that in recent years a number of companies have been willing to take on indirect debt through leases, guarantees of subsidiaries' obligations, or other devices that do not show in debt ratios as such, but which represent very real compromises with the no-debt position. I think we will see more of this kind of financing. For some reason this half-way debt, or nine-tenths debt, seems more respectable and palatable than the direct formal kind.

Turning to a separate though related area, we can expect increased managerial effort and skill devoted to achieving tighter control over and more effective use of assets. More and more top managements are and will be accepting the concept of return on investment as a primary standard of management performance. As the concept is implemented in practice, visible increases in the efficiency with which assets such as inventory are utilized in the economy as a whole should become discernible. The gradual refinement for practical use of mathematical tools, such as those employed in operations-research programs, should lend support to less sophisticated efforts to maximize the effective use of inventory and other assets.

In the area of fixed-asset investment, greater and more carefully organized effort and increasing skill in capital budgeting, together with implicit recognition of the usefulness of "present value" analysis, should have an increasing impact on management decisions, and in general should work toward more effective use of the dollars poured into fixed assets. In so doing, it should help to cushion the increases in the needs for funds for fixed-asset investment stemming from the accelerating rate of technological change that so many see ahead.

Nowhere has the growing pressure for more effective asset management been more obvious than in the handling of cash itself by many major corporations. The large corporation that has not worked out a program for short-term investment of temporarily excess cash or of liquid reserves is now more the exception than the rule—a sharp reversal of the practice ten years ago. Many medium- and smaller-sized concerns are following suit. While cash or near-cash is an important asset category and one susceptible to close management, it seems to me that the recent trend toward reducing bank balances and increasing short-term investment in bills and other less liquid instruments may well give way in favor of programs in which greater effort is made to plan financial moves so as to avoid accumulations of large amounts of liquid funds. After all, there should be little management satisfaction in earning 3 or 4% before taxes on a large amount of liquid funds carried for long periods when the average pretax cost of capital to the firm may well run 10 to 20%. In many firms I believe discerning analysis will bring to light acceptable alternative ways to provide reserves of financial strength that still conserve expensive capital. For example, firms that have become accustomed to providing their own reserves against vague or unanticipated needs through liquid security holdings may well find they can meet such needs much more economically through a combination of modestly larger bank balances and carefully cultivated reserves of bank borrowing power. In any case I am satisfied that further improvement in the management of liquidity and standby assets can and will come.

Noteworthy in itself has been the striking progress of many firms in the forecasting and forward planning of cash flows. Not many years ago one could find relatively few firms that really tried hard to forecast cash flows in any very organized or meaningful system. In the last decade a large number of companies have recognized cash-flow forecasting as a keystone of financial planning and have organized to develop detailed and comprehensive cash-flow forecasts. Although many have encountered the usual difficulties involved in any sort of forecasting of the uncertain future, the usual experience has been one of developing skills that improve accuracy or forewarn of need for revisions of projections. The practice of cash-flow forecasting should and probably in time will spread through to the smallest firms and indeed become a routine and near-universal tool of management. This trend will be accelerated to the degree that commercial banks and other financing institutions come to insist on cash forecasts as an integral part of the supporting data required on loan requests. To date, bankers generally, with striking exceptions, have either not fully appreciated the potential usefulness to them of cash forecasts or have been unduly diffident about insisting on meaningful forecasts.

Under the stimulation of rising affluence abroad and competitive pressures domestically, American companies will continue to expand their activities abroad. Many companies that have done little outside the U.S. will "go international." Like other members of top management, the financial officers of these companies will find that overseas activities bring novel and complex problems. Some of these problems will devolve from an increasing trend toward less complete financing of foreign activities with U.S. funds and more use of indigenous capital under a variety of generally involved arrangements with the foreign sources of capital.

Since I am forecasting what will be, rather than what should be, I must also note the likelihood that many companies will in the next few years build unnecessary complications for themselves in exploiting the opportunities for business abroad. Judging from much recent, all too common experience, there is strong temptation toward entry into foreign business on an "ad hoc," piecemeal basis pretty much as specific propositions come in to them. The piecemeal efforts of the U.S. firm may well offer some modest income at little investment of money, time, or effort, but at the real price of blocking off opportunities for much more rewarding programs. For example, many firms have been able to pick up some "extra income" by entering into licensing and technical advisory contracts with foreign manufacturers of similar product lines. More careful subsequent investigation has revealed that the Americans implicitly, through such seemingly attractive arrangements, have blocked themselves off from sales—in particular markets offering large profit potential—of their own products exported from the U.S. or those they could manufacture overseas.

In short, the opportunities overseas for American firms will be unusual—both in the inherent possibilities for long-term gain and for "lousing it up."

Another developing area that will be marked with progress and problems—yes, fiascos—is that of financial public relations (FPR). In recent years an increasing number of companies have inaugurated or much expanded FPR programs—that is, planned activities designed to influence favorably the attitudes of investors (present or potential) toward the company and its securities. Efforts to shape a favorable investment image have taken such diverse form as speeches by corporate presidents before societies of security analysts, efforts to achieve maximum publicity of favorable developments affecting the company's future and to cushion the impact of bad news, stepped-up and more detailed communication with existing shareholders, arranging inspection trips (complete with fulsome creature comforts) for security analysts, financial editors, or other opinion makers to impressive new facilities, and changes in the corporate name "to more truly reflect the nature of the company's operations" and perhaps to capture a bit of current glamor.

But is there real significance in this upsurge of FPR? Clearly, yes. First, FPR can claim impressive practical results. Though the impact of effective FPR on market values cannot be conclusively measured, veteran students of the market insist that a broad and effective FPR program, combined with sound stockholder-relations policies broadly, can add a multiple to the price/earnings ratio of the firm's stock. Put differently, management of a large company can increase the market, or realizable, values of its shareholders by many millions of dollars through effective FPR.

If a significant impact on share values is possible, and if other companies are playing the game, it can be argued that the management that shuns FPR, or does a poor job of it, effectively penalizes its shareholders. The case for this viewpoint seems persuasive enough —after all, isn't a basic criterion of management performance its ability to maximize realizable values for the shareholder?—to justify a prediction that more and more companies will get or will be forced aboard the FPR bandwagon.

Further, it takes no great sensitivity to recent developments or keenness in thinking ahead to predict the emergence of tricky problems as FPR activity broadens and expands. Apart from a variety of such operational problems as the choice of internal versus outside organizations to do the job, some basic management problems can be expected. Basic will be the problem of keeping FPR under control. The line between putting your best foot forward with investors (just as with customers) and organized touting of your stock is by no means a clear one. Not only can overvigorous tub-thumping mislead investors, but it can build its own captivating updraft. The management that promises, however subtly or indirectly, more than it can deliver may well find itself in a situation where to hold its shining image (and stock values) it is tempted into holding out more and more promise for the future—postponing but not forestalling inevitable investor disillusionment.

Managements that build up effective techniques and organization for shaping investor opinion should appreciate that they have in their hands a powerful weapon that should be used with particular care. Since the weapon obviously could serve the interests of market manipulation, responsible managements must take care that they avoid unwitting actions that arouse suspicion of manipulation or that cause inappropriate movements of stock prices. Let me illustrate: the president of a utility corporation in which I had recently bought some stock made a speech to the New York Society of Security Analysts in which he made a number of pessimistic predictions as to the future profitability of the company—forecasts in sharp contrast with most market expectations. In apparent direct response to his speech, the market price fell in the next few days by almost 15%. My inquiry to an analyst presumably in close touch with the affairs of the company brought an explanation that the gloomy tone of the speech had been struck deliberately as a move in support of the political campaign of a friendly gubernatorial candidate in the company's home state and wasn't to be taken seriously!

And how to handle such situations as that when the president is fired after years of FPR effort devoted to picturing him as the epitome of effective management?

Now let me resist the temptation to further wide-ranging comment and focus more closely on my announced subject: Competing for the Capital to Finance Growth. A basic query first: "Is business going to have real trouble finding the capital to finance its part in the substantial economic growth most observers anticipate for the sixties?"

For business in general I do not anticipate that difficulties in financing clearly desirable expansion will be a major limiting factor on the rate of such expansion. But for a significant segment of business, finding the funds for expansion on acceptable terms will be difficult, and management of these firms will have to show skill and imagination if finance is not going to become a controlling factor in their growth. Some of the ways they can minimize their weaknesses in competing for capital I will comment on shortly.

One of the most striking features of postwar corporate expansion generally has been the ease with which corporations have tended to finance their growth. Earlier I noted the degree of self-generation of capital for expansion within the successful firm and the widespread existence of unexploited capacity to carry debt, particularly among larger corporations. Altogether, during the past decade business seemed to make out pretty well in competition for funds with other capital-hungry sectors of the economy.

But as the money markets tightened in recent years, under the pressure of active demand and restrained supply of funds, the wide disparity in the ability to compete for capital between the stronger and weaker companies became more strikingly apparent. To a significant degree the factors that make for the disparity seem self-generative; the old observation "them what has gits" is likely to assume increasing poignancy in the sixties.

What sort of companies make up the groups at each of the extremes in the range of ability to compete for capital? Those in the top need little description—the General Electrics, IBMs, A.T. & T.s, or the newer Litton Industries and Texas Instruments—and share many common characteristics: they are well established, diversified, active in research and new-product development, and possess depth of management skill, unused debt capacity, and large internal-funds generation. Their stock enjoys a broad market, and commonly sells at a relatively high multiple of earnings. New issues of stock find a ready market.

It is important to note that the competitively strong concerns as a class have accounted for a large part of the postwar growth in productive capacity. Typically active in research and in the development of new products and processes, as noted, they have been important contributors to, as well as beneficiaries of, the national growth in economic strength and wealth. From a broad economic viewpoint, the capacity of these firms to raise capital easily may be well deserved and well placed.

Now let us look at the other end of the competitive scale—at those firms with active opportunities and desire to grow, but with attributes that make external financing difficult. This is a conglomerate group, hard to describe precisely. But it includes a large percentage of the smaller firms desirous of rapid growth. Typically these firms are not diversified: specialization in a limited sphere is central to their ability to compete. Top management is thin. Financial sophistication often is limited, and financial planning haphazard. Often the capital structure has become complicated through successive resort to whatever financing could be arranged. Unless the firm is in an area currently glamorous, equity can likely be sold only at low multiples of prospective earnings, and issue costs are high. Further, ownership-management is likely, and the owners have a decided distaste for sharing equity, particularly if absolute control must be surrendered. Commonly, the firm does not have a long record of demonstrated earning power; instead, it may be a relatively young firm, or a firm with a variable record in the past. Or it may be in the low-group-on-the-totem-pole class if it is in a highly competitive, untested industry, or one with a record of vulnerability to cyclical fluctuation. Further, the need for funds is likely to be a continuing one—to finance plant or equipment or permanently expanded investment in inventory and receivables. The firm's commercial bank deposit account is likely to be modest and active. It probably has not developed a close relationship with any financing institution other than its commercial bank.

Mere recitation of common characteristics of this "low group" makes evident many of the reasons these firms find long-term debt and equity financing difficult to arrange, costly, and subject to certain constraints (sharing of control, for example) not important to the blue-chip companies.

The picture I have painted of the disparity in the capacity to compete for the capital to finance major growth has been a gloomy one for those especially interested in the future of low-group concerns and indeed for anyone concerned lest the dynamic qualities within this group be lost to the economy through financial frustrations. The question arises, "What can management of firms in this group do to minimize inherent weakness in their ability to compete for capital and to avoid being enveloped in financial 'cul de sacs' that frustrate expansion?" The question is phrased as "what can management do" rather than "what can be done to help these managements deliberately." For it is self-help that offers the greatest promise.

First, at the risk of seeming platitudinous, I urge explicit recognition by management of finance as a likely controlling factor in continued expansion. As such, finance is an area of management that must receive management's special attention and emphasis. Unusually keen financial management must be recognized as a necessity, not a luxury to be enjoyed only by the blue-chip concerns.

More specifically, "keen financial management" in this context can well center in these areas:

(1) *Especially heavy pressure toward efficient use of assets.* Tight inventory control, for example, frequently can permit sharp ex-

pansion of volume with little additional investment. "Lazy assets" are a luxury capital-hungry firms can ill afford.

(2) *Full exploitation of measures which avoid the need for funds.* Assertion of a vigorous attitude of "is this asset necessary" can frequently disclose patterns of corporate operation which minimize the need for the firm's tying up its own capital in expensive assets. In the future, leasing of plant and equipment probably will increasingly be available as a practical alternative to ownership of fixed assets. Subcontracting of particular operations which require expensive and lightly utilized equipment is another illustration of measures "which raise funds by avoiding the need for them." As a generalization, the capital-hungry firm should investigate particularly carefully a wide range of possible alternatives—subcontracting, multiple-shift operation, and the like—before decision is made to invest in new plant facilities.

(3) *Careful advanced cash-flow planning.* The special values here should be self-evident, but it must be noted that careful cash forecasting remains the exception rather than the rule in low-group companies.

(4) *Vigorous search for sources of long-term funds well in advance of the anticipated needs.* The fact that long-term sources are not readily and freely available does not mean that they do not exist. And, as I shall shortly suggest, new sources are emerging. But they must be sought out; successful effort can be strenuous and time-consuming. So long lead-times in finding and developing sources must be anticipated.

(5) *Careful cultivation of possible sources of funds.* Obviously, this area is closely related to the search for sources. Once potential supplies of funds are located they must be "brought along." Commercial bankers report that many would-be borrowers of sizable amounts still show up at their desks only when and after an urgent need for funds has developed and they want funds immediately—

having done nothing to build the long-term confidence in their capacity so particularly vital in the banker's mind in light of the inherent risks of their enterprises.

(6) *Realistic attitudes toward the terms on which funds can be secured.* Once they have really canvased the possibilities, it is important that management be prepared to recognize the hard facts of life. Naïveté as to the cost of funds has played a part in the difficulties of many managers whose report that "financing was not available" should have read "financing was not available on the terms that we liked." This point has particular significance with reference to the obduracy of some owner-managers toward concession of control to new equity investors.

It is easier to see that keen financial management is a keystone in the ability of firms with inherent disadvantages to compete for capital than it is confidently to predict that mediocrity in financial management will disappear. But this mediocrity *need not be inherent* in the low-group companies; recognition of the importance of good financial management and steps to secure it do seem basic to the long-term success of these firms in a "touch market" for capital.

Now let us look at those sources of financing that may well become increasingly available to the resourceful low-group management. First, I predict that large suppliers will increase in importance as furnishers of credit to their customers. Routine trade credit has always been of great importance to small business generally, with the larger corporations as a class supplying more credit to their business customers than they obtain from their own suppliers. And it is a ready source that capital-hungry firms have not been hesitant to exploit. As competition among suppliers for available outlets tightens, some "de facto" easing of trade terms can be expected even if nominal terms of sale are not expanded.

More important is the increasing willingness of large suppliers to negotiate special financing deals with customers of promise. Just recently, for example, one manufacturer of an expensive consumer item publicly announced his willingness to offer continuing credit to new distributor firms in an amount up to twice the distributor's equity investment. Effectively, the affluent large manufacturer will substitute his own relatively high capacity to raise capital funds for the much lesser capacity of his customer. The trend toward greater supplier financing is not uniform across industry; it seems most likely to be important in the case of firms with all or most of the following characteristics: (1) position is strong financially, (2) fixed costs are high so that additional volume is highly profitable, (3) capacity is generous, and (4) product differentiation is not high. To firms with these characteristics, such as many chemical manufacturers, it makes real sense to use finance as an important tool in building or holding sales volume.

It is likely that more and more industrial or commercial equipment will be available for purchase on fairly long payment terms or, as indicated earlier, available on a strict rental basis. In recent months there has been a veritable rash of new "captive" sales finance companies organized by industrial firms seeking to make it easier for less affluent customers to buy their products. Armed commonly with the direct or indirect guarantee of their debts by their manufacturing parent company, these captive finance companies have found it possible to raise large amounts of borrowed money at moderate rates, so their finance charges in turn can be moderate.

Of particular interest to firms of some size with attractive prospects but some significant weaknesses as a long-term credit risk has been the increasing willingness of some important institutional investors, such as life insurance companies, to extend sizable credits providing the borrower concedes some opportunities for equity participation by the lender. The instruments for such equity participation usually have taken the form of detachable warrants to buy equity shares at a fixed price or the form of debt convertible into equity. While there are important problems for both borrower and lender in this "incentive financing," it may well grow substantially in the future and represent another alternative source of financing to many firms for whom alternatives are not abundant.

Of course, for those firms that find themselves in fields of which the investing public has become enamored as especially promising for the future, the general aura of optimism may be such that public sale of equities is possible on attractive terms, even for the low-group firms in the industry. But since the investing public is fickle in determining those fields to which it will attach glamor, such corporate good fortune may well be more the product of luck than the fruits of careful long-term planning.

Now let us turn to government programs for financial assistance in business. It is entirely likely that the present governmental programs aimed at increasing the availability of intermediate and long-term finance for firms that find it difficult to compete for capital—particularly smaller businesses—will be altered and expanded. This forecast is based on the dual premise that the present programs have structural weaknesses that will become apparent, and that programs for aiding small business particularly have irresistible political appeal. It may well be useful to review the highlights of these programs and to illustrate the sorts of change that are likely.

Since 1953, the Small Business Administration (SBA), a federal agency, has had an active program of lending government funds, often in conjunction with loans by banks, to qualifying small business. Amortized repayment over periods of 3 to 10 years is typically required. Through 1959, 18,271 loans totaling $856 million had been approved, and 1959 was an especially active year. It would appear that the SBA in practice has shown a heavy interest in security; typically it has sought a security interest in almost any unpledged assets of value. Consequently, SBA loan funds may be invaluable for the hard-pressed firm that needs to stem declines or wants to finance one-step expansion programs; but their security and repayment requirements make difficult further financing until the loan is repaid. Thus, to the firm contemplating continued expansion the SBA program has basic shortcomings.

The success of programs built around government guarantees of private loans in the home mortgage and other fields makes it likely that future expansion of government aid to business will make more substantial use of guarantees to facilitate the flow of institutional loan funds into competitively weak concerns. It is interesting to note in this context that expanded governmental support of long-term private credits to business built around the guarantee device has been recommended to the English government by the highly regarded Radcliffe Committee.

Much cussed and discussed has been the relatively recent legislative sanction for a new kind of private financial organization to invest in smaller firms—the Small Business Investment Corporations. The legislation provided that, under the supervision of the SBA, special tax concessions and government loan funds to supplement their own privately financed equity funds would be available to the SBICs. Subject to legislative rules and to regulations established by the SBA, the SBICs were to use their equity and borrowed funds for investment in smaller firms. The legislation provided that the SBICs could ask for equity participation in the form of debt convertible into equity.

It is the possibility of gain through equity participation that has particularly spurred interest in the SBICs, since the inherent costs and risks of long-term lending to smaller firms for a limited interest return alone are no more likely to appeal to these new organizations than they have to established financial institutions. Through 1959, 61 SBICs, with some $40 million of equity funds, had been licensed by the SBA. The future of the SBICs remains conjectural. Probably present regulations will be liberalized to give the SBICs greater freedom and scope of action. But at least the concept of the combined debt-equity instrument is an important and realistic contribution and the framework on which a significant new type of financing institution could be built.

Since realization of gains from the equity participation will be facilitated by the development of a market for the common shares of creditor firms, it is likely that the interest of the SBICs will be restricted largely to firms with attractive prospects for very substantial growth and public issue of securities. The number of companies with such prospects is by no means unlimited, and many of these will be able to find suitable financing elsewhere. Barring substantial liberalization of the rules under which the SBICs operate, one can expect that their support will be restricted to a relatively small number of firms, but ones which represent a particularly dynamic and promising sector of business.

Also much publicized have been the various business-development loan corporations established in a number of cities and states. Many have been patterned consciously on the lines of the pioneer in the field, the Massachusetts Business Development Corporation. The MBDC aims to meet the intermediate-term loan needs of credit-worthy firms, particularly sizable employers, who have not been able to find satisfactory accommodation elsewhere. As in the case of the SBA, the MBDC has usually insisted on strong security provisions, so that its credits are best suited to a "one-shot" need for debt money. The volume of credit extended by the development corporations has not been large, and it is hard to see their future role as more than a very modest, if useful, one.

"If you can't lick 'em, jine 'em." This succinct philosophy may well represent a practical, if not fully satisfying, alternative for many concerns with the human and technical qualifications for rapid growth but limited finances. Organizational growth through merger into a firm with strong financial capacity can provide the means for development of an enterprise, even though the corporate identity of the old enterprise disappears. There are a number of reasons why merger will represent an attractive opportunity for an increasing number of growth-minded enterprises in the future, one very much more attractive than a last resort to "going it on our own."

First, there is the basic fact, already discussed, that many large firms are limited in their expansion, not by finances but very much by management talent and by products to develop and sell. It may well be cheaper and certainly faster for such concerns to buy an organization, even one with lopsided management capabilities which must be supplemented, and a promising product line than it is to expand solely through development of its own personnel and products. Often the merger prospect's product line or capabilities can supplement and support existing lines, or alternatively can offer desirable diversification. From a financial viewpoint, if the new acquisition can be financed with an issue of stock, the acquiring firm can enrich its own earnings per share if it issues stock in a proportion less than the current price/earnings ratio of its stock in the market. Thus, Company A selling at 30 times earnings could enrich its per-share return significantly by paying for acquired Company B in stock with a market value equal to, say, 15 times the earnings of Company B.

Going it alone is likely to have real emotional and intangible appeal to individualistic entrepreneurs. But realistic assay of the costs of the funds for major expansion, barring the possibility of a highly enthusiastic market for its shares, may well make the outlook for long-term financial reward through merger highly attractive. Further, the relative certainty that adequate financial support will be available for full exploitation of their idea or product line as a division of a large company can be an important consideration favoring merger. Control over destiny of the firm is obviously surrendered in merger, but large-scale equity or debt financing on their own can also compromise control. Further, if the old management team is unhappy under the merged arrangement, they can quit without jeopardizing the financial fruits of their success.

From a social point of view, a most important *desideratum*—that worth-while new ideas or solid product lines with prospects of successful expansion find the financing support essential to their development—is satisfied by the merger, quite possibly much more completely than if the individual firm struggled along hampered in its progress by inadequate financing.

It must be pointed out that merger is a real possibility for most new or small firms only after the promise of its products or the demonstration of its manager's skills is fairly well established. Consider, for example, the new technical firm that starts out as a thinly capitalized, small firm doing research and development for the government. Such development work can often be financed by bank loans secured by assignment of prospective receipts under the contract. Now comes the time when its researchers develop the idea for a new product. This new product has promise, but it must be developed, tested, manufactured, and sold. At this stage significant but not huge amounts of capital are required to develop the product and to establish its promise. An equity issue at this stage, possibly indirectly, such as through convertible notes placed with an SBIC, may well be necessary in order to have something tangible in the way of a proven product and demonstrated market to serve as the basis for a subsequent large public offering or, alternatively, a merger.

In any case, subject only to the degree of restriction imposed on mergers by the threat of antitrust action by the government, it seems likely that mergers will represent an increasingly important, if indirect, way for the promising but capital-hungry company to insure the financing necessary for full realization of its potential.

COLLECTIVE BARGAINING AND INFLATION

E. Robert Livernash

IT IS appropriate to link collective bargaining and inflation because the results of labor negotiations since the war have tied the two so closely together in the minds of so many people. We have, in fact, developed the concept of "cost-push" inflation in response to this alliance and set up an argument, if you will, between the more traditional explanation of a "demand pull" and the much-discussed cost-push idea. Had we not had this postwar experience with its rounds of wage increases, I doubt whether anyone would have come up with the term "cost-push inflation." In other words, collective bargaining has created this new issue for our economy and our economists.

Note: Mr. Livernash is Professor of Business Administration, Harvard Business School.

We will not solve the dilemma of the relative influence of cost push and demand pull as causes of inflation in this chapter. I wish, however, to discuss initially five points dealing with this general topic. I wish subsequently to comment more specifically on the relation between collective bargaining and inflation. Let us turn, then, to some selected aspects of the inflation problem.

In the first place, we cannot get far dealing with aggregate statistics, for they really prove very little. For instance, we constantly hear that wages or earnings have advanced more than output per manhour, the commonly used measure of productivity. That is true. Throughout the postwar period, the increase of hourly earnings has outstripped the increase in output per manhour. But that fact is true of any inflationary period, for it is the very essence of inflation itself. Price levels would not be advancing if wages were not moving ahead at a more rapid pace than output per manhour. So this phenomenon is of little value to us in ascertaining the causes of inflation. While leads and lags in various statistical series sometimes give clues as to causes, they provide no clear resolution of the issue. The broad statistical trends by themselves, then, do not solve our problem.

Secondly, unions did not create the wage-price spiral. Advancing cost of living has always had substantial influence on the movement of money wages. Data on consumer price movements and hourly compensation of manufacturing employees from 1890 to 1957 show a clear short-run relationship between the two and a considerable inflationary trend over the entire period. To be sure, inflationary forces have varied in intensity over this long period, but real wages have advanced, as a trend, by the process of sharper increases in money wages than in consumer prices. The wage-price spiral is not a new mechanism introduced by unions into our economy.

Thirdly, changes in our official national cost-of-living index, which now has such a direct effect upon wage adjustments through escalator clauses, do not reflect in any simple fashion such cost push as may be inherent in collectively bargained wage increases. The consumer price index is made up of about one third food prices, one third service prices, and one third nonfood commodity prices. Food prices advanced more sharply than the other components of the index from 1946 through 1948, contributing most significantly to the inflation of that period, dropped up to mid-1950, rose markedly through 1951, but have contributed very little to inflation since 1951. These movements in food prices are influenced not only by demand but also by special circumstances within the agricultural sector of the economy. The steady and very significant advance in service prices from 1946 to 1959 also must be explained in considerable part by special circumstances growing out of the 1929–1932 depression and World War II, which influenced this sector of the economy. Virtually the entire advance in the consumer price index from 1951 to 1957 is attributable to the increase in service prices. It would be difficult to explain the advance in service prices on a simple cost-push basis. Nonfood commodity prices have behaved differently in the various subperiods of the postwar years, but on balance they have contributed very modestly to inflation subsequent to 1951. Clearly, even in the oversimplified analysis presented above, a cost-push theory will not explain adequately movements in consumer prices and their effect upon wage-price movements.

The fourth point relates to the three subinflations of the postwar years. The first postwar inflation was from the end of price controls through the year 1948. Consumer prices advanced about 33%. Shortages of goods and the overhang of the greatly enlarged monetary reserves certainly imply a major demand orientation for this period. The second postwar inflation was from mid-1950 through 1952. Consumer prices advanced about 10% during this period. Again, a defense spending and demand orientation seem predominantly appropriate. The third inflation from mid-1955 to mid-1959, during which the index rose about 9%, is much less readily attributable to demand factors. To be sure, the investment boom in 1955, 1956, and 1957 contributed some special demand impetus, but, as capacity grew relative to physical production and sales, cost push seems to have played an increasingly important part in the price increases of this period. In other words, the purposes of these remarks is not to deny the influence of cost push, but to illustrate the interaction between demand and cost and to put the cost influences in perspective.

Let us examine what happened to industrial prices and industrial output from mid-1955 and from mid-1957. Exhibit I shows the relationship by industry groupings, excluding processed foods. Commodity price data are from the BLS wholesale price index. Output measures are from the Federal Reserve Board's index of industrial production. The industries for which output and prices were matched account for two thirds of the total weight in the Federal Reserve Board index, excluding processed foods. (The chart was developed by Charles L. Schultze and is from his study paper for the Joint Economic Committee.[1])

The first point to note on the chart is how poorly output behaved during these two years. The average unweighted change in output for all the industries was a decrease of 1%. And it may be noted that this was in the face of substantial increases in capacity. Certainly there was no general surplus or excess demand for industrial output during this period. On the other hand, prices rose on the average almost 9%. There was some correlation between output and price changes, but, as can be seen from the scatter around the lines of relationship, the correlation was not high. Some of the sharpest increases in prices were in industries with declining or only slightly increasing output. The industries showing the best gains in output, which also indicated above-average price increases, were industrial

[1] Charles L. Schultze, "Recent Inflation in the United States," *Study of Employment, Growth, and Price Levels,* Joint Economic Committee (U.S. Government Printing Office, Washington, 1959), p. 108.

and commercial machinery, electrical machinery and equipment, and fabricated metal products—industries clearly benefiting from the investment boom. Closer analysis of this period would be ap-

Exhibit I. Changes in Industrial Prices and Output May–June 1955 to May–June 1957.

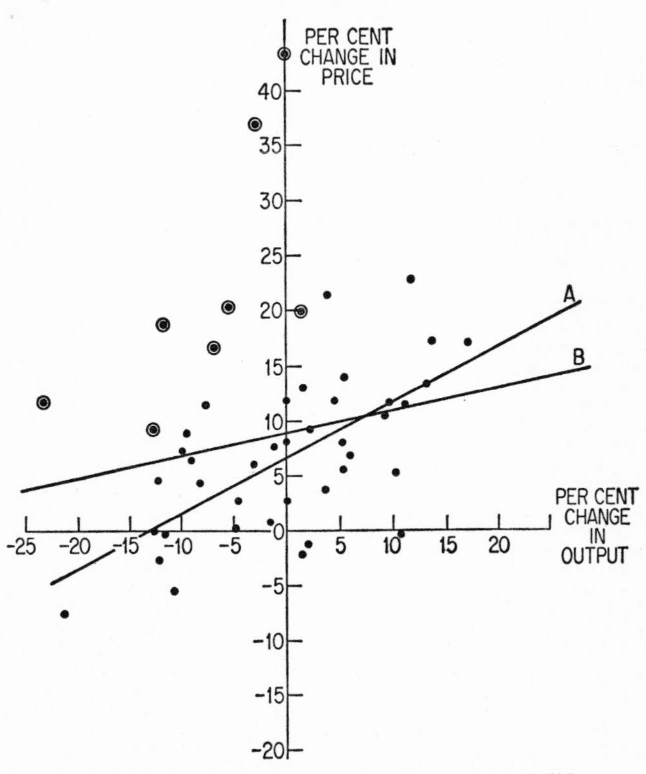

propriate, and for this purpose Schultze's study paper can be highly recommended, but judgment leans to the conclusion that cost pressures were decidedly significant.

The chart provides an introduction to the fifth and final general point which I wish to make. One of the pressures on cost during this period was the relatively insignificant increase in output per combined unit of labor and capital from 1955 to 1957. This opens a subject too complex for brief condensation. The term "productivity" is variously used in discussions of inflation. It is also variously measured. John Kendrick has presented the following table.[2]

Productivity ratios, private economy *
Average annual percentage rates of change

	1889–1957	*1919–1957*	*1948–1957*
National Bureau of Economic Research			
Real product per unit of:			
Total factor input	1.7%	2.1%	2.1%
Capital input	1.0	1.3	−0.2
Weighted manhours †	2.0	2.4	3.1
Unweighted manhours †	2.3	2.6	3.4
Bureau of Labor Statistics			
Real product per:			
Manhours worked (Census) ‡	—	—	3.6
Manhours paid for (BLS) ‡	—	—	3.1

* The NBER estimates relate to the private domestic economy, but real net income from abroad, which is deducted from private product to put it on a "domestic" basis, is a relatively minor item.

† The manhours used in these estimates are primarily manhours worked, but in some industries only manhours-paid-for data were available.

‡ There are other differences between the manhour estimates based on Census as compared with BLS data.

For the period 1948–1957 we find that output per unit of capital declined, output per manhour increased between 3% and about 3½% per year depending upon the measure used, and output per total factor input increased about 2% per year. The meaning and

[2] John W. Kendrick, "Productivity, Costs, and Prices: Concepts and Measures," *Wages, Prices, Profits, and Productivity,* The American Assembly (Columbia University, June 1959), p. 43.

application of these various measures of productivity can be debated at considerable length. A common statement is that wages can advance on the average by the increase in output per manhour without necessitating an increase in average prices. This appears to be true only with some qualifications and on the basis of certain assumptions. The first major qualification is that the term wages must be expanded to include all employment costs, including all fringe benefits. The second qualification is that this is true for the economy as a whole as a trend concept and not applicable directly to any particular industry or to any particular year. But there are also assumptions underlying the statement which must be clarified.

What have we really said in the statement that output per manhour increases at a given rate? We have said that it takes fewer manhours to produce a unit of output. We have said that labor cost per unit of output has declined at a certain rate. Employment costs can be increased, therefore, to their former level without advancing prices. But the underlying assumptions are that capital costs (and material and service costs, if we are talking about a particular industry) per unit of product have not increased and that the existing rate of return on capital is satisfactory. If Kendrick's measure of productivity per unit of capital be accepted as a reasonable estimate, it required, from 1948 to 1957, some slight increase in capital per unit of output to achieve the expansion and technological advance implicit in the gain in output per manhour. The cost of this added capital must be recovered either in higher prices or lesser wage increases if the average rate of return on capital is to be maintained. Even this implies that a constant rate of return on capital is appropriate as contrasted with the growth in real wages. Speaking more loosely, only very modest increases per year in employment costs appear consistent with constant return on capital and stable prices.

Turning more directly to collective bargaining, it should be clear from the points previously made that, in my judgment, not much of the postwar inflation can be attributed to collective bargaining. During the period through the Korean War and the establishment of the enlarged level of military expenditure, the wage-price spiral would have operated even had there been no unions. To be sure, the wage-price advance no doubt was somewhat sharper than it would have been without collective bargaining—just how much is anyone's guess. But, while it is meaningful to examine this record, it is also true that, with greatly diminished demand forces after 1955, major collective-bargaining settlements were at a level that was inconsistent with stable prices. The level of wage-fringe settlements, combined with escalator clauses, created a built-in base for continued inflation. There are various features of this built-in system which should be noted.

The key settlements in the economy have been in major industries and in the expanding sectors of the economy. The pattern influence, however, has tended to spread these wage and fringe advances widely throughout the economy. For example, railroads and coal mining, with substantial employment declines, have nevertheless shared in the advance in wage and fringe gains. This is not what one would expect in a free market. Regardless of the equity or economic logic of the pattern influence, and this may be debated, it appears that declining industries will not be significant adjustment influences in restraining the advance in average prices. While pattern forces may weaken under longer-term influences, it appears that key settlements must be held to noninflationary levels unless average prices are allowed to advance. Both wage and price behavior suggest a structural inflationary influence, a point developed by Schultze in his study, which, as noted above, suggests the wisdom of restraint in key collective-bargaining benchmark settlements.

Another feature of our built-in system of wage increases is the long-term contract and annual wage adjustments. The annual improvement factor, deferred wage increases, escalator clauses, and staggered contract expirations of labor agreements in major industries give us wage and fringe advances each and every year, regardless of business-cycle influences. The level of *this* year's adjustment is more and more established by decisions made last year and the prior year. This has not been an entirely negative development. The degree to which personal income has held up, and even advanced, in mild recessions can be attributed partially to the continuous advance in wage rates every year. Regular advances in wages may create a more stable economy than would greater annual fluctuation that is responsive to recession and recovery influences. But, again, if this process is not to create an inflationary trend, it must be restrained in periods of recovery and be at a noninflationary trend level.

Collective bargaining has made substantial progress in establishing orderly day-to-day industrial relations over the last twenty years. Contract administration is much improved over what it was in 1940 and in 1950. But it has operated during the postwar years in what has been essentially an inflationary environment. It is only now beginning to grapple with the wage-adjustment problem in a more competitive environment. In 1959, the steel settlement, albeit the result of a long strike, was made on the basis of total employment cost. It brought all employment costs, including the secondary effects of wage increases on fringe costs, within the terms of the economic package; this is an important move toward minimizing cost push. It also gave a limited escalator clause with an insurance cost offset. The over-all trend appears to be toward minimizing the cost push of key settlements.

Collective bargaining is modifying our wage and price mechanisms. Experience to date, however, is too limited to justify strong judgments as to the nature and impact of these changes. The hope is that collective bargaining can adjust to a level of gains which is reasonably consistent with stable prices and which at the same time minimizes recession influences. Balanced progress is not beyond hope of attainment. Exaggerated criticism only creates hostility and delays improved understanding of inflationary influences.

Part Three

SOME LARGER ISSUES FACING BUSINESS

ECONOMIC GROWTH AND THE WELFARE STATE

Raymond A. Bauer,
Theodore Levitt,
and Herbert E. Striner

INTRODUCTION*

THE PROBLEM of the welfare state can be divided into four main issues: (1), the benefit of the individual; (2), the problem of social cost; (3), the effect on economic productivity; and (4), the relation-

Note: Mr. Bauer is Professor of Business Administration, Harvard Business School. Mr. Levitt is Lecturer on Business Administration, Harvard Business School. Mr. Striner is a member of the Senior Staff, The Brookings Institution.

* By Mr. Bauer.

ship of retired people to people still active in the economy. Let us look at each of these very briefly.

The positive argument as far as benefits to the individual is clear. The people who want welfare benefits, whether it be health insurance, free education, subsidized housing, or whatever, make their plea, and the direct benefits to them, as they see it, seem to be so obvious that they need very little elaboration. However, it is also common knowledge by now that some people will argue that perhaps these benefits are illusory, that there are higher values that you sacrifice. If you give people too much security, they forget the nobler objectives; their characters will not develop as well as they should, and we will all get flabby. You know the general line of argument, and I am not taking sides here; I am just pointing out that there is a marked split on this issue.

This is an interesting point: in the problem of material versus spiritual benefits, you can pretty well predict the side a man will take if you know his income. Notoriously, the fellow who does not have the material benefits—or the college professor speaking for him—will argue that in order to develop man's highest aspirations, you first have to assure him ways of meeting his material needs. Once these are met, the higher needs get expressed almost spontaneously.

On the other side it is argued that when you concentrate on material needs, a man's spiritual goals become subverted. Occasionally this begins to smell like an argument for the virtues of poverty. This viewpoint, when introduced, usually comes from a person whose material needs are already met. This naturally produces a certain amount of vulnerability on the part of people who deprecate the desirability of social-welfare benefits.

Very often, the problem of welfare benefits is discussed from the standpoint of social costs. Can we afford them? I am not able to answer that question, but I do want to label it as one of the issues which will come up for discussion later.

However, welfare benefits are not exclusively a social cost. An argument can be made in many instances that they may, indeed, contribute to the productive effort of the economy. It is quite conceivable, for instance, that if health care were available on a free basis and used properly, the increase in manhours worked might offset the cost. I am not saying this is so; I am introducing it as one of the arguments for the power of welfare programs to increase productivity.

Also, certainly the social investment in education increases the productivity of the economy by increasing the skill of the available manpower. On the other hand, it might be said that if you make people secure, you deprive them of the incentive for working. That is a familiar argument which has a certain amount of plausibility because, almost by definition, if a man is infinitely secure, he is not going to move. But that is not so, because people will get bored and they will move if only in search of some sort of activity.

Finally, there is the question of benefits for retired people and benefits for those still active in the economy. This problem of retirement is a big one. It seems to me that you have to regard benefits to retired people as social costs, a pure outlay, or argue that benefits which a person gets after sixty-five may have a positive effect on his behavior during his productive years.

The only argument I can think of on the other side would be one saying a man should save and provide for his old age; we should not encourage him to be wasteful. Yet only a small percentage of people in the economy would be farsighted enough to do this. Then we should think about the possibilities of unexpected illness. Would savings cover that? And what about the larger problem of saving? Don't we want to encourage more spending?

These are some of the problems involved. Let us have some views on them.

WHAT IS WELFARE?*

I would submit that the United States has always been a welfare state, unless we have repealed that part of the Constitution which refers to the general welfare. This clause was placed in the Constitution with some serious consideration and some serious thought. What has happened is that a perfectly good word has been appropriated and misused. We tend to think of the welfare state in terms of Russia and the dictatorial powers. Perhaps what we have to do is really think of two separate terms: (1) a legislative welfare state; (2) a dictated welfare state.

In the case of the Soviet bloc, we undoubtedly have what we may term a dictated welfare state, where a minority, without really considering all of the social factors involved, determines what it feels are the proper criteria for establishing welfare programs. These programs are then developed full-scale and with a single-minded purposefulness throughout the society.

In our system we legislate welfare, through the many factors forced to the attention of our legislatures, both state and federal, showing the need for these programs. The ultimate program is a result of the interaction between the people and the individuals who are the so-called policy makers.

This distinction is important because there have been significant changes in the way we look at welfare over the years, as mirrored in the changing programs. This does not mean, let me repeat, that we have not been a welfare state all along; it does mean that our attitudes and approaches have shifted.

Let me tell you about an article I came across some months ago; I could not forget it, and it fits in with my comments on the change in philosophy that has taken place in the last few decades.

President Cleveland, in his first administration, vetoed an ap-

* By Mr. Striner.

propriation of $25,000 to buy seed corn for Texas farmers who were ruined by a drought, saying:

> I find no warrant for such an appropriation in the Constitution and I do not believe that the power and duty of the general government ought to be extended to the relief of individual suffering, which is in no manner related to the public service or benefit....

As I read this, I wondered whether this would not spell political suicide if the same statement were made today after a disaster in Texas! Cleveland would probably not be elected to a second term at the present time after a statement like that.

We have gone through several periods in our history, and until fairly recently government was more of a symbol than a force. It did very little to inject itself into society.

It has only been in the last several decades that government is no longer viewed as something extraneous or outside the total system. Rather, we recognize it as a tremendous operation, a form of industry, in partnership with labor and management as a participant in the economy. So the question of whether or not government should have a role in the economy is no longer an open one. The question is now: What is the proper role of the government and of the welfare activities of the government, aside from the usual well-accepted one of military defense?

By way of our answer, let us look at the government's impact on productivity, since that is one of the key questions in this book.

Much of the increase in productivity which we have seen recently is the result of technological innovation. At the present time, the federal government accounts for about 60% of all the scientific research and development in the United States—either on its own, or through contracts.

Through this research and development program, which we translate into technological innovation, the government has had a number of effects on the economy. It has made it possible for business to develop new products, reduce costs, improve production methods. It has accelerated the development of automation, which may have brought with it some technological overemployment because of a lack of good planning. But the list of results is too long to present here; suffice it to say that the impact has been considerable.

One of the most interesting aspects of this particular welfare program is that the government took it on partly because of pressures brought to bear by industry. In many instances, industry cannot perform the kind of research and development that it needs because of excessively high costs, or because it feels that the government can do it more easily. I could give a whole list here, going from the obvious one of atomic energy to areas where the payoff is so slight and the horizon for the returns is so distant that it is the sort of investment you could not expect industry to undertake.

For example, few people realize that the computer industry was developed on the basis of a wartime need, when the government decided that it needed a rapid means of computing firing and ballistics tables. The Ordnance people in the Army let a $300,000 contract to the Morse School of Engineering at the University of Pennsylvania, in 1942, which produced the first modern computer. As a result, we have an industry which has had a tremendous payoff in terms of the entire economy.

This is not an unusual situation. A great deal of military research and development has had clear applications in the civilian economy. The only reason we have not seen even more is that we do not have the means to communicate the sort of results that we get in military research and development into the business sector. One of the crying needs is to develop a form of communication so that business can find out what is being done in the government. To give a specific example:

> I was once speaking before a business group in Washington, which included a number of representatives from various industries.

> I began to refer to some of the research results of various military research and development projects, including the work which had been done on corrosion linings. One of the men present later expressed an interest in this. I put him in touch with the right department, and he discovered that this was research his company had been working on for two years. They were able to take over this piece of information at a great saving.

This is only one area of government activity which tends to support both business and the national economy. It is part of the new concept of government's proper role, and it is part of the new concept of the welfare state.

CORPORATION WELFARE*

I should like to talk about welfare in a narrower, more familiar sense than the one used by Dr. Striner, even though I agree essentially with his broader definition, which reminds us of a host of governmental activities designed to aid the economy. But there are some issues that need clarification when we discuss the term in a narrower sense, and I want to turn my attention to them.

We all agree that there are certain kinds of public benefits that have to be provided in some fashion. We agree that there should be some welfare. People should not be permitted to starve in the streets. We are a civilized society, and we do not want people to die from starvation, small pox, or lack of medical care.

Charity is an old, old idea. St. Thomas, for example, argued that the only justification for profits was their use for charitable purposes. Until now it has been exclusively an individual affair, and often a most glamorous one. In New York, they have charity balls for High Society. People take great pride in staying out until all hours of the morning, in order to fill the coffers of the Milkman's Fund and the Salvation Army.

A businessman cannot live long in a community without auto-

* By Mr. Levitt.

matically assigning a considerable portion of his time to public-welfare activities. Indeed, he achieves more of a general reputation and status by that kind of work than he does by performing his duties with his company. He makes more speeches, and he is involved in more activities. He ceases to be on the financial pages of the home-town paper, but he is seen more on the front pages. And if he becomes the firm's chief executive, the pace of these extracurricular activities is intensified.

Now a new dimension has been added to all this: business itself is becoming concerned with what they call the "higher values" and is contributing to all kinds of public-welfare activities; to an almost vulgar degree it is involved in such matters.

For example, companies now provide a whole host of fringe benefits to employees; there are the pensions and additional pension benefits; there are the unemployment-compensation benefits; there are recreational facilities; there are washrooms beyond anybody's obvious needs, all shined up with showers, drapes, full-length mirrors, and cosmetic trays.

There are all kinds of educational programs. There is piped-in music played into veritable crystal palaces. I say that this is a form of charity; it is a form of welfare activity. We talk about the danger of too much guaranteed welfare when it comes from the government. If it is bad for the government to do it, is it not equally bad for business to do it?

You might say that business indulges in such pursuits because of the unions and competition. But, as a matter of fact, I am not so sure. The whole welfare idea in modern times certainly did not come from the unions; it did not come from the church; and it did not come from government. It came from business itself. The welfare concept started in business and at the highest level—going back to the nineteenth century, chief executives have always been especially well taken care of by the companies.

Life insurance was bought for them and still is, along with health insurance. They are sent off on vacations. Special contracts are being made for them. There are public records at the SEC for a special compensation for widows and—on a contractual basis, not on an insurance basis—for *x* number of thousands of dollars a year if they outlive their highly placed husbands.

We argue very often that welfare business is bad because it cuts down on a man's moral fiber; it does not make people actively participate in their own future. However, if it is not bad for the chief executives on whom the whole future of the organization depends, one wonders whether it is so bad for the lower-level people.

Let me cite some dangers involved in the corporations and business generally getting involved in this kind of welfare activity. What about the danger to business itself? Is there anything wrong with business doing this, or is it the right and moral thing to do?

A business must be concerned with its existence—its major contribution to the community, to society, lies in its economic function. If a business is involved inordinately in welfare activities, its vital growth might be impaired. The most singular danger that I see is that business may lose its profit-building orientation and become oriented in directions which are going to dilute the vitality and the interests of the organization as an economic organism.

Another danger is a purely political, civil-liberties threat—namely, what happens when an individual's whole life becomes too much tied up in his place of work. You say that this is a pretty exaggerated notion. Recreational facilities, libraries, Muzak, and so on and so forth, could never destroy individual liberties.

But let me illustrate the possibility. You remember the old company towns in the mining areas. The company dominated the whole community, and this was conceived as harmful. There are some companies that are getting more and more involved in welfare activities, even to a point of real danger to the community.

Take the Olivetti company in Italy. Olivetti, who died last spring, was a man of great sensibility, a kind of a Renaissance man. He was greatly involved in the "elevation" of his employees. What we had in that community was a little town where this man started out; his headquarters are still there, and the company owns the buildings which are rented to the employees at a fairly low rate. They have a recreational program, tying in the whole community. They have concerts and arts festivals. They have special programs for children and educational programs for everyone. All is aimed toward taking care of the whole man—there is no effort to try to sell something, no party line.

This man was honored throughout the world for having done these things. The *Saturday Review* published a long article on his town. Right-wing people, left-wing people, middle-wing people—everybody thinks it was a wonderful concept.

However, what would have happened if this man had been oriented in a different direction, using his influence for some unworthy purpose? As a matter of fact, he organized a political party around this idea, and now there are forty communities in Italy that have an Olivetti political party, designed to generalize the whole idea of the way to run an industrial plant.

This is still good. But what happens if a company should gear the whole program in some offensive direction, one that we might find distasteful? What if people were being fed McCarthyism? Or taught to abhor all art that was not Jackson Pollock?

This can lead to some pretty medieval concepts, it seems to me. The point is this. The people in charge of the dispensation of welfare are given the power to distribute, and their ideas of welfare may be very different.

Let us look at the other part of the danger—the threat to the survival of capitalism if business continues its welfare activities. This can be well illustrated by the Greyhound case. A group of stockholders tried to get the Greyhound Corporation to stop race segregation in buses in the south. It filtered up through the courts and finally was passed over to the SEC, because they wanted it as a petition of the stockholders to vote on it. The SEC threw it out on the grounds that the Greyhound Corporation was in business for profit, not for social reforms. Now, everyone is arguing that the corporation should be involved in more of these welfare activities. If enough people continue arguing vigorously, one of these days the SEC is going to rule the other way. And that day will see the end of capitalism as we know it today. We will be motivated, not by gain, but by goodness; not by profit, but by service. Will this keep a business strong?

I conclude, then, with this word: there are many places where welfare is bad. And one of the worst places is in corporations.

DISCUSSION

Question: In connection with the corporation's uses of power for nonprofitable purposes, there is much agitation and picketing against Woolworth to abandon segregation of lunch counters in the south. Should Woolworth take a stand on the issue?

Levitt: It seems to me that Woolworth has a business decision to make, based on their business concept of whether they will be better or worse off by going to one side or the other. To expect business to be involved in social reform is a noble sentiment, but a highly dangerous one. It is dangerous for society and it is dangerous to business.

Do not forget that the business organization is unique. It is the only organization other than the state itself which has the power to create its own capital and its own resources. To the extent that it can do this, there is no check on the social-reform activities in which it is engaged. If it has the notion of being bountiful and good, then it can go ahead without restraint. Society might think otherwise.

You may say that society can protest through a product boycott. But what this does to total social and economic efficiency is terrible to consider.

Question: Is welfare, straight and pure, at the basis of all company benefits?

Striner: I can conceive of a number of fringe benefits which corporate enterprise has brought into existence strictly as a form of competition. If, for example, a company is in a highly competitive industry, it has to hold skilled workers or entice new skills into the plant. They are going to use the fringe benefits, all of the delightful things that have been mentioned here, as a means of attracting and holding people. And this is nothing but the old device of competition.

However, this is not true in all cases. The corporate system has been used to attain other nonbusiness objectives. You can go back to Robert Owen; this is not too new. It is a problem only if you want to keep the corporate form of government in its pristine form, unconcerned with social experiments.

Question: The term "welfare" still disturbs me. I would say there is a distinction between the welfare state and the Russian state not because the latter is dictatorial, but because it takes over entire activities of the people. There is no freedom of action.

The mere fact that our Constitution says "to promote the general welfare" does not constitute a welfare state—there are simply some things we feel the government can do better. And the fact that a company has fringe benefits should not be thought of as welfare; that is what the workers have earned. If they do not get it there, they will go to another firm. People want benefits.

If the government created a pension fund, the people would go to work for the government. But pension funds are not really welfare. When we are talking about the welfare state, we are talking about housing and education—which might well lead to controls. It is this angle that worries me—the gnawing away of our freedoms which always seems to be tied up with the word "welfare."

Striner: It is important to recognize the fact that the idea of controls for the general welfare is so pervasive even in our own system that they are often forgotten.

For example, you cannot open a radio station without government consent; there are strict regulations controlling that. Your space in the air is allocated by government. You cannot start many forms of private enterprise without a license. You cannot, realistically, open a bank unless you are a member of the Federal Deposit Insurance Company and a member of the Federal Reserve System. In many, many instances, government operates to control your freedom. You can go to any bank you wish; that is true. But all of the banks to which you go must adhere to certain minimal standards, federal and state.

But I think the significant fact of this discussion is that it illustrates the wide variety of definitions which people hold for the term "welfare." Given this situation, it behooves us to beware of spurning a particular program because someone calls it a "welfare" project. We must take the time and trouble to look at it pragmatically and see whether or not we think it is good.

Question: I would like to ask about the total costs of welfare. Often the price of security is loss of an equal amount of freedom. If we are going to buy security, if the government is going to take our money and buy security with it, then we lose the freedom to dispose of that work or that asset.

However, this neat formula is complicated by the fact that we may already have lost a lot of our freedom without realizing it due to forces beyond our control. The depression of the thirties brought that home; we thought we were a nation of individualists, but we found that forces had grown up in the world which made it impossible for a man to control his own destiny as he once had.

In a shrinking, interdependent world, what real freedom do we have left anyhow?

Bauer: The hypothetical question of freedom versus security is not a simple one because in one sense there is no freedom without some security. You cannot plan a certain act unless you are certain of some events in your environment. Very often we get into a paradoxical and unrealistic situation when we try to look at the relationship of freedom to security.

Question: In terms of the welfare state, just where should this public sector of the economy take over from what has been called the private sector?

Take a specific instance: the Forand Bill for people over sixty-five. I represent an insurance company, which has a private stake in this welfare business. Our executives are just not sure what our approach to the bill should be. On the one hand, of course, we say: "Give us a chance to supply this market with welfare. We can do it. We are doing it. We had 20% coverage ten years ago and we have 60% now; we will have 80% in ten years from now."

The bill is now in Washington and the Democrats and the medical-care proponents say that no private enterprise should be given the opportunity to do this, and that it is more equitable to let everybody pay it as part of social security, to get their payments back after they reach the age of sixty-five. Is this not encroaching in the areas where private enterprise should also have a right to provide?

Levitt: The counterargument might be that private enterprise has had that right since the beginning of time. You may say that private enterprise tends not to enter into welfare but that social and political forces are forcing the issue. But, every time such a threat comes around, ought we to wait five years for a chance to have private enterprise measure up to it?

Bauer: You are talking about a situation in which, under some sort of threat of government action, business takes steps, presumably to forestall the government action. But surely the insurance industry would not go into insurance for the aged if it were not profitable, just to keep the government from doing any medical insuring because of the theoretical considerations involved.

From the floor: Actually it is less profitable and difficult to sell; the market is hard to reach. The fact of the matter is that outside of a very few companies, and I am talking about private enterprise involved in welfare, this market was not even available through insurance up until, let us say, ten years ago and mostly in the last five years. This is not entirely a political effect or influence—it is social forces at work.

Levitt: I would like to comment on this. Socially responsible welfare activities are those activities which you would not ordinarily engage in as part of your normal profit-making strategy. If the insurance industry provides medical care from the point of view of profit-making procedure, then that is no longer welfare, charity, or social responsibility; that is business. And these are distinctions to maintain.

THE ENTREPRENEUR AND SMALL BUSINESS

Herbert F. Stewart

WHAT, EXACTLY, IS the role of the entrepreneur in this age of economic explosions? Does he simply ride it like the flotsam on the crest of a wave; does he live off it like a parasite; or does he light the fuse that sets it off? And what does it take to be an entrepreneur in this kind of world?

Whenever I think about these questions, my mind inevitably turns to three Horatio Alger figures I know who would be classified as entrepreneurs in anyone's book. Let me first describe their careers, then make some general comments on what I think it took for them to get where they are. With these three "exhibits" to look at and

Note: Mr. Stewart is Lecturer on Business Administration, Harvard Business School.

study, we will be better equipped to ponder the unanswerable questions I have just posed.

The first gentleman is named Joseph H. Davis, Jr. Joe was born in Brooklyn in 1920. He went into the Navy, came back, and graduated in 1947 from the Harvard Business School.

The first job he had was with a local instrument company where he was assistant to the president. The company had new products to be developed, and Joe was a natural. His salary was $4,500, and he worked for eight months and quit: he could not get along with the president who, Joe said, was backward, lacked vision, etc., etc.

For his second job he went to another local instrument company as sales engineer, again for product development. His job was to write reports on potential products. At the end of the first year, Joe wanted to leave. But the president said, "Wait, Joe. One of these reports looks pretty good. Suppose we put $100,000 into the project, start a new company, and give you equity in it when it reaches the break-even point? Would you be willing to do that? Of course your salary would have to go back to $4,500." Joe said yes. Eight months later, the enterprise was breaking even, so Joe asked for his equity. Said the president: "Joe, don't get impatient." Joe quit.

Then he went to teach at a local college, starting at $4,500. At the end of the first year he had earnings of $17,000: he found the golden touch in the U.S. Department of Commerce, consulting and writing reports on foreign opportunities.

One of the firms Joe consulted for was a chemical firm. The partners said, "Come with us. We will give you some equity when you have expanded sales for us." Joe went with them; his salary went down to $4,500. The business expanded, but he got no equity. In nine months he quit. Fortunately his wife was a musician and was earning income during this time. To supplement it, he also taught nights at a local university.

So at this point Joe said, "No one is going to give me anything.

There is only one way to start a business and that is to do it myself, and the way to start a business is to get an order." So he went to Massachusetts Institute of Technology, convinced a man that he could make a certain item, and got two contracts at $6,000 apiece. In his basement he did all the work, using a $200 piece of equipment bought specifically for the job. At the end of the first year, Joe and Bernie, his partner, had sales of about $80,000 and gross profits of about $40,000.

Then they thought they had better do some long-range planning—what were they going to do tomorrow? Bernie came up with the answer: "The thing of the future is an analog-to-digital converter. To finance this development, Joe and Bernie raised $150,000; at the end of the year the converter was completed but they had no money left. At this point Bernie called Joe from an aircraft company on the west coast: "Joe, I have a $3 million order, but we need to show financial ability to do the work. We need $250,000 cash in the bank." Joe asked his backers for this money, but he was turned down cold since they only saw how fast the previous $150,000 had been spent.

Joe did not sleep very well that night, but he had an idea. The next day he convinced his financial backers to put up $250,000 in escrow, subject to receiving the $3 million contract. Last year the company had about $9 million in sales. According to the stock market, the company is now worth over $10 million.

My second character is Peter J. Kanavos. Pete's father came to this country from Greece; he was a barber and died when Pete was fourteen. Pete had five younger brothers and sisters to support while still going to high school. During the war Pete worked at the Fore River shipyard, but he complained about something one day and was fired. He had saved enough by that time to go to Harvard and graduated in 1946 with a B.A. From there he went to the Harvard Business School, graduating in June 1947.

While he was there he operated a real-estate agency in Copley

Square. He also had a full-time job as night watchman of a battery company nearby until one night when he was sleeping some crooks stole $30,000 worth of batteries.

Upon graduation Pete went to New York and looked for a job. Things did not seem promising, so he came back and bought a bar and grille in Brookline Village for $46,000. Since Pete had no money, he borrowed what he needed from a barber in Harvard Square, his high-school principal and teachers, his old newspaper-route boss, the Harvard Business School faculty, and others. The bank refused him a mortgage, but he borrowed from the bank president personally. Within eighteen months he had refinanced his enterprise with a first mortgage for $20,000 at the bank and had paid off all his other debts.

Next Pete bought a package store for $25,000, taking a $15,000 mortgage and getting together $10,000 from seven people. He bought a second store that was going bankrupt, took a first mortgage of $15,000, moved it around the corner, added a delivery service. Total sales went from $800 a week to $12,000 a week in twelve months.

In real estate, Pete bought a house on Marlborough Street for $40,000; using a first mortgage of $25,000, second mortgage $10,000, and third mortgage $5,000, he remodeled and sold it for $70,000 in fourteen months. At this time he also bought a lot for $2,500 at a public auction and sold it to a gasoline company for $28,000 after obtaining changes in zoning to permit construction of a gas station. Then came a land-redevelopment project, the Dedham Shopping Plaza, which is very close to the intersection of Routes 1 and 128 outside of Boston.

He has opened or is in the process of opening shopping centers in Marlborough, Mass., Rockland, Maine, Charleston, South Carolina, Franklin, Mass., Hingham, Mass., and Roanoke, Virginia; developed industrial parks at Marlborough, Dedham, Stoughton, and Avon, Mass.; and owns the Hotel Raleigh and the Mark Monroe in Richmond, Virginia. He also has an $80 million urban redevelopment under zoning. Pete's estimated net worth is over $5 million.

My third "exhibit" is Arnold Ryden. Arnold was born in Clay Center, Kansas, in 1920, but when he was two years old the family moved to Minneapolis. He went to the University of Minnesota, concentrating initially in mathematics and engineering but later shifting to sociology. At this stage he intended to become a social worker. Upon graduation he decided to come to the Harvard Business School and graduated in 1943.

During the war Arnold was in the Army Quartermaster Corps, serving as a financial analyst and assistant negotiator in contract renegotiation. After his discharge he took a job with the Northwestern National Bank, at $300 a month. During his five years at the bank, Arnold supplemented his income by teaching accounting each morning from eight to nine o'clock at the University of Minnesota's business school. He also taught accounting and money and banking in the university's extension division.

In March 1951 Arnold left the bank to become assistant treasurer of Engineering Research Associates, Inc. ERA, a Minneapolis firm, had been formed in 1946 and was a pioneer in computers. All its business was military. This was Arnold's first exposure to technological businesses, and he saw that there was good opportunity in some phases of fast-moving technology, such as electronics, with competent people.

Some months after he went to work for ERA, Arnold discovered that the president was negotiating to sell out to Remington Rand, and it later became the Univac Division of Remington Rand. Since Ryden did not want to work for a "little offshoot of a big corporation," he began to look for another job.

Through the president of his old bank, Arnold was hired as assistant to the executive vice-president of a paint company. He remained there for nine months at a salary of $7,500, but he was given no responsibility or real duties and he left.

Next he was employed by the Minneapolis-Honeywell Regulator Company as comptroller of the aeronautics division. Two and a half years later he was fired, "without any real explanation," as he says. His salary at the time—early 1955—was $10,000.

Arnold's next job was consulting for a company in printing and school supplies, but the firm's president seemed to like only his own ideas. So, in July 1957, with some people from Univac, he formed the Control Data Corporation. To finance it, Arnold and his attorney put up $25,000. He then sold publicly 600,000 shares of stock in the corporation at $1 a share. Subsequently, he helped Control Data acquire a subcontracting company, with annual sales of almost $2 million, doing a variety of electrical and mechanical work. In 1960, its third year of operation, consolidated sales of Control Data were running at the rate of $12 million annually. Its stock was selling over the counter at $40 a share.

Arnold resigned as an officer of Control Data in October 1958, though he continued on as a director, and formed the Midwest Technical Development Corporation. The initial capital of $250,000 was supplied by him and a few business associates. In the following May, 500,000 shares of common stock were offered to the public at $3.75 a share. "We tried to get an underwriter for this issue but we couldn't, so we sold it ourselves as issuer and had several people acting as selling agents," he explained later.

Four months later, in February 1959, Arnold and a small group of associates bought a 98% interest in Telex, Inc., a hearing-aid manufacturer, for just over $1 million. Arnold became president, and annual sales rose from $300,000 to $8 million. He is now confident that the company is about to "go places" and anticipates sales of $20 million within a year or two.

What lies behind these success stories? What techniques did these three men use, what drives did they have, which enabled them to rise so fast to such significant positions in a variety of enterprises?

First of all, they all wanted to own and operate their own companies rather than work for someone else. To achieve this goal, they were willing to work hard, to hammer a career out of solid rock with their own muscles and sweat. Security as such had no appeal to them, and large, well-oiled organizations offered them no challenge. This is not to say that there are no challenges there, of course; it is just that the opportunities did not tickle their particular fancies.

Secondly, they were not afraid to borrow, nor were they hesitant about going to friends to ask for money. As one of them says, "You really have to develop a borrower's personality; ever since I was a kid, I have had one. It was easy for me to go in and ask because, after all, they can only say 'no.' "

They each had a talent for picking industries that were on the way up, capitalizing on technological advancements, population growth, and the expansion of our urban areas. Together with choosing the right industries, they selected the right associates: men who had the skills they needed to build these fast-moving enterprises. "Everything I have done in the past three or four years," explained one of the trio, "essentially revolves around taking outstandingly capable technical people and combining them with money, and as a result creating something of value."

But simply associating yourself with these talented people is not enough; you have to try to keep them with you so they will not spin off and form a company of their own. This can be a problem, as one of the three indicates:

> You want the type of fellow who is fed up with the standard organization, is willing to go out and perform and has the freedom to develop ideas on his own. But there is a certain amount of control you have to exercise over him.
>
> When we got our company going, we were able to obtain two eminent people who had experience in the particular field we wished to enter; the incentive we gave them was the stock gift. Later on, after they had gained substantial confidence, they left our company and formed another one. They are still very good friends

> of mine, but I think the lesson to be learned is that you should give such men the opportunity to make a capital gain but not so that it will ultimately cause you some trouble.

Generally speaking, our three friends believe in—and one even insists on—the key people owning a share of the company in which they work. This stipulation holds for the technical people as well as the management.

Another outstanding characteristic is ingenuity. Listen to one of them talk about one of his land-development arrangements:

> We decided to take an acreage that had been relatively undeveloped and thought we would put up 2,500 homes; so we got a huge tract of land. But we did not want to put money into the project at this point.
>
> We got hold of four real-estate companies to do the selling and told them we would give them an exclusive. We worked out terms and returns. Then we got a big builder. Next we asked the land redevelopers to round up all the developers they could. They brought in about fifty small builders who build ten to twenty homes a year, and we laid out a master plan for them from selling to building to financing. We got the money they all needed, making an arrangement with the banks that if one of them got into trouble we would come in somehow or other. The banks felt that somebody else would be behind the project, despite the fact that these fellows themselves did not have the experience and net worth behind them. So it was a happy situation for everybody.

The sacrifices these men made to their businesses were prodigious. Here is another pertinent quote:

> There is no question if you're going to go in business, particularly a new venture in which you have a very active part, that practically your whole life is going to be devoted to its success. It requires tremendous energy and sacrifices, a lot of worrying, and just plain spilling of guts.

Then, the willingness to risk—maybe even a passion for gambling—is stamped all over these men. They recognized early along the way that you do not get far in business today, in large or small companies, without taking chances. This they have done, and it has paid off.

But there is one final factor I want to mention, and maybe it is the key to the puzzle. David McClelland, professor of psychology at Harvard, has been studying achievement motivation for a number of years, and he has made an effort to know and understand businessmen at every level and from Timbuktu to Turkey. He has had this to say: "Singleness of purpose, to *achieve* above all else, may turn out to be the distinguishing success feature of the entrepreneur."

I think what we have seen in the careers of these three men supports that judgment emphatically.

COMPETING WITH SOVIET RESEARCH AND DEVELOPMENT

Charles D. Orth, III

IF WE are to have economic growth of the kind we need, our national research-and-development effort, both public and private, must be functioning at a high level of effectiveness. Many elements go into the successful operation of a R & D program, including the educational process feeding the technical people into the system, the management of laboratories, the social and economic standing of scientists, and national policies.

In this chapter I want to look at our R & D, compare it with that of the Soviets, and explore some steps that American businessmen might take so that we may compete more effectively with our op-

Note: Mr. Orth is Assistant Professor of Business Administration, Harvard Business School.

ponents and, more important, do the job we must do to meet our needs at home.

My major thesis will be that a number of forces in our society are operating in such a way that the number and quality of creative technical people who might potentially be available to staff our engineering and scientific corps is being seriously depleted. The diagram shown in Exhibit I outlines these forces. My second basic point will be that there is strong evidence that the Soviets are doing a better job than we are at educating and using technical talent and that, despite some comments to the contrary, this is cause for serious concern.

The first sputnik set off a round of concern about the potential technical strength of this country, especially in comparison to the Soviets. In this reaction it was not hard to find a considerable amount of panic and hysteria, leading to a whole series of unhelpful and unwise recommendations. James Killian, then president of Massachusetts Institute of Technology, made a speech shortly after the first sputnik went up in which he mentioned two of the steps which he specifically thought we should not take in our effort to compete with the Soviets technologically.

The first one was to copy them, to operate the same way they do. Clearly, since our political and economic systems are so different, we certainly should not try to duplicate them. In effect, he said, we should stick to our own course and do those things which reflect our particular genius and best meet our own needs.

The second warning he issued was that we should not get caught up in an educational numbers game. Our problem, he said, is one of quality as well as quantity, and we need first-rate talent in other fields, not only in science and engineering.

In short, he was trying to remind us that we need to maintain our balance, though not at the sacrifice of a sense of urgency about a highly alarming situation.

Exhibit I. Factors Blocking More Effective Use of the Potential Technological Strength of the United States.

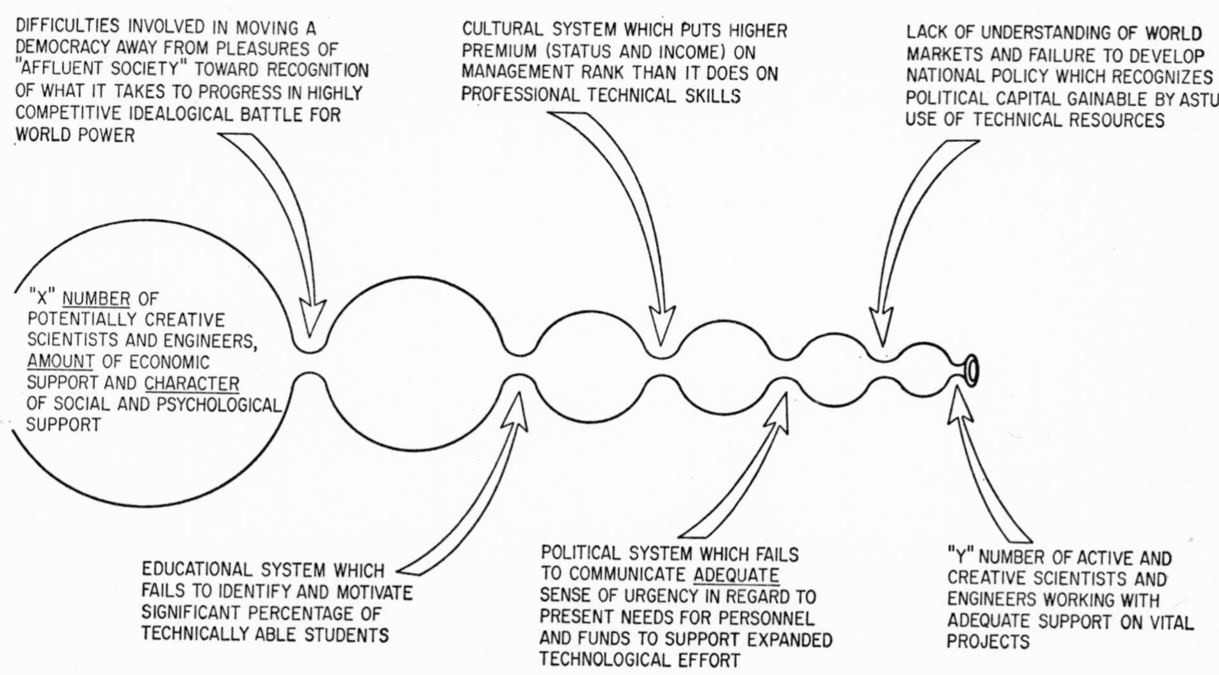

DIFFICULTIES INVOLVED IN MOVING A DEMOCRACY AWAY FROM PLEASURES OF "AFFLUENT SOCIETY" TOWARD RECOGNITION OF WHAT IT TAKES TO PROGRESS IN HIGHLY COMPETITIVE IDEALOGICAL BATTLE FOR WORLD POWER
CULTURAL SYSTEM WHICH PUTS HIGHER PREMIUM (STATUS AND INCOME) ON MANAGEMENT RANK THAN IT DOES ON PROFESSIONAL TECHNICAL SKILLS
LACK OF UNDERSTANDING OF WORLD MARKETS AND FAILURE TO DEVELOP NATIONAL POLICY WHICH RECOGNIZES POLITICAL CAPITAL GAINABLE BY ASTUTE USE OF TECHNICAL RESOURCES
"X" NUMBER OF POTENTIALLY CREATIVE SCIENTISTS AND ENGINEERS, AMOUNT OF ECONOMIC SUPPORT AND CHARACTER OF SOCIAL AND PSYCHOLOGICAL SUPPORT
EDUCATIONAL SYSTEM WHICH FAILS TO IDENTIFY AND MOTIVATE SIGNIFICANT PERCENTAGE OF TECHNICALLY ABLE STUDENTS
POLITICAL SYSTEM WHICH FAILS TO COMMUNICATE ADEQUATE SENSE OF URGENCY IN REGARD TO PRESENT NEEDS FOR PERSONNEL AND FUNDS TO SUPPORT EXPANDED TECHNOLOGICAL EFFORT
"Y" NUMBER OF ACTIVE AND CREATIVE SCIENTISTS AND ENGINEERS WORKING WITH ADEQUATE SUPPORT ON VITAL PROJECTS

In this book a good many authors refer, first, to the need for an expansion of our research and development qualitatively as well as quantitatively. Secondly, they point to some of the unfortunate consequences of our current "affluent society" which are making it difficult for us to do so. The editor of the *Bulletin of Atomic Scientists,* Eugene Rabinowitch, put the problem in these words:

> ... the world which we have been fitting our children to live in no longer exists; it has gone with the wind, torn to pieces by the gale of a worldwide triple revolution, social, racial and scientific. Since the reforms of the New Deal, the aim of our society—which at times seemed close to realization—has been idealized in the great American dream—the dream of a permanently and universally prosperous nation, slowly but steadily growing in wealth, in fairness to all its members and in equitable distribution of the technologically advanced industry and agriculture; the remaining evils of poverty and racial discrimination seemed destined to slow disappearance....
>
> Unfortunately, it was not fated that parents, who had caught a glimpse of this enviable state, should bequeath it to their children. Instead, the world, and an America inextricably involved in it, has entered an era of instability, of breath-taking changes, of terrifying dangers and blinding promises—a world about which only one thing can be said for certain; that it will look different ten years from now from what it looks today, and different twenty years from now from what it will look in ten years. We are educating a generation whose main aim in life will be security in an age which is abundant in everything but security.[1]

This comment brings us to a consideration of our educational system, which fails to identify and motivate a significant percentage of technically able students. A statement by the President's Science Advisory Committee entitled "Education for the Age of Science" outlines the issue very clearly. In that document, these paragraphs struck me as particularly significant:

[1] *Bulletin of Atomic Scientists,* November 1958, p. 345.

> Tragic individual losses occur when able youngsters live in communities whose aspirations do not demand or whose pocketbooks cannot afford the educational opportunities in secondary schools that these young people need and deserve. The nation loses as well as the individual student. There is probably more attrition of potential talent at this level than in any other part of the educational system. We strongly urge that measures be evolved to discover and provide financial support for bright students whose needs cannot be met in their local communities, and to make it possible for them to study in more adequate schools.
>
> It is scarcely possible to put the matter too strongly. The potentially great scientist, scholar, physician, or educator who ends up through no fault of his own as an underling at a task below his native endowment, represents an indefensible national loss.[2]

Exhibit II (pp. 236–7) is a rough schematic diagram of the Soviet and the American educational systems. There are several features of them which I think are especially worthy of our attention. In the first place, the Soviet system is arranged to cull from their advanced educational system those who are clearly not going to benefit by it, and to identify and give special training to those who will profit from this kind of academic work. This process starts early. After kindergarten, they have a primary or four-year school system. Those youngsters who are identified as not being very educable at the kindergarten level terminate their education at the end of this primary school, or at the age of eleven or twelve.

The children who can benefit from slightly more education go on to the incomplete secondary or seven-year school. Those who clearly have a potential for going considerably higher complete the full ten-year school system. And note that it is a ten-year system instead of a twelve-year system, as in the United States.

From then on, many young people who did not complete the ten-year curriculum go to the so-called technicums. These institutions

[2] Government Printing Office, May 1959, p. 14.

Exhibit II.

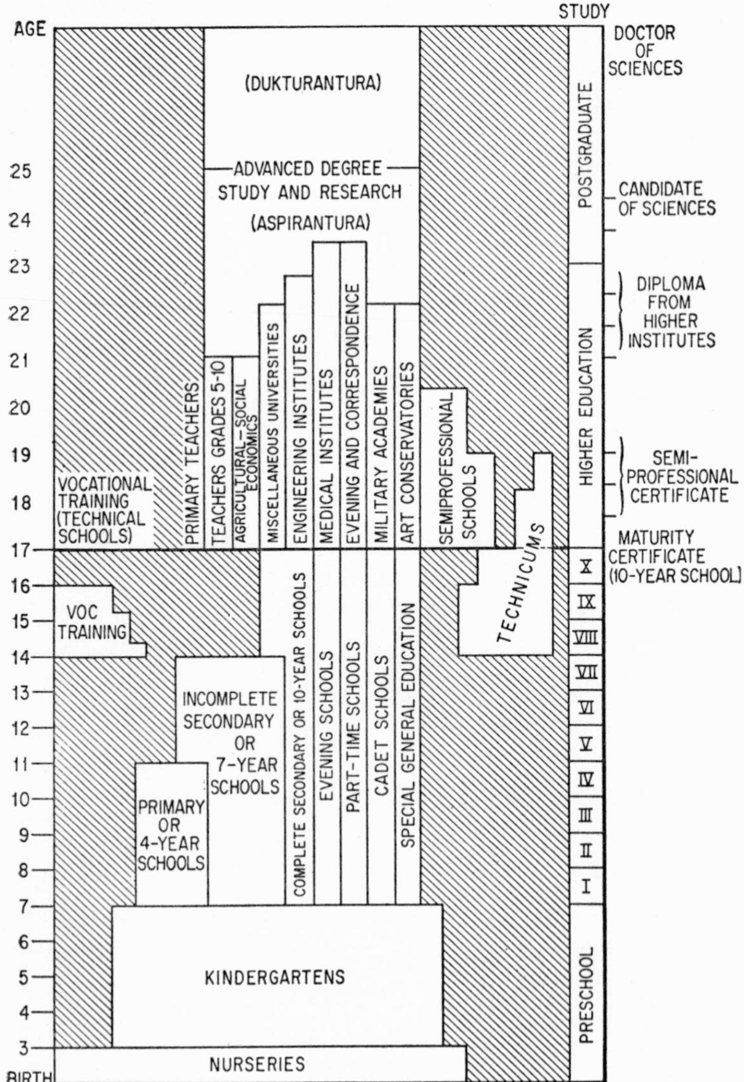

EDUCATIONAL SYSTEM
IN THE SOVIET UNION
AGE
STUDY
DOCTOR OF SCIENCES
(DUKTURANTURA)
POSTGRADUATE
ADVANCED DEGREE STUDY AND RESEARCH
(ASPIRANTURA)
CANDIDATE OF SCIENCES
DIPLOMA FROM HIGHER INSTITUTES
HIGHER EDUCATION
SEMI-PROFESSIONAL CERTIFICATE
MATURITY CERTIFICATE (10-YEAR SCHOOL)
VOCATIONAL TRAINING (TECHNICAL SCHOOLS)
PRIMARY TEACHERS
TEACHERS GRADES 5-10
AGRICULTURAL—SOCIAL ECONOMICS
MISCELLANEOUS UNIVERSITIES
ENGINEERING INSTITUTES
MEDICAL INSTITUTES
EVENING AND CORRESPONDENCE
MILITARY ACADEMIES
ART CONSERVATORIES
SEMIPROFESSIONAL SCHOOLS
TECHNICUMS
VOC TRAINING
INCOMPLETE SECONDARY OR 7-YEAR SCHOOLS
PRIMARY OR 4-YEAR SCHOOLS
COMPLETE SECONDARY OR 10-YEAR SCHOOLS
EVENING SCHOOLS
PART-TIME SCHOOLS
CADET SCHOOLS
SPECIAL GENERAL EDUCATION
KINDERGARTENS
NURSERIES
PRESCHOOL
BIRTH
3 4 5 6 7 8 9 10 11 12 13 14 15 16 17 18 19 20 21 22 23 24 25
I II III IV V VI VII VIII IX X

Exhibit II.

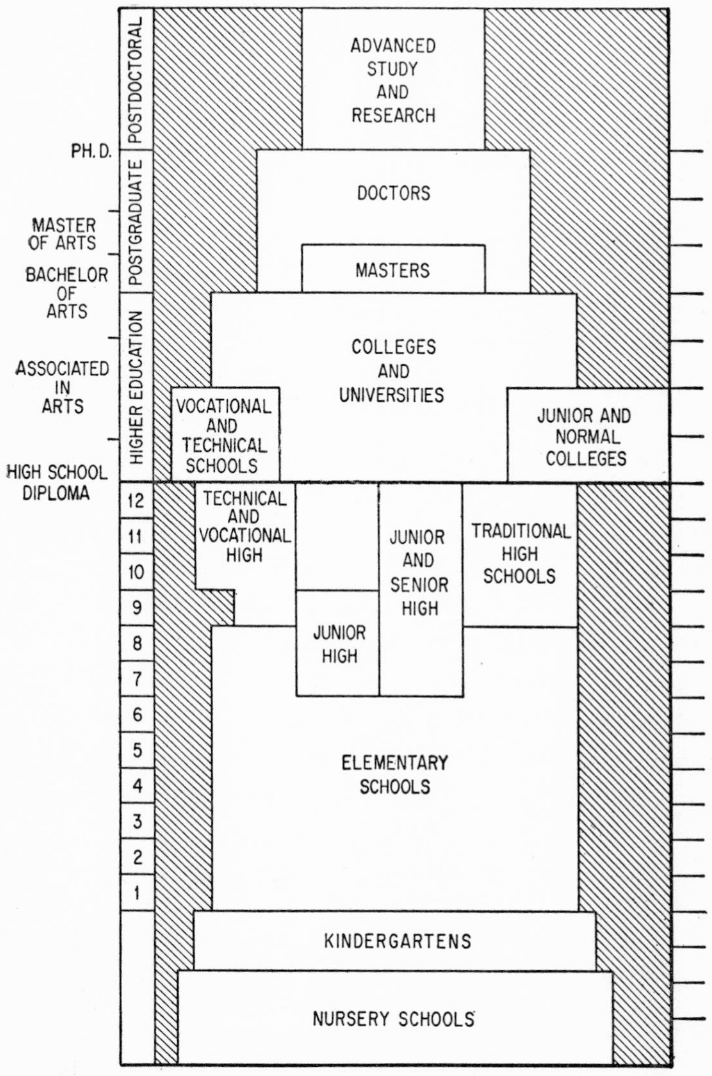

Source: Adapted from *Education in the USSR,* U.S. Department of Health, Education and Welfare, Bulletin No. 14, 1957.

are unique to the Russian system. Each year they graduate 200,000 technically able eighteen-year-olds who become laboratory assistants, engineering helpers, and so forth. Some observers have said that we have less than one quarter of the people in this category that we need in this country; we are graduating 15,000 a year, two thirds of whom come from nonaccredited institutions. The Soviet Union, on the other hand, clearly has an adequate supply because of this method of training.

To give you an idea of the magnitude of the need here and why it has increased so immensely, in 1940 it took 17,000 manhours to design a fighter plane. In 1960, it takes 2 million manhours to design one. An engineer today is part of a team that requires five technicians. At the present time, we are graduating only one eighth of the needed number of engineering technicians. Over and above the technicians, the Soviet Union is producing more scientists yearly than are all the Western countries put together.

But what about quality? Some observers have claimed that the Russian scientists are not as good as ours; it seems clear to me that their people, at the very least, are no less well trained than their opposite numbers in the United States.

In thinking about our educational system in terms of the quality of the product, here is a statement by Dael Wolffe, the executive officer of the American Association for the Advancement of Science. The objectives of an educational system should be:

> ... to provide the conditions that will encourage and assist each student to develop his talents to the highest possible degree. If this is accepted as a guiding principle any degree of failure represents a waste of educational opportunity. Judged by this standard, the amount of waste [to be found in American high schools] is great, indeed. Among the reasons for this waste, these two must be listed as of high importance:
>
> 1. The general level of aspiration on the part of teachers, administrators and parents is too low, too far beneath the potential level of achievements of the students.

2. What is expected of students is too uniform and does not adequately recognize the great diversity of their talents.[3]

Wolffe then went on to describe an experiment designed to improve math courses. He noted that "between sixth grade arithmetic and ninth grade algebra comes a lull in the child's occupation known as junior high math." He described a class of twenty-three average or below-average youngsters in a seventh grade math class which was given a course taught by an excellent teacher and included such topics as factoring and prime numbers, nonmetric geometry, approximation methods, and probability. That last subject, incidentally, is one that many graduate business students find difficult.

Obviously, the ability of these youngsters had been underestimated before this experience. They learned the material; they found it interesting; and they responded to the challenge of being expected to work on material that was hard but possible to do. At the university level—note Exhibit III—the total number of hours spent at Kharkov State University is not quite twice that of our leading technical institution. Furthermore, the hours spent on physics, math, and chemistry are again nearly twice the number of hours spent at MIT. So, in effect, we are not just talking about quantity; we must also face the question of quality in comparing these two educational systems.

Each boy and girl in the Soviet Union who completes the ten-year school course—and there were 1.3 million of them in 1950 as against 1.6 million high school graduates in the United States—has had 4.4 high school years of math and 5.9 high school years of science. In contrast, it has been estimated that 23% of American public high schools offer neither physics nor chemistry. Only one out of five American high school students takes physics, and only two thirds take any algebra. Only 29% of pupils take eleventh-grade algebra.

[3] "Educational Waste," *Bulletin of Atomic Scientists,* November 1958, p. 364.

Only 13% take twelfth-grade trigonometry and solid geometry. Only 32% of eleventh-grade pupils take chemistry. And only 24% of twelfth-grade pupils take physics.[4] Clearly, this is a very con-

Exhibit III. The Physics Course at Kharkov State University Compared with That at Massachusetts Institute of Technology

	Lecture hours	
Subjects	*KSU*	*MIT*
Higher mathematics	584	270
Chemistry	100	225
Physics	1,560	870
Extra physics (subjects at choice)	804	300
Electronics	36	105
Electrodynamics	120	0
Electric circuit theory	0	60
Marxism-Leninism	250	0
Political economics	140	0
Philosophy	140	0
Drafting	52	0
Foreign language	240	0
Pedagogy	68	0
Methodology of teaching physics	60	0
Physical training	136	0
Humanities	0	360
Military science	0	180
Freshman elective	0	45
Total hours spent in course	4,290	2,415
Hours spent on physics, maths, and chemistry	3,356	1,830

Source: John O. Bocris, "Higher Education in the Soviet Union," *Current History,* V, no. 35 (1958), 25.

siderable gap. The sheer amount of technical training which is built into the Soviet school system is far greater than it is here.

[4] For these and other comparative figures, see Alexander Korol, *Soviet Education for Science and Technology* (Cambridge, Technology Press, 1960).

When you know these numbers and statistics, it is rather hard to keep the sense of balance which Killian urges us to maintain. I hope that these figures communicate the sense of urgency that some of the other contributors to this book are discussing.

I have been particularly interested in the sociocultural system within which our scientists and engineers operate. My research in this area has turned up some disturbing findings. We have found, in effect, that the value system of the American business world is antagonistic to the idea that the status of our professional technical people should be raised. The manager or businessman in our industrial system is accorded high status; he is the elite of our society. But the scientist who goes into this system rapidly finds that if he, too, wants to be part of the elite, he must also be a manager. As a result, these men—and unfortunately some of them are our most competent scientists—tend to leave the bench where their technical training is doing us real good and start trying to move up the ladder of the administrative hierarchy.

Many companies have tried to solve this problem by establishing what they call *parallel ladders*. But unfortunately the value system is so built in that the scientist quickly recognizes that this parallel ladder is not really there at all. In actual fact, there is a ceiling—both a salary ceiling and a status or prestige ceiling—on the professional in American business. To some degree, of course, this also holds true of our governmental laboratories. It even holds true—but not nearly so much, of course—in our universities. Unfortunately, because the top people in our universities are not paid at the same rate as their counterparts in industry, they will leave the academic life for industry, for the wherewithal with which to support their families. This leaves us with an alarming shortage of research people in our universities.

Let me contrast this situation with what is going on in the USSR. The Russians are determined to win the race for scientific supremacy, and they do not count the cost. They pay their scientists and engineers salaries that seem fantastic when compared to other Soviet incomes and with what we pay our scientists and engineers. Senior professors in universities, research scientists, and top engineers are a major segment of the Russian elite. Their incomes are frequently six to ten times the average industrial wage. In the United States, six to ten times the average industrial wage would be $25,000 to $40,000 a year. Housing and other privileges are correspondingly lavish.

While preaching equality, the Soviets use capitalistic incentives far more boldly than we do. Indeed, practicing engineers and scientists have been complaining about the exalted status of professors and top research people, and salary scales are now being adjusted to place a greater premium on practical results.

In Exhibit I, I included two other influences—besides education and status—which are harder to document; but I think they exist nevertheless. One is the political system, which fails to communicate an adequate sense of urgency about the present need for personnel and funds to support expanding technological effort. By this comment, I do not mean to question democracy as a system. I do want to point out, though, that it is far easier and far less time-consuming for the Soviets to move to meet a need such as we are facing than it is for us to convince everybody that we have a job which should be done.

The second is the last little box: our lack of understanding of world markets and our failure to develop a national policy which recognizes political capital gainable by the astute use of technical resources. One of the interesting examples I have run up against in this area has to do with machine tools:

> The Russians are producing about four times as many machine tools today as we are. In comparison, we are almost handmaking our machine tools. Needless to say, with that kind of production, only a 5% diversion of that production to overseas markets would

> represent a very sizable ability to penetrate those areas, particularly in comparison with our ability to do so.
>
> The Soviets sell to a country where there are very few machine tools; they train the people to use them by sending in Russian technicians; the calibrations and operating instructions of these machine tools are in Russian. It is pretty clear to see that it is going to be a hard market to crack for a Johnny-come-lately.

What are the reasonable steps that a democracy can take, given this situation, to enable us to make better use of the potential number and quality of the creative scientists and engineers that we do have?

For one thing, are we using our resources—human and physical—to their full capacity?

It seems to me that we have two problems here. One is the apparent shortage of scientists and engineers, and the other is the attitude toward training those we have. I recall in the fall of 1950 that *Life* came out with a big spread on the surplus of engineers in this country. Shortly thereafter, the registration of engineering students fell off rather markedly. And, in turn, there was a reaction to that in the next year or two with people angrily complaining that we did not have enough technically trained people. Just recently I read an article about the colleges being upset because everybody was going into physics and the higher scientific disciplines rather than into engineering.

On the other hand, we hear many stories of large corporations that hoard engineers. They hire them by the gross, put them in the drafting room, and let the poor devils sit there drawing a modest salary with little prospect of any increase. They are like horses in a corral, kept in case the firm gets a contract. Then the company feeds into the contract the cost of the stable they have been keeping.

What might we do to eliminate such confusion, to evaluate our situation and come up with plans so that, in effect, we can tell the young people coming into high school today what the needs are, what the chances are if they decide to major in math or physics or chemistry?

Perhaps part of our problem lies in the shortage of good engineering management. Maybe the status question is an element in the imbalance; a highly trained man goes on up to administration because he is dissatisfied, even though he may be totally unqualified to do so. Thus, you lose a good technical man, a scientist, and gain a poor manager. Somehow we have to supply people who can motivate our technical personnel. We have to supply objectives that will make it attractive for them to stay in the forefront of the field in which they are working. We have to give them the supporting services that they need—the technicians, for instance.

Currently, the vocational or technical high school in this country is a low-status school. Very few people will be caught dead in one of them; as a result, we simply have nothing like the Soviet technicums, high-status schools, in this country. Therefore, we do not get the necessary number and quality of high-grade technical people to support our engineers and scientists.

Some people say that the answer lies in the fact that in Russia they start weeding out the fit from the unfit at an early age, and they go right through the system with this approach. Thus they get a much better, workable educational scheme. But is it politically possible to do that in this country, where we hold dear the fundamental concept that, potentially at least, everybody is as good as everybody else in everything?

Others suggest that raising our standards all along the line—in the secondary and elementary schools, in higher education, in industry, and in the research work that the nonprofit institutions are doing—might go a long way toward helping close the gap. Maybe more self-policing by teachers and scientists similar to the methods adopted by doctors would be effective. But how can you raise standards if the people are not capable of meeting them? So you are faced with the old chicken-and-egg dilemma.

Another line of argument runs that you must raise the status of the scientist and the teacher of science. But how do you change the status level of a group in a society? How, for instance, do you go about giving teachers and university people more prestige? You cannot force a new set of values like this down people's gullets: it has to emerge somehow from the society itself.

It is true that in Russia they have made a planned, conscious effort along these lines. Their scientists wear white collars; they have chauffeurs; they are extremely well paid, equipped with the facilities and assistance they need, and given all manner of special privileges. So theirs is a combination of monetary and social status.

There are, of course, a number of other approaches to the problem of smashing these various vicious circles in which we find ourselves. But to me the missing ingredient at this stage of the game is leadership. I do not subscribe to the prevalent notion—prevalent among businessmen as well as others, I might add—that the furnishing of this leadership is the sole responsibility of the government. I do believe that our political leaders should supply the sense of urgency, based on their more intimate knowledge of the facts, without which we do not seem to be able to get off our national haunches and get going.

But informed and thoughtful businessmen who have watched the postwar world unfold should need no more urging. It is time for us all to search out ways of meeting this serious deficiency of capable scientists and science teachers. We can put our brains together with those of the academic scientists and educational administrators to work out ways in which industry can strengthen the training of both teachers and practitioners in this field to the mutual benefit of the business and the school system or college. I know it can be done because I have seen it done: companies supply needed equipment, provide on-location training with modern facilities, hire teachers for scientific projects during summer vacations, and even plan out systems which permit teachers to work for them part-time and in the classrooms during other segments of the year.

But perhaps the most important single contribution we can make is closer to home: better management of R & D. This means more attention to the concerns and needs of scientific personnel in industry, more effective recognition of their work, better communications with other functions in the company, far better evaluation procedures, more satisfying projects, and more appropriate working conditions.

Unfortunately, our business schools are not playing a proper part in this effort. We are only beginning to pay adequate attention to this sensitive and tricky matter. But whatever the sins of the academics may be in this regard—and they are many—the business manager who faces the problem every day has to plead guilty to many more of them. It is about time that businessmen took a serious systematic look at their own R & D efforts and improved them, in the interests of the nation as well as in their own.

THE STRATEGY AND TACTICS OF ECONOMIC COEXISTENCE

Raymond Vernon

MY FIRST intensive exposure to the problem of living with the Soviet Union in the economic field goes back about fourteen or fifteen years, when I was working on trade matters with the Department of State. One of our concerns then—a lesser one, on the whole—was how to coexist with the Soviet Union in the international-trade and international-payments field.

I can remember our appraisal of the Soviet Union's role in those days. For a very brief period after the war, some held a vision of a brave new world with a great deal of trade between the capitalist countries and the communistic countries. But this period passed

Note: Mr. Vernon is Professor of International Trade and Investment, Harvard Business School.

swiftly into oblivion, and a sober view of our relations with the Soviet Union emerged—a sober and, I may say with all the accuracy of hindsight, a somewhat distorted view. As we observed the Soviet economy around 1950 we said in our wisdom, "Well, the Soviet Union is committed to the objective of autarky, of self-sufficiency, so it simply cannot get into the position of trading too much." We reasoned that a country which plans its own development and plans its own growth cannot rely on foreign markets to sell its production because foreign markets are undependable.

Similarly, a reliance on a foreign source of supply is dangerous because, first, there is a political risk of being cut off from the source of supply and, second, no one can know what world prices are going to be. And so again we said in our wisdom, "You can be pretty sure that foreign trade won't amount to much in the Soviet Union."

Then we argued that a state apparatus is not an effective one for engaging in foreign trade because such trade typically requires speed of reaction, a willingness to make contact with the outside world, and a sensitivity to individual markets that a government agency really cannot acquire. Thus, we assumed, the Russians would be as clumsy as bears if ever they got into the foreign-trade field and would be discouraged from participating heavily in that activity.

Finally, we reasoned, the Soviet Union may be growing, but it is not going to have any surpluses available for foreign aid for some time to come. In terms of foreign aid, then, we can probably wash the Russians out for a generation.

That was the early fifties. Contrast that picture to 1960's, when the popular impression runs something like this: here is a giant monolith, a great trading state, capable of ignoring the problem of profit or loss in international transactions, and therefore able to buy and sell at will as its political requirements dictate or as the economic requirements (though not profit-and-loss requirements) suggest; capable of using an extensive foreign apparatus for marshaling information on markets and prices; capable of ignoring the question of protecting home industry; capable of taking the fish, cotton, rice, or wool that she acquires in her trade and cramming it into her shops and her households, simply through planning techniques. What a powerful trader—very much unlike the picture in the 1950s!

And as for aid, the Russians can always squeeze the necessary amount out of their local economy. They have no appropriations process, no problem of dealing with their congress each year. They can always reduce consumption a little or home investments a little, and they can pour out the aid to the extent that politics require.

This may be a slight caricature, but it is roughly the picture which today we are being invited to accept by a variety of popular journals. The truth, of course, lies somewhere in between, and our first job is to achieve a balanced appraisal of our adversary, to see where his strengths and weaknesses lie, and to try to evaluate them in a sober, realistic way. So let me devote a few words to that objective.

In the first place, we do not generally appreciate the extent to which Soviet trade has a substantial economic, nonpolitical, base. A curious thing has happened within the Soviet bloc: in a sense the Soviet planners have become a victim of their own theories. They had always assumed that the road to the most rapid growth was through industrialization. Since the first of their five-year plans, they had tended to neglect raw materials and agricultural development. If this was true of the Soviet Union, it was even more true of the rest of the Communist nations in Europe. The result has been a growing scarcity of raw materials within the bloc, and, latterly, a rather significant effort to make this up by imports of raw materials.

There is a kind of irony in all of this. The Soviet Union claims to be the friend of the undeveloped areas and would appear to be helping them along in their development process through trade and aid. But the Soviet Union's demands of the underdeveloped countries encourages them to remain in the business of producing raw materials. When American firms perform this role, it is said to be a capitalistic plot to keep the underdeveloped areas in bondage.

There is another "economic" aspect of Soviet foreign trading. Soviet development is a "lumpy" process, in the following sense: up to a given year and up through a given plan they rely upon, say, natural fibers to clothe their people. Then they make a decision to move into the artificial-fiber field. When they take the step, it is a giant one, involving a major investment in a new chemicals industry in one fell swoop, with all the interrelated plans and processes.

There are many advantages to making the move in one giant step, especially in fields where existing technology is simply being copied by the Russians. There are economies of scale in planning, economies of scale in production, which are achieved by this gigantic uneven process of development. But this method means that the Russians do not have the capacity for producing all the plants to make the product they are interested in—and they do not want to build that much capacity because it will be too much in terms of their ultimate replacement needs.

In a case of this sort, however, it is only the get-going capacity which the Soviets are short on, not the capacity for supplementing or replacing the machinery once it is in place. You can anticipate, after the first get-going purchase of chemicals machinery, that they will no longer be in the market for such machinery.

Therefore, trade does meet two real economic needs for the Soviet bloc: it helps them to overcome their raw-materials deficit; and it enables them to buy some of the machinery which goes into the creation of a new industry. Since they must sell in order to buy, they typically offer products for the world market in which they have a very great comparative advantage.

This is the basic pattern of Russian purchases and sales. I would not suggest for a moment, however, that there is no political element in their buying and selling. Of course there is—a rather considerable one. When the Egyptian cotton crop could not be marketed, the Russians stepped in quickly and picked up large quantities of cotton. When Iceland discovered that her fish was being embargoed in British ports and realized that she could not sell to Western Europe or the United States because of protectionist restrictions in the latter countries, she took the Soviets' well-timed offer to buy a third of her fish catch. There are many instances of this kind involving swift action, dictated in part by political considerations, to pick up otherwise unsalable commodities in one country or another around the world.

Another example of the intrusion of politics into Soviet international economic activity is, of course, the sale of Soviet-bloc industrial plants to the rest of the world. They have delivered bottling works, canning factories, textile mills, and many other plants during the last decade. These moves have not necessarily been costly for the Russian economy because typically the plants did not involve complex technology or advanced designs and may well have been in ample supply in the Soviet economy.

But, despite these instances where a considerable dose of politics has been present, it is probably right to say that the pattern of trade between the Soviet bloc and the rest of the world is based heavily on the bloc's economic needs. Given this conclusion, we have to get rid of some notions which have been cluttering up our thinking and getting in the way of our strategy.

One of the most persistent is the belief that Soviet sales are primarily designed to disrupt capitalist markets and to create economic disturbances in Western countries through the dumping of products. The evidence hardly supports this view.

It is true, of course, that there are three or four known cases in which the Soviets have seemed to be dumping goods. Tin is the classic one. The Russians dumped a great deal of tin on world markets and pushed down the price dramatically over a brief period of time. But what was the aftermath? The Soviet Union made overtures to the International Tin Committee, which is in the business of stabilizing tin prices. There were negotiations between the committee and the Soviet Union, and thereafter Russia agreed to accept a limited quota on sales in world markets. She now has agreed to sell no more than 13,000 or 14,000 tons of tin a year and appears to be living up to her agreement.

Let us take aluminum, which is another well-known case of dumping on the part of the Soviet bloc. The Soviets did push hard at world aluminum prices for a while, but they have now reached an agreement with other producers in accordance with which they are restraining sales of aluminum on world markets.

Let us take diamonds. Russia recently discovered new large deposits of diamonds inside her borders. What did she do? She promptly made a marketing agreement with the De Beers syndicate, the prototype of monopoly capitalists. Under this cozy agreement, the USSR will restrict her sales of diamonds on world markets and will work in harmony with her monopoly-capitalist friends.

In short, Soviet behavior seen in retrospect looks to be what one would expect from a slightly clumsy seller learning the business—one whose channels of internal communication have not been perfected to the level at which they will ultimately arrive, but one which has every intention of trying to maximize the foreign-exchange reserves through the sale of the products it has to offer in world markets.

What is our net appraisal of the effect of Soviet trade in world markets, or the potential effect? In the first place, we must not summarily discard our judgments of 1950 or 1951. The autarkical character of the Soviet economy means that its trade may never have the relative importance to its economy that, for example, United States trade has to its economy.

It is also wise to continue to assume that as long as the Soviets are committed to a planned economy, to a performance economy and not a market economy, they will not allow a very considerable part of the goods they use or produce to be involved in international trade. On the other hand, there is still some room for Soviet trade expansion, since at the present time their trade only constitutes something on the order of two and a half billion dollars a year each way.

Another myth which we should dispel is the stubbornly held notion that the Soviets are infinitely wise and skillful in their foreign programs; that their international economic efforts usually win them converts while ours produce little. Actually, their trade efforts have proved a mixed blessing: Russia has sold tires to Indonesia that have failed to last through five thousand miles of wear; she has sold jeeps to the same country with glass which fractures under tropical heat. From time to time Russia, Czechoslovakia, or East Germany has sent generators to Egypt and other places which have burned out almost as soon as they were installed. Having bought cotton from Egypt, the Soviet bloc has been found reselling some of it on world markets, depressing the price and irritating the Egyptians. She has gone through much the same procedure with Burmese rice, and the results were similar.

Russian factory installations in India have generated bitter complaints over the clannishness of the Soviets, their unwillingness to talk with the Indians, and their summary vetoing of Indian plans.

In Egypt there have been similar complaints. Egyptian engineers have bridled at Soviet alterations in their Aswan Dam plans, changing their diversion tunnels into ditches, altering their generator specifications, never consulting with the Egyptians as the changes were made.

In Burma you hear the story of the delivery of Soviet cement two weeks before the monsoon season, after a six-month delay, and the sequel of its ruin on the docks. Burmese officials were irate.

In Afghanistan, the wail has been over the fact that the Soviets were delivering so much less than they were buying, forcing the Afghans to finance the trade balance.

None of these incidents has endeared the Soviet Union to its trading partners. In short, we must not assume that, simply because Soviet trade is growing, Soviet influence is growing along with it. The relationship between trade and influence is substantially more complicated than this. On the other hand, I do not mean to say that we can count eternally on Soviet clumsiness in trade matters. The Soviets are learning; they are getting better at it every year. Shoddy goods, bad deliveries, poor handling of trade balances—these are not growing phenomena, relatively speaking. In all prudence we have to assume that the level of Soviet effectiveness will be rising in time. But for the present, we have an enemy in the trade field who is far from infallible.

Now let us briefly turn to the Soviet aid program. Of course, it is almost entirely political in its character and, on the whole, is growing. The Soviets are handing out something on the order of $500 million to $1 billion a year in the form of various kinds of credits. That figure is increasing, and one can reasonably estimate that it will be $1 or $1.5 billion in the years ahead—getting within shooting distance of the programs which we call foreign economic aid.

In one way, the Russians have an advantage over us. Because they are guided by more than the acquisitive instinct, they have greater flexibility in the fixing of interest rates and prices. Indeed, the whole concept of interest is an anti-Marxian concept. In general, they offer a low interest rate: 2% or 2½% is typical as against what is getting to be 5% and 6% for United States money or international agency money.

Unlike our programs, the Soviet Union tries to maintain the claim that "there are no ideological strings attached to our aid nor need there be." Superficially, its claim seems justified. When the Soviets lend money to another government they do not raise questions about the role of private enterprise in the country concerned. When we lend money to another government, questions regarding the system of economy with which we are dealing are very much involved.

But while Russia pretends that there are no strings attached to her aid, the record speaks differently. She has lowered the boom on various countries at different times when they have behaved "badly" in political terms. She withdrew her aid from Yugoslavia as a political gesture. She withdrew certain trade arrangements with Finland on similar grounds. She cut off trade with Iceland at one point. In her recent agreement with Cuba, a provision is said to exist to the effect that each country would support the other in political positions before international agencies and in their foreign policies. These were all political weapons.

Most of the world knows better than we do that Soviet aid has political strings attached. As you watch the behavior of Nasser and Sukarno and Kassim and Nehru, the only way in which you can interpret their ambivalence, their ropewalking, their desire to be wooed but not won, is by assuming that they realize that their transactions with the Soviet bloc obviously involve political strings.

The important point here, once again, is that we are not dealing with an unerring and invulnerable adversary. We are dealing with a human mechanism which is trying to perfect a difficult technique—how to win friends and influence people. The adversary has certain advantages. He can act a little more rapidly than we; he does not have a congress to deal with. But by and large he is a lender who is trusted rather less than the United States is trusted; his political objectives are quite obvious to the people who are borrowing. Accordingly, he must not be viewed as an infallible monolith whose tactical superiority over us is self-evident.

Now let us turn to the United States picture, to our own policies and practices. The foreign economic aid of the United States is running to something like $2.5 billion a year. This is a gross figure and represents about .4 per cent of our gross national product. Our net foreign economic aid, after one calculates the repayments which countries are beginning to make on old loans, is running to only about $2 billion a year.

This does not mean, as some people have assumed, that we are shelling out $2 billion worth of gold each year. What is happening, in effect, is that in one form or another—sometimes in the form of wheat, cotton, and tobacco which we cannot use, sometimes in the form of capital goods which we might not otherwise have produced, sometimes in the form of dollars or gold which do not immediately return in payment for purchases—we are giving to the rest of the world something on the order of $2 billion net per year.

Meanwhile our private investors are doing a rather good job. They, too, are investing abroad approximately $2 billion a year in plant and equipment. But these American private investors lately are being paid back in foreign exchange even more than they are investing in fresh foreign capital.

The outflow of fresh capital has been on the order of $2 billion. The inflow of dividends, royalties, and interest has been some $2.5 billion. In balance-of-payments terms, seen from the side of the United States, our outflow of private investment can readily be viewed as something which contributes to stability in the United States balance of payments. Over the long pull, it helps to retain the gold and foreign-exchange reserves in the United States. So any assumption that our outflow of private investment is harmful to us in the sense that it generates a gold flow is much too simple a way of looking at a complex phenomenon.

What is more, any assumption that our private investment simply represents the export of jobs, because it means that new plants are being built abroad to produce goods that once were produced in the United States, is too simple to stand up for very long. The process of overseas foreign investment is more subtle than that. Nobody really knows what the job effect is. Though the obvious result in some cases is to reduce exports to the United States, there are some offsetting effects that are not so obvious. In some cases, for example, we know of companies which have produced only two or three items of a much broader line for sale overseas. Having begun to produce abroad, these firms have begun to develop foreign markets for their full line and have found themselves obliged to round out their product line by exports from the United States. In other cases, managers of American plants in foreign markets have found that the need to import their intermediate products from the United States generates new exports of such products.

In general we know that our best customers are the most industrialized countries of the world. One might begin with the presumption that the more a country industrializes the more exports we will be making to that country, while at the same time accepting more imports. But there is no necessary predetermined balance in the flow of trade with other industrialized countries.

One may well ask whether United States aid endears us to the world. Is the presence of American firms and individuals abroad an asset or a liability in the generation of good will for this country? Once again, the answer is complex. The image which the foreign investor projects in most countries is decidedly a mixed one. In Brazil, for instance, one large American company is generally looked on as an entirely indigenous investor entitled to respect and even affection. Another American company operating in Brazil in the same product line is looked on as a hostile outsider.

If you try to trace the reason for the different reactions, you discover that it has to do in good part with the way in which these companies staff their plants, carry out their labor policies, and so on.

One firm handles itself well in the country and the other handles itself badly.

The United States has long since passed the stage when some of its foreign investors were buccaneers, buying and selling governments overseas. To the contrary; by and large, American companies operating overseas are sensitive to the fact that they are dealing with sovereignties, that in the long run they must operate in a way which is consistent both with their own interests and with those of the country involved.

Furthermore, we should not overlook the fact that the role of private enterprise is increasing in many underdeveloped countries, though it is decreasing in some. One sees, for example, in India, Argentina, Pakistan, and Brazil, indications of an increasing respect for the vitality and utility of private enterprise. These countries seem more and more willing to share the task of development with private enterprise in a way which gives greater scope for enterprise and which confines the government task to areas in which the government can perform best.

In short, the possibilities for private enterprise overseas and international investment clearly are not diminishing. They may well be increasing. Private investment is not the echo of the past, fading out of the world picture. We are not faced with the inevitable ascendancy of socialism and its certain dominance.

Nonetheless, one can well ask: "Couldn't U.S. foreign economic policy be greatly improved? Couldn't our programs be better conceived and better executed to ensure that we will come out ahead in the struggle between us and the Soviet bloc?"

The answer is yes. There are many steps we could take to strengthen our position on the world scene and to strengthen the chances that our way of life will endure longer than that of the Soviet Union.

First, there are some obvious things that can be said. The widespread notion among Americans that they really cannot afford more foreign aid is one of our most dangerous contemporary myths. The concept that the United States, operating at a $500 billion gross-national-product level, cannot part with more than $2 billion of its gross product to achieve a critical economic and political objective is sheer nonsense.

Whether or not we can increase our aid in light of our balance-of-payments situation can of course be questioned. For the long run we certainly can, but the short run is not as clear. The impact on our foreign-exchange reserve position of $2 billion of foreign aid is not $2 billion, as I pointed out earlier. It is an uncertain sum—perhaps $600 million or $800 million. In my view, this is a sum which is easily manageable in our present balance-of-payments position.

I have heard people say that in giving aid, especially government aid, we may be undermining private enterprise abroad. With this view I am unsympathetic. On the contrary, in many instances it has seemed to me that the effect of our aid has been to widen opportunities for private enterprise overseas. There is a very complex relationship between government expenditure in undeveloped countries and the opportunities for private enterprise, all of which suggests that at a given level of development government spending may be indispensable to the growth of private enterprise.

Then, too, we have to bear in mind that our ideological adherence to private enterprise is not totally simon-pure, as other countries well know. In many cases, for instance, American companies have asked foreign governments to go into partnership with them. I am not the least bit critical of these operations. As pragmatic people, as people who are always attempting to discover new methods of operation and to adapt existing ones to changing conditions, we must never exclude the possibility that we may find ourselves at times in partnership with government enterprise. Nor should we assume that this is a slippery slide which leads in the end to socialism. History would deny that premise.

Turning from our investment and aid policies to our trade policies, there are further points which can be made. On the whole, we are not a terribly protectionist country. Fifteen years of intensive tariff negotiations have done much to lower a once-high tariff. But as we have lowered our tariffs, the number of exceptions to the general rule of liberal trade has increased. Lately, the exceptions have become more prominent than the rule.

We are restricting imports of lead, zinc, petroleum, textiles, agricultural products, and a variety of other items, in ways which are inimical to our own foreign interests. Unfortunately, the major impact of these restrictions is on the underdeveloped countries, and it is as much political as it is economic. This unhappy situation would not be so important were it not for the fact that one can foresee the possibility of revolution in world trade just around the corner. The possibility of bridging oceans with air freighters in a period of five or six hours constitutes not a difference in degree for foreign trade, but a difference in kind. It opens up vistas which until recently were not envisioned even by the most prophetic. Already some of these possibilities are being realized. For example, more and more women's garments are being sewed in far-off places like the Philippine Islands, Japan, Puerto Rico, and then being shipped back here for sale. More and more engraving is being done abroad for printing jobs which eventually are completed here. More and more electronic components are being manufactured overseas for products which are assembled here. Until recently it had not been possible to conceive of producing components abroad because the transport time excluded any possibility of receiving and incorporating the product in time for marketing. This has been especially true of products which have to be available and ready for the market within a limited time, such as consumer electronics and clothing. But modern transport technology has changed all this.

Of course, not all products are candidates for the increased international trade made possible by these transport innovations. They have to be of relatively high value to absorb fairly heavy transport costs. They must be produced by a technology which can be internally contained within the four walls of a plant and does not have to rely extensively on the external economies of the area in which it operates. They must have a rather significant amount of labor-cost content left in them, so that halving the cost of labor means a real price advantage in the final market.

Whenever you find products with those characteristics—and there are many of them—you will probably find a substantial potential for export from undeveloped areas. I anticipate the growth of trade in such items—unless the developed countries stop the process. If they do, it is hard to see how countries like India, Pakistan, and Nigeria will generate the export growth they need for their essential development.

Here is one of the great challenges to the United States and to the other industrialized countries of the world. We must prepare to accept more and new types of imports in order to make room for the industrializing underdeveloped countries. This probably means that we will have to go into the business of domestic adjustment programs to facilitate the movement of workers out of one industry into another. The question of whether or not to adopt such a program is sure to be a minor issue in the domestic politics of this country.

If it were not for the fact that expansion of exports by the underdeveloped countries will lead to more exports by the United States, the political problem and the economic problem of added imports would be insoluble. But the whole purpose these countries have in expanding exports is to earn the currencies with which to buy goods. This fact is what makes a solution possible.

My second area of concern is with our approach to trade with the Soviet bloc specifically. I do not regard this problem as the greatest one with which the United States is currently confronted, nor do I believe that it is as important as the aid question or the trade matter which I have just described. But it is reasonably clear that the United Kingdom, France, Germany, Japan, and all the rest will trade with the Soviet bloc to an increasing degree over the years despite any pressure we may exert to keep them from doing so. All our efforts to restrict trade with the Soviet bloc in the past have done us little good; I suspect they will be even less effective in the future.

So our approach to commerce with the Soviet bloc must change in the sense that we must express ourselves as willing to engage in trade where there are gains to be had, and then must coordinate our activities with the other free countries of the world to bring those gains to a maximum. As matters now stand, the Soviet bloc is in a position to enter into bilateral bargains one at a time with Britain, then with France, then with Italy, then with us. It can use its monopoly power, to the extent it exists, to exact the best possible bargain from each of us. This makes no sense. There is no reason why the free-world countries should not coordinate their efforts to trade with the Soviets in an effort to achieve the best possible negotiated deal from a bargainer who is in a position to bargain well.

Such a step would not be easy. There are all kinds of technical difficulties in the way of developing such a coordinated trade agreement, but I am satisfied that it is worthwhile to make the attempt.

Finally, we have to help the underdeveloped countries get into a position in which the Soviet Union cannot practice trade blackmail upon them. We have to help the Icelanders and the Finns, the Yugoslavs, the Egyptians, and even the Cubans so that if and when the Soviet Union threatens to cut off trade with these countries in an effort to exact some political concession, these countries will be in a position to say, "All right—cut off the trade. We can stand the gaff."

In short, there must be some kind of emergency machinery available in the free world which permits us to say to underdeveloped countries: "If the Soviet Union stops trade with you, there will be *ad interim* markets for your goods and foreign exchange available to you. You will have a decent period within which to reorient your sales back into the free-world markets and away from those of Soviet bloc."

One last point: much more important than any particular device, any isolated measure or gimmick, is the development of a state of mind among us that we are not on the losing side in our transactions with the Soviet bloc and in our negotiations with undeveloped countries. With this confidence, we also need the willingness to evolve and experiment, the willingness to break down some of the self-imposed restraints and tradition-ridden concepts to which we cling. It is perfectly clear that in the end there has to be some kind of change if the Soviet Union and the United States are both to inhabit the earth. The evolution will not be solely on the part of the Soviet Union in an effort to make its system compatible with ours, but also an evolution on our part to make our system and objectives compatible with those of the rest of the world.

At the same time, we must be clear about the objectives that are vital to us and those that are expendable. Right now we know what we want to avoid, even though we do not know exactly what we want to achieve. We want to avoid the development of a situation in third countries, countries outside the Soviet bloc, which is irreversible in terms of the choices they can make for the future. We want to prevent a situation in which a Communist machine takes over control of a country.

My assumption is that this threat is most serious not by reason of overt military action on the part of the Soviets but by reason of internal subversion or by the use of perfectly legal, nonsubversive processes. I assume, too, that the threat is generated by a sense of frustration, a sense of lack of alternatives, a sense of lack of growth. The rekindling of the hope and expectation of growth abroad must be our primary aim.

DISCUSSION

From the floor: Professor Vernon, I came here to learn and not to talk polemics. I am afraid I must disagree with you on some points, such as your statement that we should not fear the Soviet thrust in business or the Soviet political thrust in the world.

As international vice-president of a management-consulting firm, I travel continuously, and I am definitely afraid of what I see in the world. I think we are losing ground day after day after day. We are suffering not only from the political penetration; it is the business penetration which follows that is doing the damage.

Our basic weakness can be laid to our personnel policies, both in government and in business. We tend to consider a man capable of handling an international situation because he happens to speak a foreign language or because he has a slightly inquisitive mind. But these are not adequate qualifications for the highly demanding job of overseas service. So the fact is that we have thousands of international bums both in our State Department and in business.

Vernon: One major purpose of my discussion was to point out that extreme views could be misleading views today. We dare not assume that there is something inherent in our private-enterprise system which automatically makes us superior in performance to the Soviet Union. Neither should we accept the philosophy that our system has to be inferior because we are dealing with a ruthless, monolithic, wise, overwhelmingly powerful foe. Both positions are nonsense. The Soviet Union has the strength of the monolith and the weakness of the monolith. It is learning rather fast to build its strength and suppress its weaknesses. But the weaknesses are there.

Of course I would want better recruitment of people overseas. Of course I would want more wisdom and flexibility. But I would still expect occasional lapses, or worse, because it is the nature of a huge program operating in untried fields under constantly changing circumstances that errors will be made.

From the floor: You say that we should not fear this monolithic power, which is not a monolithic power, too much. Nevertheless, when you get down to a specific situation, you ask yourself: how is a private company, which is engaged in business for profit, to compete with a government, such as Russia's, that does not have to take commercial considerations into the picture? I speak of a specific situation in India. The Russian government has offered crude oil to India for payment in rupees, and at a much lower price than commercial prices stand now. How on earth can a private company compete with that sort of thing?

Vernon: This is a tough question, without an easy answer. When conditions ease for India in terms of dollar supply, she will be less disposed to enter into bilateral agreements with the Soviets. Moreover, the Soviets are limited; they cannot expand their foreign-trade component substantially because they cannot allow it to get too large relative to their total economy, as I mentioned before. So you can conceive of the Soviet Union's increasing its trade 50% or perhaps doubling it, but you could not conceive of its being a world trader like the United States.

Then there may be a third answer. There is a possibility that in exceptional cases there ought to be some mechanism for subsidy on the part of the United States government or preferably a group of governments, to be used whenever some kind of major political problem hangs in the balance. It may well be that at some times in some places the offer made by private companies should be backed by a subsidy. I am, I confess, chary of such an approach, and I do not know how it would stand up on close examination. But I think we should look carefully at the possibility.

POSTSCRIPT: SOME THOUGHTS ON GROWTH, ECONOMIC AND PERSONAL

Stanley F. Teele

IN ORDER TO avoid the risks of oversimplification, I shall undertake no summary of the rich intellectual fare in this volume. There is, however, one final point to which I should like to direct your attention.

At least three times during the conference, I had a man say to me, in differing words but in essence, "I wonder whether there would be any possibility of my shifting from business to teaching. Before I am through, I should like to do something really socially useful." Now, I am deeply interested in recruiting men for the teaching profession. Moreover, there are at least a dozen different good reasons that I can see why a man might wish to leave business in order to become a teacher. Any one of these deserves full respect. But, on the other hand, I must reject the implication that being an effective business manager is not a way to perform a socially useful function. The plain and simple fact is that in a society like ours effective business management is of the utmost social consequence, and it is important for business managers to believe this deeply and firmly. Alfred North Whitehead, in an oft-quoted statement, summed this up nearly thirty years ago when he wrote that a great society is a society in which its men of business think greatly of their function. My basic proposition, then, is that the first requirement for personal growth is a deep-seated conviction that what one is doing has real significance.

This thought emboldens me to return to a theme which I stressed in the volume commemorating the fiftieth anniversary of the Harvard Business School in 1958.[1] There, as the original structure of my remarks, dealing with the business manager of the future, I made use of the three Rs. I expressed both the hope and the expectation that the business manager of the future would be more rational, more responsible, and more religious. At other times since, I have sought to elaborate the concept of a more rational manager and of a more responsible manager. I should like here to call your attention again to the more religious manager. I use this word advisedly, confident that none of you will suppose I take it in any narrow, dogmatic, or sectarian sense. Rather, by "religious" I mean an awareness of the ethical dimensions of the problems we face and a clear view of the ultimate values and goals by which we chart the course of our lives, personal and professional. What I am seeking to do is to emphasize the importance of knowledge about and belief in the basic values on which our society was founded and by which it has developed.

If we identify these values and do our jobs in terms of them, we need have no fear that our careers as business managers are not socially useful.

All this is given added urgency by our continuing nonmilitary

[1] *Management's Mission in a New Society,* Dan H. Fenn, Jr., ed. (New York, McGraw-Hill Book Company, Inc., 1959), pp. 41–47.

competition with the Soviet Union. In this nonmilitary area, our success may well depend on the clarity with which we are able to sort out what is really important and lasting in our own ideology from that which is false and transitory. We have made genuine progress in the last two and a half years in achieving a better perspective on this kind of competition with Russia. We have begun to see that emphasis on material progress alone as the measure of success or failure is not only inadequate but dangerous. But, in spite of our progress, we continue to be in danger of falling into a trap of our own making. The world's reaction to our tremendous material progress has been so overwhelming that we tend to believe this to be the true measure of our greatness and potential greatness, and we hear ourselves saying that affluence is the most important contribution which we have made and can make to the world. In our hearts we know better; we know that the demonstration, imperfect as it may be, of how 170 million people can live together in peace, with basic goals of human dignity, morality, and justice, is our real contribution.

Recently—and increasingly in the last few years—we have heard a great deal of discussion about our national purpose and goals. Directly and indirectly we have debated the relative importance of material values and more intangible objectives, and argued over precisely what these more intangible purposes may be. Currently, this search is being brought to a focus by the President's Committee on National Goals and by a series of articles in various national publications offering the views of leaders from various fields of endeavor.

As I observe this great debate, I cannot help thinking back to the formative years of our country and being struck once again by the overwhelming impact that the ideas of a relatively small group of men had on a receptive populace and, consequently, on the course that we set as a people. Though our society has become vastly more complex during the intervening years, I am convinced that the beliefs and values held by our leaders are no less significant today in determining the direction that we shall take. Consequently, it seems to me of the utmost importance that the leaders in the field of business, which is so central in our society, should have strong convictions about the nature of that society and demonstrate them in deed as well as in word.

Thus, when I urge every business manager to appreciate the social importance of effective performance in his job, to take pride in his role in our society, I then wish to go further and urge him to exercise his leadership in the nation-wide effort to sharpen an understanding of our goals and strengthen our belief in them.

Those of you who have seen the study carried out by the Harvard Business School Boston Alumni Club, and published by the Greater Boston Economic Study Committee,[2] no doubt shared with me a concern over the finding that so many graduates of business schools, not this one alone, take no active part in public affairs. And—to me, far worse—they seem to show very little interest in such matters. The zeal which the typical Communist Party member shows for his faith may seem ridiculous and all out of proportion. It is certainly a far cry from the pleasant, passive attitude revealed by the Boston study. That attitude is also perilous: we must have more zeal, more conviction, and more understanding.

This thought brings me back full circle. For if the businessman is to function effectively as a leader in public affairs, help us see and articulate our national goals, and take pride in his career as a manager, he must pay attention to his own beliefs and values. He must, if you will, refurbish his religious sense and do it with wisdom and with knowledge. This pursuit, to my mind, is the most important part of personal growth. In an age of rapid change, of explosions, it becomes a vital necessity.

[2] "A Profile of an Executive Group in Greater Boston," 1960.